ANGIE ZELTER defines herself as a 'global [...]
her life work as experimenting in findin [...]
resisting unethical and unsustainable pr[...]
ing to re-create with others the broken t[...] .. ... planetary web of
life. She specialises in initiating nonviolent direct action campaigns and
has been arrested over a hundred times in Belgium, Canada, England,
Malaysia, Norway, Poland and Scotland, serving 16 separate prison sentences totalling 20 months.

In 1993 she initiated a campaign called the Citizens' Recovery of
Indigenous Peoples' Stolen Property Organisation which confronted the
major timber importers and agents of Brazilian mahogany and of British
Columbian red cedar. After a series of 'open' letters she organised a series
of 'ethical shoplifting' actions whereby activists took timber from shops
and timber yards to the local police stations, handing them in as stolen
property and asking that they be returned to the rightful owners – indigenous people in Brazil and Canada. Protracted office occupations and
negotiations led to some substantial changes in timber buying and environmental awareness in the firms involved.

In 1996 she was part of the East Timor Seeds of Hope Ploughshares
action which disarmed a Hawk Jet, causing £1.5 million worth of damage and preventing it from being exported to Indonesia where it would
have been used to continue genocidal attacks on East Timorese villages.
After 6 months in prison she was acquitted by a jury along with the other
three women in a court victory which helped put the control of arms sales
on the political agenda.

In the '80s she founded the Snowball Campaign which encouraged
several thousand people to cut the fences around us military bases in the
UK and four years ago she initiated the practical disarmament campaign
Trident Ploughshares which has brought the issue of the UK's weapons of
mass destruction back onto the public and political agenda. Based on
international humanitarian law, the campaign encourages people to
engage in practical acts of nuclear war crime prevention. In 1999 she was
acquitted at Greenock Sheriff Court in another high-profile jury trial
after joining with two other women to disarm a Trident-related research
barge in Scotland.

All royalties from sales of this book go to Trident Ploughshares.

'This fine book should be read by everyone, especially those who have the slightest doubt that the world will one day be rid of nuclear weapons. From Mothers Against The Bomb (usa, 1950s), to the Greenham Women, to the World Court Project and now the brilliant Ploughshares movement, those who have campaigned literally to save our lives are the true heroes of my lifetime. Angie Zelter's informative and powerful book is a manual and inspiration for the most important of all human struggles.'
JOHN PILGER, Investigative journalist and author

'I'm now totally convinced that Trident is theologically and morally indefensible, strategically irrelevant, illegal in terms of international law, and a colossal waste of resources that could be creatively used for the common good.'
REV NORMAN SHANKS, Leader, Iona Community

'Protest has always been central to the Scots constitution. In the 1320 Declaration of Arbroath, the community told the king that sovereign power comes from bottom-up and they'd depose him if he forgot it. Today the Scottish people roundly reject defence by threatened genocide. Trident is held not in our names. Given Britain's supposedly spiritual constitution and given international law, Trident is the treason. That is why Trident Ploughshares carries such deep authority. It presents a naked moral challenge. It names, unmasks and engages the Powers. It calls the nation from fear and hate to learn to love.'
ALASTAIR MCINTOSH, author of Healing Nationhood

'We must never allow ourselves to think that defence issues, and nuclear weapons issues in particular, are only defence issues. Questions about how we defend ourselves are not merely questions of strategy: they are also questions of right and wrong. The strategic questions are difficult and important, but they are not as important as the questions of right and wrong. This book deals with some complex technical issues, but always in a context of pointing towards what is decent and good and what is not. To deal with some of the matters in the nuclear debate you need a big brain, and this book will help, but even more you need a big heart. Reading this book will help you to play your part in keeping human life human.'
THE VERY REV DR ANDREW R C MACLELLAN, Moderator of the General Assembly of the Church of Scotland 2000/2001.

'...the reader is forced to think about the survival of the planet, the legality of weapons of mass destruction, and the duties and rights of the humblest of citizens in trying to ensure the planet's survival. I suspect that 100 years from now, the themes raised in this book will continue to provide sustenance for the legal imagination... I commend this work to all who seek nuclear disarmament... and to all who would like to explore the cutting edges of International Law and Criminal Law'.

ROGER S CLARK, Board of Governors Professor, Rutgers University School of Law, NJ

'Angie Zelter's campaigning courage and commitment to justice reflect a spirit of defiance that has echoed in Britain through countless generations.'

CONOR GEARTY, Professor of Human Rights Law, Kings College, London

'...crimes against International Law are committed by men, not by abstract entities.'

The Nuremberg Tribunal

'...murder does not cease to be murder merely because the victims are multiplied ten millionfold.'

SIR HARTLEY SHAWCROSS, UK Prosecutor, Nuremberg

'...nuclear weapons are the enemy of humanity, ...biological time bombs whose effects transcend time and space, poisoning the earth and its inhabitants for generations to come.'

GENERAL LEE BUTLER, Commander in Chief of The United States Strategic Command

'...if humanity and the dictates of the public conscience demand the prohibition of such weapons for some states, it must demand the same prohibition for all states.'

GARETH EVANS QC, Australian Foreign Minister

'...the shock troops of the sane in the war against insanity.'

KURT VONNEGUT, Message of Support for Trident Ploughshares Big Blockade at Faslane, 2001

'Homo Sapiens appeared on earth in the last flick of an evolutionary eye, and in the very recent past has modified the world in ways that may give the species a prize for rapid extinction. It is, surely, within our power to demonstrate that the particular forms that higher intelligence took will not prove to be a lethal mutation. Elimination of nuclear weapons from the earth is a fundamental step in this direction. The nonviolent activists who are dedicating themselves to realizing this goal deserve our sincerest thanks and strongest support.'
NOAM CHOMSKY, Message of Support for Trident Ploughshares

'It's not as simple as good and bad, right and wrong, moral and immoral. It's how to recognise the humanity in all of us, our hope in the future, our desire for a better world.'
JANE TALLENTS, Local Heroes Affinity Group

'This is the story of global citizenship in action, a story of people's power and the right of individuals to prevent their state from committing very great wrongs. This book is about the women and men who are taking responsibility to prevent mass murder. It is about people's disarmament. I hope it will inspire you to join us.'
ANGIE ZELTER

Trident on Trial
the case for people's disarmament

ANGIE ZELTER

Luath Press Limited

EDINBURGH

www.luath.co.uk

First published 2001

UK TRADE DISTRIBUTION
Scottish Book Source Ltd., Scottish Book Centre,
137 Dundee Street, Edinburgh EH11 1BG ++44(0) 131 229 6800

US TRADE DISTRIBUTION
Midpoint Trade Books, Suite 102, 27 West 20th Street, New York, NY 10011
++(1) 212 727 0190

OTHER TERRITORIES, OTHER LANGUAGES
Please contact Luath Press ++44 (0) 131 225 4326

The paper used in this book is acid-free, neutral-sized and recyclable.
It is made from low chlorine pulps produced in a low-energy, low
emission manner from renewable forests.

Printed and bound by
Bell and Bain Ltd., Glasgow

Design by Tom Bee, Edinburgh

Typeset in 10.5 and 9.5 point Sabon by
S. Fairgrieve, Edinburgh

Title page illustration by Cinders McLeod, www.broomielaw.co.uk

Contents

INTRODUCTION   11

FOREWORDS

Conor Gearty, *Professor of Human Rights Law,*
Kings College, London   17
Roger S. Clark, *Board of Governors Professor, Rutgers*
University School of Law, Camden, New Jersey, USA   23

Resistance and Hope Rap – Brian Quail,
Local Heroes Affinity Group   34
Message from the Muse – David Mackenzie,
Local Heroes Affinity Group   38
A Little Nuclear Crime Prevention up the Goil –
Angie Zelter, *Pheasants Union Affinity Group*   39

CHAPTER 1   PEOPLE'S DISARMAMENT   47
Cutting up the Convoy – Susan van der Hijden,
Jubilee 2000 Affinity Group   56
The Brown Envelope – George Farebrother,
Dialogue and Negotiation Affinity Group   62

CHAPTER 2   THE LEGAL BATTLE AT GREENOCK   66
Citizens Inspect Aldermaston – Marguerite Finn,
Woodwoses Affinity Group   71
With a Little Help from our Friends – Alison Crane,
Midlands Affinity Group   75
The Art that Art Conceals: Profile of Judith Pritchard,
Midlands Affinity Group – David Mackenzie,
Local Heroes Affinity Group   77

CHAPTER 3   THE LORD ADVOCATE'S 4 QUESTIONS   79
Commotion – Sheila Mackay,
Gareloch Horticulturalists Affinity Group   85
Wheelchairs and Websites – Mark Leach,
Ceilidh Creatures Affinity Group   88
Melangell – Kath McNulty,
Melangell Affinity Group   91
Trashing Trident – Rachel Wenham,
Aldermaston Trash Trident Affinity Group   94

CHAPTER 4 SETTING THE LEGAL CONTEXT 98
Confronting Fears – Sue Davis,
Muriel Lester Affinity Group 124
Prison Thoughts 1 – Marcus Armstrong,
Waterbabies Affinity Group 127
Prison Thoughts 2 – Helen Harris,
Aldermaston Trash Trident Affinity Group 129

CHAPTER 5 ANSWERING THE LORD ADVOCATE 132
ANSWER TO QUESTION 1 132
An Iona Perspective – Norman Shanks,
Dialogue and Negotiation Affinity Group 137

ANSWER TO QUESTION 2 138
We're all in the Same Boat – Jane Tallents,
Local Heroes Affinity Group 150

ANSWER TO QUESTION 3 151
Belgian Nights: Koen Moens, Titanic Trident!
Affinity Group – David Mackenzie,
Local Heroes Affinity Group 152

ANSWER TO QUESTION 4 153
Sentenced to a Comfy Chair – Joan Meredith,
Northumbrian Affinity Group 159

CONCLUSION 160
Resolving Culture Conflicts – David Heller,
Faslane Full-timers Affinity Group 165
Decommissioning in Baggy Pants – Roger Franklin,
Midlands Affinity Group 168
Supplement – Marlene Yeo,
Midlands Affinity Group 172
Dear Bailiffs – Angie Zelter,
Woodwoses Affinity Group 174

CHAPTER 6 CHALLENGE TO THE SCOTTISH JUDICIARY 175
The Japanese Connection – Astrid Ubas,
Peace Pagoda Affinity Group 204
International Mosquitoes Buzzing Around
Trident – Katri Silvonen,
Titanic Trident! Affinity Group 207
For Mother Earth in Action – Bernard De Witte,
Titanic Trident! Affinity Group 211

CHAPTER 7   THE SCOTTISH HIGH COURT GIVES ITS OPINION   214

Letter to the Court – David Mackenzie,

Local Heroes Affinity Group   238

The Dragonrider – Kreb Dragonrider,

Druids Against Trident Affinity Group   239

Disarming the Bases with Music – Emilia Benjamin,

Venus' Birds Affinity Group   243

Strike the Little Bell – Maire-Colette Wilkie,

Adomnan of Iona Affinity Group   246

CHAPTER 8   OURSTORY   252

Trying to Disarm the Vanguard Submarine
– Ulla Roder,

Douglas Water Affinity Group   292

From out of the Horses Mouth – Brian Quail,

Local Heroes Affinity Group   297

Contacts   300

Acknowledgements   301

Names of Trident Ploughshares Pledges on 30 March 2001   303

Index   306

Introduction

ON 8 JULY 1996, in prison at Risley in England for a peaceful act of civil resistance against violence, I received inspiring news which was to profoundly affect the next five years of my life. I was informed of the historic decision of the International Court of Justice (ICJ) at the Hague in Holland – the Advisory Opinion on the Legality of the Threat or Use of Nuclear Weapons. The ICJ is also known as the World Court and is the judicial arm of the United Nations used to adjudicate disputes between nations. The 1996 Advisory Opinion explained that the threat or use of nuclear weapons would generally be contrary to the rules of international law applicable in armed conflict. The ruling put the burden of proof on the nuclear weapon states to justify how their nuclear weapons could be deemed lawful. How, for instance, could a 100 kiloton nuclear warhead with its known effects of massive blast, heat and radioactivity however accurately targeted, discriminate between a legitimate military target and nearby civilian women and children and their hospitals and schools? The ICJ also stated that there was a legal obligation on all nuclear weapons states to actually achieve nuclear disarmament, not just talk about it.

There was very little public debate of this landmark opinion and no doubt the UK government, amongst others, hoped that it would remain this way. However, in prison as I read the Opinion, the seed was planted for what came to be known as 'Trident Ploughshares'. In this book I have given a personal account of this civil resistance campaign of people's disarmament. I have interspersed my own story with some factual background, flavouring it with profiles of some of the people and groups who have pledged to prevent nuclear crime – those who engage in practical and peaceful acts of nuclear disarmament. I have let them have their say in their own words to show the variety of different perspectives that is our strength.

I have also put in some of the detailed legal arguments against Trident and explained the background to some of the struggles in the courts. Because we come from many different backgrounds and have different beliefs and politics, not all of us want to use legal arguments in our own defence in the courts. For some the moral case against Trident is so clear they feel the legal arguments are an irrelevance. For others there are compelling political reasons not to respect a legal system that they see as working on behalf of the powerful and rich. Others want to confront the system head on through the system's own institutions. However, we have all come together in this campaign and respect each other's differences and know that the way forward is to responsibly confront our society on as many different levels and in as many different ways as possible.

We have therefore based our campaign upon international law and the Advisory Opinion and are challenging the legitimacy of the UK nuclear forces – which are deployed on nuclear powered submarines called Trident. We are invoking the Nuremberg Principles that came out of the Nazi War Crimes Tribunal held at the end of World War Two at Nuremberg and contrasting these with the Royal Navy's use of the Nazi defence of obedience to the state.

Without intense public pressure to abolish all nuclear weapons, the nuclear weapon states will ignore the Advisory

A Trident submarine, with tugs, inside the high security boom at Faslane
Credit: David Mackenzie

Opinion and continue to abuse their power by maintaining and developing their weapons of mass destruction. Rather than trust the empty promises of the nuclear weapon states, Trident Ploughshares issued an ultimatum to prime minister Tony Blair to either implement international law by disarming all British nuclear weapons or the campaign's members would do it themselves. Not content with a mere campaign statement, Trident Ploughshares has organised people to make a personal pledge to disarm the nuclear weapon system themselves. These Pledgers will continue with this task until the government takes over the disarmament work and fulfils its promise of complete nuclear disarmament.

Our practical people's disarmament campaign has led to spectacular actions which challenge the whole legal system. To take just one example, on 8 June 1999 three of us completely emptied the research laboratory barge, *Maytime*, throwing its contents into Loch Goil in Scotland and explaining our right to do this under international law. The acquittal of the 'Trident Three' at Greenock Sheriff Court on 21 October 1999 by direction of Sheriff Gimblett caused a political and legal furore that may yet end in nuclear weapons being kicked out of Scotland.

This is the story of global citizenship in action, a story of people's power and of the right of individuals to prevent their state from committing very great wrongs.

May 2 1998 – Conway Hall, Public Launch of Trident Ploughshares, Angie Zelter.

Today we are publicly launching our Ploughshares project here in London. Other friends and supporters are holding simultaneous press conferences in Hiroshima, Gothenburg, Gent and Edinburgh. We are especially pleased with the Japanese support and hope that through our connection with their personal suffering following the nuclear devastation at Hiroshima and Nagasaki we can be sustained in our struggle here to dismantle the British nuclear threat, at least.

The majority of British people are in favour of nuclear disarmament – with 59% believing that Britain would be better off without nuclear weapons and 87% believing that Britain should negotiate a global treaty to rid the world of nuclear weapons. The vast majority of the international community is likewise dedicated to the complete elimination of all nuclear weaponry. In an era which hopes to progress towards global sustainability, ethical foreign policies and respect for human rights, we know that nuclear weapons must be dismantled.

We know within ourselves that it is deeply immoral and inhumane to threaten mass destruction with weapons that will leave genetic abnormalities and environmental damage for many future generations. We also know that we have a responsibility for what our society does in our names. And, as Richard McSorley once said, 'The taproot of violence in our society today is our intent to use nuclear weapons. Once we have agreed to that, all other evil is minor in comparison. Until we squarely face the question of our consent to use nuclear weapons, any hope of large-scale improvement of public morality is doomed to failure'.

Trident Ploughshares 2000 activists have squarely faced this question, acknowledge that we do not feel 'defended' by nuclear weapons, feel ashamed at the threat of terrible mass destruction and are determined that as 'global citizens' we will take our responsibilities seriously and start the practical work of dismantling the system.

Trident Ploughshares 2000 have formed a Dialogue and Negotiation Team that has written to the Prime Minister Tony Blair asking the British government to start serious and meaningful steps towards abolishing their nuclear weapon system. We have suggested a set of 9 steps that could be taken by Britain to show a genuine commitment to nuclear disarmament and a safer more ethical world. We have stated that:

Trident Ploughshares 2000 will be prepared to halt our direct activities as long as we are satisfied that genuine progress towards disarming Britain's nuclear capability is being made, but we will resume if undertakings are reversed or unreasonably drawn out or postponed. We regard the following visible and verifiable elements as indispensable to genuine commitment by the government to a process of de-nuclearising Britain.

i) The British Trident submarine system must immediately be taken off 24 hour patrols.

ii) No new Trident missiles are to be purchased from the United States.

iii) All British nuclear warheads must be removed from their delivery systems and stored separately by 1 January 2000.

iv) No further deployment of US nuclear weapons in Britain. Britain should work with its NATO allies for withdrawal of all tactical nuclear weapons from Europe.

v) Trident missiles are to be returned to the United States and the warheads to be returned to AWE Aldermaston/Burghfield by an agreed date.

vi) Commitment to a timetable for the decommissioning of British nuclear weapons as fast as is feasible and safe, with a target date for completion of 2010 at the latest.

vii) Agreement not to replace Trident or seek to acquire nuclear weapons again.

viii) Conversion of Britain's nuclear production sites towards the decommissioning of nuclear weapons and facilities and safe management and disposal of nuclear materials

ix) Active and constructive British involvement in efforts to reduce nuclear weapons globally.

This public launch is part of our attempt to be as open and accountable as possible to the public and the government. We are using this opportunity to give a list of the names and addresses of all of those global citizens who have committed themselves to peaceful, safe and nonviolent attempts to disarm the British nuclear Trident system. We now have 49 people who have completed their training workshop, have signed the Pledge to Prevent Nuclear Crime and the Nonviolence and Safety Pledge and are ready to commit themselves.

Many more people are in the process of completing their training and by August 11th we hope to have at least a hundred people ready to start the disarmament process by safely dismantling Trident.

The public launch of our campaign was on 2 May 1998. That August over 100 people were arrested for their disarmament work. In the following three years we have increased the pressure for the disarmament of nuclear weapons, engaging many people in active debate about the ethical base of our society and its legal system and explaining how nuclear weapons undermine its very foundation. We have challenged our political, legal and religious institutions to join us to dismantle the nuclear system.

Our legal system here in the UK is based on a common understanding of what is right and wrong. Ignorance of the law is no defence and every member of our society is expected to know the law – whatever our level of our education or intelligence, whether we can read or write and despite the jargon, Latin phrases and complexity! We are all expected to know what is lawful and what is unlawful because the law is meant to be based on common humanity and common ethical values.

It is obvious to all that taking another person's life is wrong. This is reflected in the legal system – making murder a crime. Why then does our state have nuclear weapons which if used would cause the death of perhaps millions of innocent civilians? Is this not mass murder? Is it not a crime?

The answer is, of course, it is a crime which is why ordinary people are working together to stop it.

This book is about the women and men who are taking responsibility to prevent mass murder. It is about people's disarmament. I hope it will inspire you to join us.

Angie Zelter
Norfolk, June 2001

Foreword 1

Angie Zelter's campaigning courage and commitment to justice reflect a spirit of defiance that has echoed in Britain through countless generations. History shows that open rejection of the prevailing status quo (and therefore its law) has long been this country's key to political change. In medieval times, of course, it was often the only way in which power could be transferred from one prince to another. The basis for the United Kingdom's contemporary constitution – the sovereignty of Parliament – was constructed out of the conscious lawlessness of seventeenth century rejectors of the then all-powerful Stuart state. That sovereignty was later only prised open for the people by the courageous rebelliousness of the masses, willing to risk brutal repression for the sake of the democratic ideal. Even as recently as the Edwardian period, politically energised women broke laws, served jail sentences and starved themselves to secure a right to vote that now seems as normal as the air we breathe. The Irish breached the law with bloody profligacy so as to force the formation of their own independent state, just as did many colonies in the decades that followed the second world war. If laws were to demand obedience merely on account of their being laws, we would still be in thrall to the successors of Edward the Confessor; in the past law breaking has been the oil that has kept the ship of state on the move, the blood that has coursed through the nation's body, ensuring its vigour and protecting it from political arteriosclerosis.

The law has of course rarely assisted such political activists. Even where it does, as Angie has recently seen first hand, the forces of the State have the power to intervene. We should never allow ourselves to be surprised that the law is on the side of the powerful, even where this seems to require a flouting of that very law. The history of political struggle in Britain is a history of legal actions lost, hostile judicial rulings incurred, and the constant legitimisation of executive excess. The role of the law is rarely to empower; more often it is to restrict and control. It is the case that, now and again, the rhetoric of the rule of law with its talk of justice and fairness can be made to work in a campaigner's favour, drawing attention to a great wrong, publicising a just cause, perhaps even securing an acquittal. But just as one swallow does not make a summer, so one success should not change the underlying scepticism with which it is right that those intent on political change should view the courts.

In some cultures and at certain historical moments, disobedience to the law does not need to involve bloodshed. This is the exception rather than the rule. The brave colonels who sought to kill Hitler in 1944 had not first tried to persuade him to resign. Nelson Mandela did not order his followers to march arms aloft in the direction of apartheid South Africa's murderous enforcers of the law. But Martin Luther King did. Discerning the moral force of his argument, and the receptivity to it of the America that lay beyond the deep South, he commended to his 'sit-inners and demonstrators' a course of 'sublime courage, ... willingness to suffer and ... amazing discipline in the midst of great provocation' (*Letter from Birmingham Jail (1963)*). Backed by a liberal press, by the majority of the American people, and in the end by the legislative power of Congress allied to the controlled violence of the executive branch, King succeeded in changing America for the better. The democratic form of American government made his campaign of nonviolent lawlessness possible: he and his followers were not murdered on the streets, the press was not censored into nonexistence, the rulers of the nation had to respond in some way to the crisis that unfolded before them.

If disobedience to the law is possible in a society with a democratic form of government, is it ever justifiable? Luther King could point to the widespread suppression in the deep South of the African-American's right to vote. At his 1962 trial on the charge of inciting a strike by African workers, Nelson Mandela considered himself 'neither legally nor morally bound to obey laws made by a Parliament in which [he had] no representation'. Neither situation pertains in a country in which every person, with very few exceptions, has the right to vote and in which a secret ballot to choose the government of the country is held on a regular basis.

The idea of democracy has a substantive as well as a merely formal dimension, however. Of course persons are elected to the

UK Parliament which then makes laws which it is said reflect the wishes of the people as mediated through their elected representatives. Sometimes this model still works effectively. More often however it does not. This is not because of the Party whip system which ensures that one of the major Parties – and therefore the Government – can always rely on the Parliament of the day to do its bidding. Without the development of Parties, the Labour parliamentary movement would have been still born and the socialist achievements of the twentieth century would never have happened. The problems with Britain's contemporary democracy go far deeper than anxieties about executive power; in fact they centre on the very opposite: the relative powerlessness of both the executive and the legislative branches to achieve necessary political change.

Our politically activist ancestors fought hard for the right to vote because they believed that voting mattered. For much of the twentieth century, this was indeed the case: Parliament could and did pass the laws that it wished in order to help realise the vision of the country that it had been mandated by the electors to achieve. Parliament's sovereignty was a real fact and made the political struggle to achieve power over it a campaign that was worth waging. It was a fight that could be fought on equal terms, with no one side able to inundate the process with money and thereby twist the result in a certain way.

None of this is any longer the case. A plethora of international and regional agreements, protocols and (sometimes secret) multilateral deals have dramatically hedged the power of parliament, making its capacity for action slight and its debates therefore increasingly irrelevant. Britain's modern executive government in the United Kingdom may still control the legislative branch but the room for manoeuvre that it has to pass laws remains sharply restricted nevertheless. It is not parliamentarians that ministers have to listen to but the high priests of the global economy; not local communities it must greet but representatives of powerful foreign governments; not deputations of councillors who must be heard but rather delegations from international economic organisations. Huge inflows of money have poisoned what is left of Britain's parliamentary tradition, with the desperate search for campaigning cash having become our contaminated democracy's main driving force.

The outward signs and forms of democracy remain while the power we traditionally associate with democratic government has inexorably ebbed away. We still have elections, a (relatively) free press and a lively political culture. But the focus is on trivialities: did this or that government minister walk to the meeting or take his car? Will this or that spokesperson get promoted after the election? How does the Chancellor get on with the Prime Minister? Is so-and-so a liar or does he cheat on his wife? Around this swirling noise, key decisions are being made, about weapons, about trade, about the kind of country Britain should become, but these deliberations are not occurring within the democratic process and are as a result rarely if ever noticed in the frenzied, hyperbolic discourse that passes for today's political debate.

It is into this space between the form and substance of democracy that 'direct action' and nonviolent disobedience to the law has inserted itself with growing success in recent years. Angie Zelter has been a prime agent of this change though there have been many others, generously celebrated in this book. The wider public has watched, admired and applauded while protestors have through their actions forced attention on key issues of deep importance that would otherwise have gone by default. Many members of the general public have been inspired to become involved in such campaigns. Juries have done their bit by acquitting defendants when the opportunity has arisen. Through direct action, many concerned British citizens have closed the gap between their private and their public selves, discovered a new sense of purpose and recovered for themselves some of the excitement that earlier generations felt about the vital importance of politics.

Disobedience to law is a double-edged sword. The powerful usually have no need of criminality because the forces of the state are at their disposal. But the more radical a government, the more it tackles genuine inequality or seeks to achieve radical change, the more it risks lawless subversion from the extreme right. This was apparent in the United Kingdom last year when reactionary forces, mimicking the protests they had for so long scorned, sought to destroy a government that had taken action against its own, narrowly sectional interests. The 'direct action' of today may be wholly moral but there is also tomorrow to think of, and the day after. A properly functioning representative democracy, of the type for which previous generations of campaigners believed they were fighting, is still something towards which, in deference to their struggle, we should all seek to strive.

At a time of rational apathy and excusable cynicism about our jaded democratic institutions, direct action which is morally driven, disciplined and carefully thought through is a reminder to us all of the seriousness of ideas and of the value of political engagement. There remains however also an urgent need to reform our political structures, to close the gap between the wishes of the people and the inclinations of their elected representatives, and to re-empower our representatives to take decisions that are in their people's best interests. Then the power of Angie Zelter's arguments might make it possible to have her ideas transformed into clear and unambiguous domestic law. We may be at a low point in democracy's long history, but there is no reason why what goes down should not – given the will and the energy – come back up. In this way direct action is inevitably and rightly linked with democratic renewal and reform.

Conor Gearty
Professor of Human Rights Law, Kings College, London

Foreword 2

1. *Stealing and doing malicious damage to the Queen's stuff*

I teach International Law and Criminal Law for a living. This remarkable book is about some fundamental issues in those areas. At the narrow level of mundane fact, the book is mostly about three determined women, members of Trident Ploughshares through which they had pledged to take direct action against what they saw as nuclear crime. In what follows, they are sometimes called 'the Trident Three', sometimes 'the defendants', and sometimes 'the respondents'. They dumped some equipment (computers and such like) belonging to Her Majesty's Government overboard from a barge into a loch in Scotland. Charged with 'malicious damage' and with theft (before a Sheriff and a jury in Greenock, Scotland), they defended on the basis that they were trying to prevent much greater evil. Two were represented by lawyers; one was '*pro se*' – she represented herself (very ably). One quickly realises that the equipment was part of the stealth infrastructure for the Trident nuclear-armed submarines on duty under the oceans. Then the reader is forced to think about the survival of the planet, the legality of weapons of mass destruction, and the duties and rights of the humblest of citizens in trying to ensure the planet's survival.

International customary law is said to be part of the law of Scotland, as it is part of the law of England and of the United States. Enforcing it, however, especially against the government, is a dodgy business. The citizen who seeks declaratory or injunctive relief is likely to find that the government is immune, or that the citizen does not have 'standing', or that the matter is not fit for a court in that it is 'not justiciable', or that it is not yet 'ripe'. (I suspect that on this type of judicial reasoning, the matter is not ripe until the bombs are in the air. Cranking up injunctive relief is then, I fear, too late.)

Thus, international law is not much good as a sword; how about as a shield? That was the premise of the defendants: the fact that they were acting to stop breaches of international law meant that they were acting within the law. Either the international principles themselves provide a defence, which can be read into Scottish law, or domestic law notions such as the defence of necessity are malleable enough to encompass such principles.

Theft and malicious damage in Scottish law are common law offences; that is to say, there is no statute defining them, or at least none referred to in these proceedings. The judges all know what they are, because they regularly read past decisions of the courts, in Scotland, and even in England and other Commonwealth countries. (United States decisions are not as welcome but not entirely beyond the pale, although I suspect they are often seen as aberrational.) Nobody in the appellate proceedings seems to have focused too much on what the *prima facie* elements of the two offences might be, apart from latching onto the rather obvious 'malice' in 'malicious damage'. The lay person might be forgiven for thinking that those who, like the defendants, act out of the purest of motives (as the Sheriff was prepared to concede) in endeavouring to hinder what they believe to be unlawful actions carried out in the name of Her Majesty are not acting maliciously. (There are, perhaps, related arguments that might be made about 'colour of right' in relation to theft.) Alas, as the High Court reminds us, malice is really a legal term of art meaning intentionally or recklessly. The Trident Three were more than reckless, they were acting perfectly intentionally. So much for the absence of malice. We are left then with possible defences – excuses or justifications – to these offences, defences, that is to say, other than a denial of the Crown's basic story. Such defences depend on the judges too. 'Excuses' are a kind of 'Oops, sorry!' which is personal to the accused. 'I did it, but I am not really to blame. It was an accident or I didn't mean it.' (Denying malice might be seen as a kind of excuse.) Justifications, on the other hand, involve toughing it out. 'Too right I did it, but it was for a greater public purpose.' There are few justification cases in Scotland or elsewhere in the precise territory into which the accused sought to travel and all depends, as you will see, on the will (and creativity) of the judiciary.

The defence sought to bolster its case with expert testimony concerning the nature of the Trident weapons, nuclear diplomacy and the legal position concerning nuclear weapons, the latter involving the testimony of a highly qualified American professor of international law. The Sheriff who sat at the trial concluded that, in the particular stance of the case at the end of all the evidence, the defendants were entitled to succeed on their justification arguments as a matter of law. She entered a verdict of not guilty without sending the case to the jury. If I understand the structure of Scottish law on which she proceeded, the prosecution carries the burden of persuasion to negative any defence raised by the accused. The accused may have an evidentiary burden, the burden of going forward and raising an issue, but then the prosecution must negate it beyond reasonable doubt. The accused does not have to prove innocence. The Sheriff was faced with a situation where all the testimony on justification was on the part of the defence. The defendants had met any evidentiary burden which lay upon them. In the absence of rebuttal by the Government, there was not even a jury question.

This decision of the Sheriff was not directly appealable. Principles of double jeopardy, or *non bis in idem*, preclude entry of a conviction or even a re-trial after such an acquittal. The Crown, using a peculiar Scottish procedure known as a 'Lord Advocate's Reference' asked, however, for certain issues of law, said to arise in the case, to be ruled upon by the Scottish appellate court, the High Court of Justiciary. (The Crown, the losers below, thus became 'the appellants', the defendants became 'the respondents' at the appeal stage.) As the defence pointed out, the questions were not precisely the ones that arose at trial. They were badly worded and sometimes tendentious (and the respondents responded in kind), but the Court answered them (and some variations on them) anyway. The answers supplied in what is called 'the Opinion of the Court' were not favourable to the respondents or to those who would assay similar endeavours in Scotland. The High Court went to some pains (constrained by the peculiar procedure?) to avoid regarding itself as bound by the facts as seen by the trial judge. It proceeded on the basis of 'hypothetical' facts, to the undoubted disgust of the respondents who had made a great effort to establish the 'real' facts. I think, however, that the High Court accepts that the burden of persuasion is on the prosecution, although sometimes in the Opinion they seem to be requiring a lot of the defence. My hunch is that if the High Court judges had been able to second guess the precise holding of the trial judge they would have reversed her, but that course was not available to them. I suspect also that, if they could, they would have rationalised such a result by asserting that the testimony about Trident simply did not relate to a substantive defence that was 'open' to the accused. The defendants, on this line of reasoning, would have failed to meet an evidentiary burden of raising an appropriate issue. The acquittal, as I have noted, stands in the present case, but the next activist in Scotland beware!

The question of admissibility of some of the evidence was much debated in the Lord Advocate's Reference. The expert evidence as to international law, the High Court holds, should not go to the jury, although in appropriate cases the judge might inform herself by listening to experts. Judges know, or can be enlightened, about the law. Juries should hear it directly from the trial judge, not from a professor, said the court. This does not dispose of the other expert material on weapons and on diplomatic developments involving nuclear weapons that was admitted by the trial judge. The High Court's opinion was not sought as to that and the admissibility of such material falls to be decided on another day. There is a cautionary moral here: litigants who seek to push the envelope may find themselves equally cut off by rulings on what is admissible as a matter of evidence as by rulings on what is an area of substance into which they may enter.

I turn to a few thoughts about International Law and about Criminal Law which were stimulated for me by these proceedings. They do not purport to cover all the issues raised in this rich tapestry of a case.

2. *International Law*

On July 8, 1996, the International Court of Justice answered a question posed to it by the General Assembly of the United Nations, namely: 'Is the threat or use of nuclear weapons in any circumstance permitted under international law?' The question was asked because people all over the world got behind an initiative called the World Court Project and forced their governments, kicking and struggling in many cases, to act. The opinion of the court was complex; so too were the fourteen additional separate opinions offered by each of the judges who participated in the proceedings. The argument before the International Court had ranged over many of the fundamental issues in modern international law: the laws of armed conflict, including rules relating to weapons that are indiscriminate in their ability to distinguish between combatants and non-combatants, or which cause unnecessary suffering; international human rights law; international environmental law; and the basic sources and structure of international law. Three of the fourteen judges were of the view that any use or threat of use of nuclear weapons would be unlawful in all circumstances. Seven judges, who with the casting (second) vote of the President of the Court constituted a majority, held that it would 'generally' be contrary to the laws of war to use or threaten to use the weapons in question. The seven were, however, not sure whether that use 'would be lawful or unlawful in an extreme circumstance of self-defence in which the very survival of a State would be at stake.' Four judges were not prepared to go even as far as 'generally'. While they conceded that a threat or use of nuclear weapons could only be made when it was compatible with the requirements of international law applicable to armed conflict, they believed that each individual case has to be considered against the relevant standards and that no general rule is possible. On one significant matter, the Court was unanimous: 'There exists an obligation to pursue in good faith and bring to a conclusion negotiations leading to nuclear disarmament in all its aspects under strict and effective international control.' That obligation is based on the 1968 Nuclear Non-Proliferation Treaty but has now become one of international customary law. At the Non-Proliferation Treaty Review Conference in 2000, the government of the United Kingdom joined in the consensus 'unequivocal undertaking by the nuclear weapon states to accomplish the total elimination of their nuclear arsenals.'

I was privileged to be one of the lawyers who argued the nuclear weapons case in the International Court on behalf of the government of Samoa, a small state which sees its security as tied fundamentally to the rule of law. A distinguished British lawyer, representing Solomon Islands, another small state, pointedly asked the court whether it was true 'that laws are spider webs through which big flies pass and the little ones get caught?' Is it true that the law does well with dealing with small-time murderers, but if the scale is large enough it cannot cope? I like to think that the earnest effort of all fourteen of the judges to answer the question reflects their understanding that a credible law (domestic or international) must speak to all levels, the lowly and the mighty. The law has something to say even about a weapon with the awesome power to destroy us all. But saying is not enough. How can one ensure that law of this ilk is obeyed? What is to be done when the fox (the state) is guarding the chickens (the people)? I am sure that the British lawyer who asked about the flies, and all the rest of us who argued at the Hague for the illegality of nuclear weapons, had no illusions that the court's opinion would act like a magic wand and miraculously wish away all the existing weapons and ensure that no-one again let the genie out of the bottle. (How can one talk about such issues without depending on metaphor?) We knew that more action, by governments and by lay people, would be necessary. Law is like that. It provides a normative framework for action and for shaping understanding of some types of complex phenomena. But it does not execute itself. People at all levels of society, including legislators and judges, are needed to do that. But how to galvanize the government into action? Can the national courts be persuaded to help? Or would they rather not? Do I detect a note of pique in the opinion of the Scottish High Court when it comments that 'in addition to their claimed aim of physical prevention of what was being done by the Government in relation to Trident, the respondents appear also to have had, and still to have, the quite different aim of obtaining from a British court a finding that the Government's conduct was criminal.'? Is that so terrible?

A Trident submarine apparently patrols the seas armed with forty-eight warheads, each about eight or ten times more powerful than the weapon that obliterated Hiroshima, weapons that are capable of quickly being aimed at some potential enemy who is no doubt well aware of this. They represent a powerful statement, a threat even. How can this rather specific threat (and the first strike capability that accompanies it) be compatible with the 'general' rules in the International Court's Opinion about not using nuclear weapons? Is not Trident inherently unlawful? How could any possible potential use of it meet the requirements of the ten person majority of the International Court of Justice? It may well be that a (different) majority of the court was not prepared to say that 'mere possession' of nuclear weapons was illegal. But Trident's mobile deployment goes far beyond possession. It is patrolling and ready to fire; its capacity is known rather precisely. What, moreover, does the continued deployment of such armed submarines, and work on their stealth infrastructure, say about the British government's commitment, underscored by the International Court, to negotiating nuclear disarmament? I'd come out the same way the defendants and their witnesses came out. The High Court, however, reached the conclusion after a lengthy discussion of the Advisory Opinion that they were 'not persuaded that even upon the respondents' description of, or hypothesis as to, the characteristics of Trident it would be possible to say *a priori* that a threat to use it, or its use, could never be seen as compatible with the requirements of international humanitarian law.' So much for a finding that the government's conduct was criminal!

For many of the judges and lawyers involved, this must have been a scary but horizon-expanding effort to exercise the legal imagination, to think about the unthinkable. The trial judge seems to have had some sort of epiphany in the course of the proceedings. It led her, in addition to entering an acquittal, to write a careful and eloquent report for the appellate Lords, to which the latter, who had no such epiphany, barely deigned to make reference. Angela Zelter, the *pro se* defendant, was unkind enough to make reference in her creative argument before the learned Lords to the Justice Case which took place in the second round of trials at Nuremberg (brilliantly dramatized in Stanley Kramer's 1961 film, *Judgment at Nuremberg*). The decision there has some fairly strong stuff on the obligation of judges in the face of abuse of power. It follows the learning of the first Nuremberg trial that international obligations must sometimes trump domestic law. I don't find any reference to it in the opinion of the Court. The Scottish Lords even toyed with the idea that the legality of Trident was not justiciable, even in criminal proceedings, that it was for the politicians to decide what international law requires when armaments are at issue. Reluctantly, however, since the Crown apparently did not mind if they weighed in, they addressed the issues, albeit in my view coming to the wrong conclusion (namely that it was all perfectly legal).

3. *Criminal Law*

I come to the Criminal Law. The Nuclear Weapons Advisory Proceedings were addressed specifically to the issue of when a state may use or threaten to use nuclear weapons. The Nuremberg Tribunal, in a catchy aphorism, made the point that 'crimes against international law are committed by men, not by abstract entities'.

Personally, I have no real problem with the notion that both the state and those who act in its name may act in a criminal fashion and even be subject to appropriate sanction. But sanction is not the only way to deal with breach of the law. Sometimes self-help and even Samaritan-help is in order. Ah, but when? The Nuremberg and Tokyo Tribunals insisted that some things may be criminal under international law even if they are consistent with the domestic law of the place where they are committed. On occasion, a citizen, at least one in high office, has an obligation to object and object strongly.

What is a person to do if she sees the state and its agents engaging in acts that appear to be illegal, if not downright criminal, under international law? Take something concrete like the deployment of the British Trident submarines. If, as the High Court did for the purposes of argument, one accepts the defendants' analysis of Trident, two lines of legal argument suggest themselves. One emerges particularly from the Tokyo war crimes trial, the other from basic principles of criminal law that appear in most legal systems.

Speaking of the responsibility of those in charge of prisoners of war, the Tokyo Tribunal said, at one point:

> If such a person had, or should, but for negligence or supineness, have had such knowledge [that ill-treatment was occurring] he is not excused for inaction if his office required or permitted him to take any action to prevent such crimes. On the other hand, it is not

enough for the exculpation of a person, otherwise responsible, for him to show that he accepted assurances from others more directly associated with the control of prisoners if having regard to the position of those others, to the frequency of reports of such crimes, or to any other circumstances he should have been put upon further enquiry as to whether those assurances were true or untrue.

How far does this obligation extend? The Tokyo trial was about the responsibility of the top civilian and military officials. It did not speak to the criminal responsibility of the populace in general, since the decision had been made that only selected top people would be prosecuted. Is there a duty on ordinary people (like the Trident Three) who know (or have reason to know?) that what seems to be a crime of state is going on? If there is no duty, for breach of which a citizen might be haled before an international tribunal, might there nonetheless be a right or a privilege to act? The responsible citizen presumably barrages her MP with questions and advice, complains to the authorities including the police, writes letters to the editor, runs for political office even. The accused here did this. What if it all fails? Should the citizen act, however quixotically, to stop it? The High Court certainly puts a damper on this line of argument. After a discussion that hardly does justice to the international material, the court pours scorn on the idea as it concludes that 'customary international law does not entitle persons such as the respondents to intervene as self-appointed substitute law-enforcers with a right to commit what would otherwise be criminal offences in order to stop, or inhibit, the criminal acts of others'.

If international law won't work directly, how about the more familiar Criminal Law notions of necessity? Someone is coming at me with a hatchet, screaming murder. I kill him first. I commit no crime. The law says that I am justified. I do not have an obligation to kill him (I could cheerfully accept my fate), but I do have a privilege to do so. The same is true if the hatchet-wielding one is aiming for my neighbour. The Good Samaritan is as justified as the person saving her own skin. It gets more complicated if the actor is mistaken. The hatchet is really a toy and the whole event is a practical joke. But most legal systems even allow some leeway for error, at least reasonable ones, an excuse perhaps, rather than a justification. Finally, think about this: I see someone about to jump off the bridge to certain death. Suicide (or attempted suicide) is no longer a crime. I tackle him and save him, at least for today. Most legal systems regard me as justified. He has a right to kill himself; I have right to try to stop him.

How far does justification based on some sort of necessity go? Think of Trident. Is someone trying to stop its deployment acting, at least arguably, in defence of the vulnerable population of a potential enemy? Of neutrals who may be destroyed willy-nilly? Preventing all of us from global suicide? What if that person believes that what she is doing is justified by such considerations and a law professor in a suit is prepared to say on oath that her belief is at least a reasonable one?

Generations of law students on both sides of the Atlantic have grappled with the question whether (individualised) self defence or defence of another may be generalisable into a wider category of necessity, and if so, how wide. The case they study is The Queen v. Dudley and Stephens, from late Victorian England. Castaways at sea killed and ate the weakest among them, the cabin boy. The court said that Englishmen did not do that sort of thing (patently false since there were other similar incidents) and the death sentence was duly pronounced. The Executive exercised the prerogative of mercy and Dudley and Stephens served only six months. The public seemed to be adamantly in favour of the accused. Does the case stand for the proposition that there is no general defence of necessity, or only that it did not apply there? The beauty of the common law is that no one knows!

Scottish law, it seems, has a doctrine of necessity which is wider than self defence. The High Court Lords were not prepared to commit themselves to its exact parameters, but at least they knew it could not apply here. There was, for example, the question of imminence and the connections between what is threatened and what is done. Eating the cabin boy certainly buys time for rescue, but what of imminence? Who is to say? Are the sails of rescue just beyond the horizon? The cases tend to say that the danger must be imminent or at least that the necessity to act arises on the present occasion. In the hatchet case, the hatchet is poised. Is Trident poised in the same way? Should it make a difference, as the High Court seems to think, that the Trident Three spent time contemplating their actions? Is spontaneity all-important? On the connections: killing the hatchet-wielder stops the action. The Trident Three were committed to nonviolence where people are concerned – they were not about to kill the captain of the Trident whose finger was near the nuclear trigger. Dumping the computer may or may not stop the action for the time being – probably not. (One hopes the security on the backup systems was better than that the Three encountered, that is to say, none!) It must represent some inhibition on the enterprise. Close enough? The High Court raises the barrier of effectiveness: 'Moreover, there is not the slightest indication that the damage which the respondents did, and which they apparently claim was necessary as a means of averting or perhaps reducing danger or harm, had or could have had any conceivable impact upon the supposedly immediate risk.'

4. *Concluding thoughts*

Dudley and Stephens lost in the Queen's Bench Divisional Court, but history and the power of public opinion were much kinder to them. I suspect that a hundred years from now, the themes raised in this book will continue to provide sustenance for the legal imagination, the way the case of Dudley and Stephens has done in the past century.

These are not ordinary cases. The Trident Three do not stand alone. Many others are pushing the limits as they attack pieces of the Trident infrastructure and other manifestations of nuclear madness. The Trident Three were not the first people with enough faith in the power of international law to give it a run for the money. They won't be the last. Those of us who would like to leave a world to our progeny are indebted to them for trying. I commend this work to all who seek total nuclear disarmament (regardless of what they think of the Trident Ploughshares tactics) and to all who would like to explore the cutting edges of International Law and of Criminal Law.

Roger S. Clark
Board of Governors Professor, Rutgers University School of Law, Camden, New Jersey

Resistance and Hope Rap

by Brian Quail, *Local Heroes Affinity Group*

Resistance is private and personal.
It is the quiet and unremarked daily rejection
of all that degrades and debases.
It is the silent and solemn persistence
in not surrendering to the system.
Resistance is keeping our inner vision
clear and intact.

Resistance is public and political,
It confronts the bloody face
of militarism and money.
Defies Moloch –
pitiless idol of power and wealth
ever hungry for sacrifice,
for our children's' blood.

Resistance is Rosa Parkes saying;
'I'm black, but I will not sit in the back
of the bus – I'm sitting right here in the front.'
Resistance is Dan Berrigan
burning draft cards for the war in Vietnam,
saying 'I'm burning cards
because I'd rather burn paper
than burn people'.
And the folk shouting:
'Hell, No, we won't go!'.
Resistance is the rose red flames
that burnt Jan Palach in Prague,
and the Buddhist monks in Vietnam.

Resistance is not just then
and for heroes,
Resistance is now too
and it's for me and it's for you.
Resistance is boycotting Nestle and Nike
and Gap and Adidas and BAe

and all the rest of the rich racketeers.
It is saying No! to consumerist crap
No! to terminator seeds, No! to GM
No! to racist immigration laws
And No! to vouchers for refugees.
Resistance is calling out
'Free Mumia Abu Jamal'.
Resistance is Faslane Peace Camp
saying we're staying,
tunnels and tree tops telling
Evict the base, not the camp.
Resistance is blockading Faslane gate,
it is cutting the cagewire at Coulport.
Cold Hell where Creation is defiled,
and the Creator reviled.
And we are shouting:
'Hell, No, we won't glow!'

Local Heroes planning their actions. From left to right – Eric Wakllace,
Una Campbell, David Mackenzie, Jane Tallents,
Brian Quail, Barbara Macgregor, El Stobo

Resistance is patient and slow and unhurried
It is the long talking and walking with friends and family
And talking too with the folk that call us fools,
tools of foreign tyrants and troublemakers.
Resistance is reaching out
to peace-people and to polis,
to punters and passers by.
Resistance is global and it's local;
It's Seattle and Sighthill.
It is Prague and Partick.
It is Davos and Drumchapel ...
Resistance is obedience to the me in you,
and the you in me,
to the god within.
Resistance is disobedience
to the gods of metal,
to the voices that howl hate,
to the prophets of profit,
to the seekers and preachers of power,
to the merchants of murder,
to the buyers and sellers
in the temple of hope ...

... HOPE

Hope is no half-hearted holy optimism about the far
future.
It is not sentimental sloganising like
'Always look on the bright side'.
Hope is not an expectation or an anticipation
   that we will live to see the results of our labours.
The seed never sees the flower ...
Hope doesn't claim somehow things will get better
   – they may well get worse.
Hope is what is left when everything is gone
   – including hope.
Because hope lives in the here and now.
She speaks to the living present.

Hope affirms the meaning and value
of the now-life in all its fullness.
Hope does not gaze wistfully into the future.
She cherishes the present
Because Hope is not a time song,
Hope is a love song

So I am telling you:
If you are not saying no,
you're saying yes.
Silence is consent,
silence is complicity.
Stand up and be counted
Don't spectate – participate.
Don't be paralysed by analysis.
Walk the talk.
If not you – who?
And if not now – when?
Get active – not radioactive.
Don't spectate – demonstrate.
Don't sit on the fence – cut it
like all those women did
at Greenham Common.
Remember Rosa Parkes.
Get your butt to the front,
And the front is Faslane.
Experience empowerment.
Live liberation through participation.

Resist Trident – Celebrate hope

We will overcome!

Message from the Muse

by David Mackenzie, *Local Heroes Affinity Group*

You dropped me so suddenly
'I'm off,' you said, 'there's work to be done
And no time for the long soaking in trances.'
You felt I'd understand – but you did worry
when they said: 'Have you written anything recently?'
 – and no guarantee I'd still be behind
the familiar green door when the struggle was done
and you all came home.

Daft bugger! I've been out there from the start,
Just waiting.

A Little Nuclear Crime Prevention up the Goil

by Angie Zelter, *Pheasants Union Affinity Group*

We painted the last of our banners, checked our equipment, and took our last walks in the beautiful Scottish hills. We had a wonderful treat of a meal with our favourite food and some wine. We made the last calls to our loved ones – how long would it be before we saw them again? Ulla had come over from Denmark some days before and I had left my home in North Norfolk to join Ellen in her cottage for the last of our preparations. We were almost ready for our act of disarmament and we were all nervous in our different ways about what lay ahead. Would we succeed in our plans? Would it make a difference? Whether we succeeded or not, we knew we would be imprisoned for some months and possibly for several long years. We were avid to experience our last moments of freedom to the utmost – the pleasure of getting up and walking out of doors, looking into the starlit sky, hugging friends – the little things we took for granted every day and which would soon be denied to us.

June 8 dawned a brilliant sunny summer's day. Ulla went ahead with two friends to check on the weather and conditions on Loch Goil. We received a phone call to say conditions were perfect. Ellen and I, helped by another friend, who was driving us to Loch Goil, packed the inflatable boat, engine, petrol, jackets, sandwiches and tools into the van – we were off. I sat holding the engine upright worrying about whether it would start properly. I had checked it on land and it had been fine, but the previous two times I had tried it out on the water it had failed to get going. However, the friend who had donated it to us and had once more serviced it for us, had assured me that it 'would work alright on the day'.

Our timing had to be just right as we did not want to attract attention by hanging around too long by the side of the loch. Nor did we want to leave other vital support people exposed too long – David was to be in position with a camera hiding by the side of the loch with a good view over to *Maytime*, the barge which was our target. This floating laboratory, run by the Defence Evaluation

Preparations – from left to right: Ellen Morley, Angie Zelter, Ulla Roder
Credit: David Mackenzie

and Research Agency, is a vital part of the nuclear weapon system as it measures and reduces the magnetic, acoustic, thermal, radar and visual signals that Trident submarines make, guaranteeing their invisibility in the water.

We were all nervous. The Ministry of Defence police patrolled from time to time and had a land-based security office right opposite David's hide-out – they would be able to see us very clearly as we crossed the loch to *Maytime* and then there were the security cameras on the barge itself. During our two previous reconnaissances there had been a heavy police boat and car presence. It was, however, up to luck now – we had done all we could to prepare.

We arrived at the edge of the loch at 7pm on the dot and there were Ulla and friends, pretending to be tourists enjoying the summer evening. A quick hug all round, and then to work. Out came the boat and equipment. We had to inflate it and get it loaded and launched, and the engine locked on. The lifejackets were tied on and we each slung in our tool bags. We waved goodbye to our three friends as if we were off on an innocent boat trip up the loch and I started the engine. It worked! Relief all round. Half way out to the barge the engine shuddered but with a little coaxing it strengthened again. How I wished we were as well resourced as the police were, or even Greenpeace! There were no police patrols about so we made our way straight to the barge where Ellen and Ulla scuttled up the ladder and started to try various doors and openings.

I tied up the boat and was immediately drawn to a window on the side. Amazingly it opened – we later found out it was the only unlocked window on the barge! Calling the others in a low voice, I clambered onto a side rail and up and in through the window. It led into the main research laboratory – the biggest room in the barge – and was full of computers and equipment. As I looked around I realised that it made no sense to smash them up where they were – the cleanest, safest and quickest way to disarm this laboratory was to throw everything into the loch. I unplugged a computer and lugged it over to a larger window which I was able to open from the inside. Meanwhile, Ulla had joined me. We decided that Ellen should stay on the outside so we could hand the equipment to her through the window – she had the joyous task of throwing everything into the water. As she explained, in one of her letters from prison later, it was a wonderfully liberating experience: she felt as if she were getting rid of the 'building blocks of oppression: Trident, the 'free' market, the exploitation of children, unbridled militarism, the all-pervading violence of society, third world debt'.

I had no time to enjoy it at that stage, I was still nervous and worried, conscious that we might only have a few minutes more before being discovered and I wanted to do as good a job as possible of disabling the lab before being stopped. After all, we were inside the laboratory that tests how to make and keep Trident invisible when patrolling the oceans. However, we were not invisible. Surely, they would find us soon!

I was sweating profusely and getting out of breath. Some of the equipment was heavy and had to be lifted shoulder high to get up through the windows. After a while, we slowed down a bit. Ulla climbed out and helped Ellen put up the banners, so that David could get some good pictures for the press. The one we had finished painting only the night before said 'Stop Nuclear Death Research – DERA = Deadly Efficient Research for Annihilation'.

The other two had been made by Ellen's permanent affinity group who call themselves 'The Gareloch Horticulturalists'. One was beautifully painted and showed rainbow coloured people pushing Trident into the sunlight with the words 'Bringing Crime into the Light' and the other said 'Constructive Deconstruction' and 'TRIDENT PLOUGHSHARES 2000 Opposes Research for Genocide'.

Ulla then started work on disarming other bits of equipment around the barge, including the cranes and winches used to control the model submarine. I continued to work inside, slowly clearing the room of all equipment for the two outside to tip in the loch. Next, Ellen and Ulla climbed in and between us we emptied all the cupboards and trays and went into the other rooms on the barge to complete the job. We threw overboard all the computers, phones, faxes, documentation, manuals, discs, spare parts – everything moveable, except for first aid and safety equipment.

David, described the scene later in the following words, 'It was riveting to be on the shore and take it all in, the small scurrying figures, the sharp clang of metal, the frequent heavy splashes of sinking hardware and the delicate fluttering of hundreds of sheets of paper.'

On board *Maytime* – from left to right: Angie Zelter, Ellen Moxley, Ulla Roder
Credit: David MacKenzie.

There was a metal cage in the corner where I discovered the expensive electrical control box for the model submarine, used in the testing. It took a good half-hour to cut our way into this with our bolt-cutters, to check there were no live electrical connections, and to smash and cut the cables and switches. That felt good and I began to realise that we were going to have time to do it all thoroughly. There was no indication that we had been seen at all despite the noise.

Having completed our work inside the barge we left it clean and tidy (it felt a bit like housework) and lay out on the now empty work-tables a copy of our joint statement, video, handbook, and pictures of the terrible destruction of Hiroshima and Nagasaki. We had spent a great deal of time writing our joint statement to explain what we were doing and why. We hoped to use it in the court case and wanted it to accurately reflect our motivation. After introducing ourselves and explaining our intentions we had written,

8 June 1999 – *Maytime* Laboratory, Joint Statement of Ellen, Ulla and Angie.

We wish to make it quite clear that our actions are not politically motivated (although we realise they have a political dimension). Our actions are based primarily on the legal and ethical premise that the UK's Trident nuclear weapon system is a system preparing for the mass murder of innocent civilians over untold generations and we believe that the Trident system is ethically unjustifiable as well as being unlawful in international law. As loving, feeling, human beings we feel responsible for trying to do everything in our power to prevent the Trident system from being able to operate with the proviso that our actions are safe, nonviolent, open and accountable.

All three of us have spent long years trying the many conventional ways our society has devised for the righting of great wrongs. After having educated ourselves and thought about the issues, hearing the different viewpoints, and concluding that nuclear weapons are terroristic weapons of mass destruction that could never be used ethically or lawfully we have demonstrated against them, written and published articles and educational materials, arranged public meetings, leafleted the general public and military personnel, signed petitions, held vigils, lobbied Parliament and spoken to our constituency Members of Parliament. When our attempts to get our parliamentary representatives to act on our behalf have failed we have even gone to the courts, the police and other official institutions in our societies and asked for their help to bring the government to court to hear our legal arguments on the unlawfulness of British preparations to use nuclear weapons. On an international level we have supported similar initiatives including the successful NGO led campaign to ask the ICJ to advise on the legality of all nuclear weapons. Applying this general Advisory Opinion of the World Court to the UK nuclear system it is quite clear that any use of one of the UK's 100 kiloton warheads would be unlawful. We have tried all manner of ways to stop this terrible threat to ours and others' lives and environment but have failed. Each person or institution that we have encountered along our way have agreed that nuclear weapons in general are terrible, that the world would be a better and safer place without them, but each have denied their own personal responsibility, saying the responsibility lies with another. We do not agree. Each of us must take responsibility and not just pass it on to someone else. Therefore we can see no alternative to taking direct disarmament action ourselves. We have thus, each in our separate ways, come to this point, where we have decided to disarm equipment essential to the full deployment of the UK's Trident submarine based nuclear weapon system.

We do it now, when our countries (Denmark, England and Scotland are all a part of NATO) are at war in the Balkans and the threat of nuclear war is probably higher than it has been for a very long time. We have read with horror of suggestions that nuclear bombs could be dropped at targets in Serbia and that if we have nuclear weapons then this is the time to use them. Russia has already responded with counter threats of using nuclear weapons. Whatever the conflict, it is always wrong to use nuclear weapons. We do this act of disarmament now in a time of war in order to take responsibility as global citizens to try to prevent the possibility that nuclear weapons would be used.

We will attempt to disarm the floating laboratory complex in Loch Goil so that it will not be able to contribute to the active deployment of Trident with its weapons of mass destruction.

After detailing what we hoped to be able to disarm we continued,

We will disarm this equipment with sadness and regret for the people who have invested so much of their personal time and energy in these technical experiments and who may feel that we are attacking their personal work. We justify our actions as being necessary however, because these experiments are part of the complex nuclear weapon system that enables the UK to threaten terrible mass destruction that affects us all. However well-intentioned the technicians of DERA or of the Ministry of Defence may be, it is nevertheless absolutely inexcusable that their work should put all of our lives at such risk. The long-lasting effects of the radioactive fallout across national borders and through to unborn generations from any detonation (either accidental or in self-defence) of Trident's nuclear warheads are a threat so immense that our thoughtful, calm, considered and reasonable disarmament action of this part of the nuclear system is a very responsible remedial action. The technicians and scientists involved in the work at the DERA facilities could much better give up the Trident connected work and be involved in building up their research and support work for peaceful projects that are of benefit to the whole global community.

Our disarmament work is done in a spirit of love and compassion. We understand that it may not be viewed sympathetically by the authorities but hope that it will help the nuclear disarmament process.

We left this statement inside with our other offerings and clambered outside to consider our next steps. There was another nearby research barge which we had hoped to disarm in a similar manner, but we discovered that by this time our inflatable had lost much of its air and would not be safe to travel on. We therefore decided to try to launch one of the life-rafts to enable us to cross over to the other DERA barge, *Newt*.

We followed the instructions and were rewarded with a huge whoosh of released compressed air, which filled the life-raft. It was great fun. I had always wanted to release one to see what happened and this was an excellent excuse to indulge my curiosity. Unfortunately it landed upside down, and as we did not want to struggle in the water to get it turned around we went to the front of the barge to release the other one but this one failed entirely to break open.

By this time the light was beginning to fade and the sunset was glorious. We decided we needed a well earned rest and a chance to think. So we sat on the top of the barge and thoroughly enjoyed the picnic Ellen had packed for us. I had been rather disparaging about it as she had packed it that morning, thinking to myself that we would have no time for such luxuries as food and drink. In the event I was delighted she had ignored me and we were able to celebrate our success so far and have a party, grinning at each other in the beautiful light.

We are pretty sure that it was the press release our supporters had sent out just after 9pm that eventually alerted the security people to the fact that they had a problem 'up the Goil', but it still took a while before they reached us. We had decided to dismantle a communications antenna on the roof of the barge and had discovered another locked room on the side of the barge. We were back at work trying to drill into this room when the police finally showed up about 10.30pm. We walked up to their boat as it came alongside, helping them tie up, smiling and telling them we were quite peaceful and friendly and had been engaged in a little nuclear crime prevention, would they like to join us? With smiles all round, they asked us to get into the police launch and so began our arrest and remand.

A while later we heard another boat arrive and a surprised and angry voice rang out, 'What have they done to all my stuff?' It was the barge master!

CHAPTER ONE

People's Disarmament

TRIDENT PLOUGHSHARES IS ONE of the latest campaigns in a long and honourable line of citizen's initiatives to try to rid the world of nuclear weapons. It is dedicated to peaceful acts of practical disarmament. The whole campaign is based on international law and the basic human right to life. People from many different nations come together as 'global citizens' and begin the task of peacefully dismantling the nuclear system. It has begun with the UK nuclear weapon system that is called Trident and which is based at Faslane in Scotland. Disarmament by Trident Ploughshares involves the safe destruction of fences and equipment essential to the nuclear weapons system, just as disarmament does when it is part of an 'official' international disarmament agreement. It is not criminal damage but practical and lawful 'people's disarmament'.

Of course, the UK government and its institutions do not see it this way. Since Trident Ploughshares began in August 1998, there have been over 1,220 arrests, mainly at the blockades and disarmament camps, held **dedicated to** every three months, at Coulport and **peaceful acts of** Faslane in Scotland. There have been over 110 trials completed and over 1,200 days **practical** have been spent in prison, not including the **disarmament** days in police custody. Although around £15,000 worth of fines have been imposed so far, only a very small proportion of these have been paid as most disarmers are refusing to pay.

We now have 179 'global citizens' from 15 different countries, who have pledged to prevent nuclear crime and have taken part in a two day workshop on nonviolence. Having citizens from other countries joining in our disarmament work with us, appearing in the courts and spending time in our prisons, has been much harder for the authorities to deal with. The government and the courts like to pretend that British nuclear weapons are a purely British affair, but find this position untenable when foreigners appear in court to explain why they feel threatened by Britain and are joining with many other nationalities as 'global citizens' and have pledged to peacefully disarm British Trident.

The Pledge is based upon our right, under international law, to take nonviolent, accountable, and safe actions to disarm the British Trident nuclear weapons system. The Pledge and the common training form the basis of our ability to co-operate safely and easily with other Pledgers when we come together in the peace camps. We may not know each other but we know we share a common basis for action.

PLEDGE TO PREVENT NUCLEAR CRIME

I am aware that the UK signed the Non-Proliferation Treaty in 1968, Article VI of which stated that each of the parties 'undertakes to pursue negotiations in good faith on effective measures relating to cessation of the nuclear arms race at an early date and to nuclear disarmament, and to a treaty on general and complete disarmament under strict and effective international control'. Over thirty years have now passed and the UK still continues the nuclear arms race and nato is still a nuclear alliance containing three of the major nuclear powers. The Trident system is an escalation in the UK's nuclear capability having three times the range, being far more accurate and being able to hit eight times as many targets as the Polaris system it replaces.

I am also aware that on 8th July 1996, the President of the International Court of Justice (which is the highest legal body of the United Nations), Mohammed Bedjaoui, stated, 'The nuclear weapon, the ultimate evil, destabilises humanitarian law which is the law of the lesser evil. The existence of nuclear weapons is therefore a challenge to the very existence of humanitarian law, not to mention their long-term effects of damage to the human environment, in respect to which the right to life must be exercised'. The Court confirmed that the Declaration of St. Petersburg, the Hague Conventions, the Nuremberg Principles, the Geneva Conventions, and the Genocide Convention all apply to nuclear weapons. It stated very clearly that the threat or use of nuclear weapons is generally contrary to international humanitarian law. The Court could find no lawful circumstance for the threat or use of nuclear weapons.

I believe that the Trident nuclear weapon system is illegal, dangerous, unjust, polluting, a terrible waste of resources, and deeply immoral. I think Trident poses a threat rather than a defence.

It is the duty of every citizen to uphold the law relating to nuclear weapons and under the Nuremberg Principles carefully, safely and peacefully to disarm any nuclear weapon system that is breaching humanitarian law. I am also aware that most national legal systems, including the UK's and other NATO countries' legal systems, allow serious damage to be done to objects if the damage is done in the belief that this would prevent serious crime from taking place. I believe that the damage Trident Ploughshares activists intend to cause to the UK Trident system will stop the ongoing crime of threatening to use nuclear weapons contrary to humanitarian law.

As a global citizen with international, national and individual responsibility, I will endeavour peacefully, safely, openly and accountably to help to disarm the UK nuclear weapon system. I will do this by actively joining with others in the Trident Ploughshares Project. This means that until the UK Government guarantees to completely disarm the British Trident system, then I pledge either, personally, to enter Faslane, Coulport and any other Trident related facility, or to help and support other Trident Ploughshares activists to enter these places, in order that I or others can dismantle the system in such a way that it can not be used to threaten or harm living.

Our plans, motivation and organisational structures are open to the public, the government and military. A freely accessible web-site contains all our materials including our *Tri-Denting It Handbook*. Every three months we send updated lists of all Pledgers to the government, along with continued requests for dialogue and negotiation. We continue to

> how can a 100 kiloton nuclear warhead ever be used in a way that can distinguish between a military target and innocent civilians?

ask awkward questions – like how can a 100 kiloton nuclear warhead ever be used in a way that distinguishes between a military target and innocent civilians – to which we have received no satisfactory replies to date.

At the beginning of the campaign we formed a Dialogue and Negotiation Team which produced the first open letter to the Prime Minister on 18 March 1998 and has sent letters every three months since then. This group contains people connected at an international level with the Conference on Disarmament, the

Middle Powers Initiative and the New Agenda Coalition, so that the information and the requests made to the UK government are in line and consistent with the international peace movement.

We encourage parliamentarians to sign our Petition of Support, around 80 have now signed including 13 from the new Scottish parliament, 9 from the Welsh Assembly, as well as 18 MEPs. We network with other organisations such as the World Court Project, CND and Global 2000 in our lobbying work and have kept up a constant stream of parliamentary questions which are now yielding some useful answers. Our parliamentary supporters help get answers to our letters, ask questions for us and are beginning to join our disarmament actions. Tommy Sheridan, the Scottish Socialist Party Member of the Scottish Parliament, George Galloway, an MP from the Labour Party, and Caroline Lucas, a Green MEP, were arrested with us at the Faslane Blockade in February 2001. Tommy had taken part in a similar blockade a year previously and had already been sent to prison for five days for non-payment of fines just before Christmas. He was given a great deal of support by his constituency for having the guts to stand up for his beliefs.

Similar to the Pledge to Prevent Nuclear Crime, which each Trident Ploughshares Pledger signs, the Petition of Support applauds the Pledgers' attempts at safe, nonviolent, active and practical disarmament. It is a good indicator of the general support the campaign is getting. Rowan Williams, the Archbishop of Wales, has signed along with other bishops and religious leaders. During the February 2001 blockade over 30 church ministers were arrested for their ethical blockade. Quite a number of academics including law professors such as Richard Falk and Conor Gearty have signed our petition. In February 2001 Ian Hamilton QC, a respected Scottish criminal lawyer, joined us at the blockade and was arrested for 'breach of the peace'. Well-known authors, actors and musicians have signified their support for us along with over a hundred non-governmental organisations and many thousands of individuals. This wide spectrum of support from many different parts of society prevents us from being easily marginalised.

We have written to the police and heads of the judicial system, suggesting to the Attorney General and Lord Advocate that they should arrest all of us for signing the Pledge if they think we are conspiring to commit crimes but that in our opinion it is the government and military who should be arrested for grave breaches of international humanitarian law.

We work in this safe, open and accountable manner because we want our methods for opposing Trident to be consistent with our vision of what we would like to see in its place.

Our careful reliance upon nonviolence and open accountability have led to very good relations with the general public and with the civil police, who note the embarrassment of the Ministry of Defence as we regularly breach the high security areas, gain access to military police boats to do citizens' war crime inspections and swim onto supposedly secure nuclear submarines.

Radical resistance to and confrontation of evil systems is undertaken with good humour and respect to the individuals within these systems. I am sure that our strict guidelines of no alcohol or drugs whilst engaged in disarmament work has helped tremendously in ensuring that our disarmament actions are seen as serious and considered work and that good personal relationships, essential in any real peacemaking, are encouraged.

The Ministry of Defence Police's annual report stated in 1999, 'The largest policing event of the year was that of the Trident Ploughshares 2000 fortnight of activity in August'. It goes on to say that over a five week period an additional 500 officers, above normal tasking levels were deployed. This shows it would not take much to overstretch them considering that they only have a total of around 4,000 officers for the whole of the UK! However, more importantly, the report uses phrases such as 'declared open actions' and also states 'Throughout the period, activists pursued various forms of nonviolent direct action to express their feelings against nuclear weapons and the Trident programme in particular'. It is significant that in court the majority of police witnesses readily agree that we are peaceful and courteous – they have certainly got part of our message. The other part – that they should be arresting the military personnel for engaging in conspiracy to commit mass murder – is proving more difficult for them to take on board, though I am sure we have some hidden support for our views!

All Trident Ploughshares Pledgers must be in affinity groups and agree to the safety and nonviolence groundrules, but there-after work as autonomously as they wish. Pledgers have chosen disarmament actions which range from blockades, to fence-cutting, to swimming onto the submarines and destroying equipment, to dismantling a research lab, to painting war crime warnings on military equipment and handing out leaflets to military base workers urging them to 'Refuse to be a war criminal'. We encourage as much diverse and active disarmament work as possible as long as it is safe and peaceful. We also encourage decommissioning work at as many different Trident related sites as possible. Our hand-book lists around 35 different Trident related sites in the UK and

Refuse to be a war criminal

we have carried out crime prevention activi-ties at 8 so far, concentrating on Faslane, Coulport, Aldermaston and Barrow.

The majority of the disarmament actions have caused minimal damage for maximum court clogging disruption. There have been at least 10 attempts at substantial disarmament damage in the last 18 months, with four groups managing to complete their actions causing hundreds of thousands of pounds worth of damage and delaying the operations of Trident related equipment. In February of 1999, Rachel and Rosie swam out to *Vengeance* in Barrow and destroyed the testing equipment on the tower. In June 1999, along with Ulla and Ellen, I took a boat to the floating laboratory, *Maytime*, in Loch Goil and threw all the research equipment into the loch. Susan and Martin, in November 2000, after cutting through security fencing, managed to disarm one of the nuclear convoy vehicles held at Wittering. Most recently on 27 April 2001, Ulla swam out to *Vanguard* at Faslane and painted 'useless' on the side of the submarine.

We call all of this damage 'disarmament' and 'nuclear crime prevention'.

The majority of disarmament actions however have taken place at Faslane naval base, and involves people in blockades and fence cutting. The effect of all the cases at Helensburgh District Court, which have arisen from the actions at Faslane and Coulport, has been cumulative. One of the magistrates has admit-ted that the large number of people involved in disarmament is overwhelming the court system which is why so many administrative mistakes are being made and why so few people are being called to court.

More and more local people are getting involved. And the ample sprinkling of foreign nationals keeps the international perspective to the fore, stopping the whole campaign from becoming stultified by parochialism. The global impact of threatening to use weapons of indiscriminate mass murder has been stressed in many different ways and in many different languages. A happy side-effect of this international co-operation has been welcome employment for local linguists in translating the proceedings for foreign activists whose knowledge of English is just not up to the muttered, half-audible, legal jargon of the prosecuting lawyers.

The media have been slow to report the emerging public discussion, awareness and concern at the ongoing nuclear arms race. They thought the nuclear arms issue had gone away with the ending of the Cold War. However, Trident Ploughshares Pledgers in many different and compelling ways have been exposing the destructive horror of Trident's nuclear warheads, the undermining of international law, the plans for the next generation of nuclear weapons and the expansion of UK bases to provide criminal support for Star Wars.

There have been four major Trident Ploughshares jury trials so far – three in England and one in Scotland. These have resulted in three acquittals, one hung jury, and two re-trials. There continue to be large numbers of district court cases in Scotland. As the pressure on Aldermaston rises, a build up of cases is beginning in the Reading/Newbury area.

Each of these trials is important because they confront the state and the legal system where they are most vulnerable – on a major law and order issue. This is why our campaign is causing such political and legal ripples.

Traditionally the law has been used against the people rather than the state – predominantly against the poor and against ethnic minorities, especially black people. Yet now, the people (the Trident Ploughshares Pledgers) have turned this around and have openly challenged the whole legal basis, and thus legitimacy, of the armed forces – one of the pillars of the state. They are demanding people centred law not state or corporation centred law.

Such a challenge has, of course, been mounted time and time again over the last 55 years of anti-nuclear campaigning. Nuclear weapons have always been unlawful and the Shimoda case in Tokyo in the 1960s showed clearly that the Hiroshima and Nagasaki bombings were war crimes. However, few citizen's campaigns have used the law in such a clear, pointed and consistent manner as Trident Ploughshares. Trident Ploughshares has based its whole campaign on international law and has used it to delegitimise nuclear weapons and legitimise our own actions and has done it in a highly public and confrontational manner so it cannot be ignored. We have kept the moral arguments to the fore by emphasising the links between morality and law. Trident Ploughshares uses the ICJ Advisory Opinion of 1996 as the legal foundation to encourage implementation of this Opinion and to pressurise our governments to uphold international law.

Our argument is very straightforward. Nuclear weapons are weapons of mass destruction and thus cannot be used with any precision or any pretence at righting any wrong. It is basically mass murder on a catastrophic scale with the potential for escalation to the use of thousands of nuclear weapons, which could put an end to all life on earth. Law is based upon morality and is respected in so far and only in so far, as it conforms to common human morality. Governments, soldiers and armed forces gain their legitimacy and power from the law. What distinguishes a soldier from a common murderer is that he has been given legal permission to undertake certain kinds of killing on behalf of society. This legalised killing is carefully controlled by laws – the most important of which are international humanitarian laws, which outlaw indiscriminate mass murder. The acquittals at Greenock and at Manchester cleared us of criminal intent and at the same time clearly pointed out the criminal intent of the British nuclear forces.

The acquittals have encouraged many more people to join in the disarmament work and to feel confident about saying they are preventing crime not causing it.

Trident Ploughshares is an example of ordinary people's power to create peace. The longing for peace and creativity is within each of us and is a real and vital power that just needs to be tapped to spring forward and take us into a new world. The present world can be seen as full of conflict, pain, misery and other injustices. We are told it is human nature – that men are greedy, egotistical, power abusers and that it is idealistic to expect a better world. However, there are many facets of our complex human nature which include the capacity to love and co-operate, to create and be joyful. It is up to each one of us to decide which parts of our nature to nourish and develop. It is up to each of us to perceive the world in all its aspects – which includes the kindness, comfort, excitement, wonder and beauty of loving, giving people. If we want peace then we have to perceive, work and live peacefully and in the process we can and will change our world. We have to live the kind of world we want. People's disarmament is a creative process of taking the power that belongs to each of us and using it for the benefit of all. It is a reclamation of love and life.

Many of us have been deadened, hardened and disempowered by state institutions and structures that are arranged hierarchically and are based on holding and wielding power over people. These structures stress that decisions must be made by 'experts' and determine who these 'experts' are. They pretend that these 'experts' or 'decision makers' are unbiased, neutral and objective. Ordinary people confronting such power are often accused of being simplistic – because they use intelligible language that can be understood; emotional – because they listen to their hearts as well as their minds; and misguided – because they believe that humans given the right environment can behave wonderfully. They are criticised as being naïve, idealistic, of not living in the real world.

It is not surprising that many people have either lost hope or feel unable to confront the wrongs that surround us. What is remarkable however, is the number of people reclaiming their power and deciding to use it wisely and lovingly; who are confronting the hypocrisies and injustices and saying 'not in my name'; who feel that a vote every four years and the tyranny of majority decision-making is not good enough – that we have to go forward to a realisation of consensus that includes everyone in community decision-making and recognises diversity as a strength. Such a process values everyone – there is no 'out' group – no enemy. We all gain or lose together. These are life guidelines completely different from those guiding the military.

Trident Ploughshares is based on taking power back and transforming it into processes capable of enhancing fundamental human morality. We are not ashamed but proud that our message can be understood by a five year old. This is our message – killing is wrong. Mass killing is wrong.

Threatening mass destruction is a denial of our own humanity and is suicidal. When something is wrong we have to stop it. Trident is wrong and so we must stop it. Dismantling the machinery of destruction is thus a practical act of love.

Cutting up the Convoy

by Susan van der Hijden, *Jubilee 2000 Affinity Group*

The first time I seriously started to think of doing a Ploughshares action was during the European Ploughshares Hope and Resistance Gathering in May 1998. I had heard about Ploughshares actions before, mainly from articles in Catholic Worker newsletters. The Catholic Workers movement started in the 1930s when Dorothy Day, anarchist turned Catholic, met Peter Maurin, a French philosopher. Day was looking for a way to combine her old anarchist ideas with her new faith and Maurin showed her how radical the first Christians were and how radical the church could be if it put its own theories into practice. Together Day and Maurin first started a newspaper and then several 'Houses of Hospitality' where hospitality was given to those who needed it.

From the beginning the movement was strongly pacifist and not a year has gone by without one or more of its members being jailed for peace protests. One group strongly influenced by the Catholic Worker is the American Plowshares movement. There are now about 150 Catholic Worker houses that keep in touch by newsletters. One of those houses is in Amsterdam and I moved into it in 1993.

The group has three Core Group members at the moment and about 14 guests who stay from one night up to several years. Most of these are refugees without permits to stay who are not entitled to money, housing or health insurance from the government. We never ask them why they came to Europe unless they want to tell us. After a few days or weeks (or sometimes never) we become friends and hear the horrific stories of how our housemates ended up here, stories of war, rape and hunger. An Eritrean woman forced to spy on her class-mates or be tortured, an 18 year old boy whose whole family was murdered by rebels while he visited the neighbours, a Palestinian man who has nightmares every night of the fighting he saw in Lebanon. It goes on and on. One night a family of four knocked on the door, the oldest child is just four and autistic. They were thrown out of the flat they had illegally rented and had nowhere to go. One of our frequent guests is a six-teen-year-old child soldier from Liberia who sleeps in the parking garage near our house. There are many more such stories.

Living with people who suffer so much made me angry and left me wanting to do something to stop this injustice. The cause of injustice is found right here in the West in our greedy con-sumerism and unscrupulous arms sales. I was already attending vigils against the arms trade, signing petitions, holding stalls, handing out leaflets. I even joined a direct action, painting slogans on the wall of a refugee prison, together with Kees Koning who did the first Dutch Ploughshares action in 1989. But I was still too scared to let myself be arrested and climbed back over the fence when I was done.

In 1998 that changed. The protests that I had done didn't impress the authorities at all, they took no notice and I was ready to go a step further. The Hope and Resistance gathering showed me the tools I needed to prepare for a Ploughshares action and also introduced me to the Trident Ploughshares campaign that had just started. In August that year I went to the first Trident Ploughshares camp and helped out in the information tent where I got to know even more people and ways to resist war and nuclear weapons. The final nudge came when I went to Preston in October to support the 'Bread not Bombs' trial and was inspired by what happened there.

Back in Amsterdam I wrote letters to people whom I knew from the peace movement to come to a first meeting. I wanted to do an action in the Netherlands against a Dutch arms manu-facturer. We had a few meetings but the 'goal' was too vague and no-one except me could afford to get arrested. Then I got a letter from Martin. I had told a mutual friend of my plans and he told Martin to write to me. Together we went to a Trident Ploughshares training weekend where we met four others who also wanted to do an action and had already done some research on the nuclear weapons convoy. We met about every six weeks for nine months and then decided to split up again as our views on prison, court and spirituality differed too much.

Martin and I initially looked at doing an action somewhere else but decided to go for the convoy in RAF Wittering as this seemed the most accessible. We were also running out of time, as the last fully loaded convoy was to go up to Scotland in November. That decided the date for us. We had to do it before the convoy left Wittering to pick up bombs at Burghfield on 6 November 2000. I came over to stay in England at the beginning of October. We found people who wanted to support us just in the nick of time. The last support roles were filled in the days before our action. We invited our supporters to a friend's house on 2 November for a meal after which Martin said mass. We packed the car and drove to Wittering. At midnight we arrived at our drop-off point near the fence of RAF Wittering. Our driver and one of our supporters helped unload our equipment and wished us good luck before we nervously disappeared in the bushes. The hole in the fence, which we had used before to check out the base, was still there. We crawled through and sat down on an old piece of farm equipment. The only sounds were the cars coming by and an occasional dog barking in the distance. We said a prayer asking for God's blessing for our action and to thank him for being able to do this. Then we set off again. We carried most of our tools in our backpacks except for a nine-foot ladder, which we had wrapped in black bin bags to camouflage it a bit. We crossed an open field to a patch of prickly shrubs. There we took the bags off as they were very noisy in the wind and got caught on bushes. Through the bushes we came to a grassy patch of about 30 feet with a brightly lit fence on the other side. The dog barking was louder now but we decided it came from the guard-dog kennel and not from a dog moving about. The second fence also still had an old hole in it which we crawled through and then quickly walked towards the shade of a big bunker. This fenced-in area was full of these old bunkers possibly for the old nuclear bombs that were used on planes. Now there was only one fence between us and the nuclear convoy. The other two were chain-link but this one was weld-mesh. We had never been past this one but had heard of others who had climbed it. After lying on the ground for a bit, listening out for possible guards, we extended our ladder and put it up against the gate in this fence. We chose the gate because there was a small gap in the razor wire on top of it. We shoved the wire even further apart and squeezed through. The area we were now in had little pre-fabricated offices in it. Some were lit but there were no people around. Here we used our mobile to let the support people know that we were close to our goal.

Although this area was also fenced in we knew that the gate between here and the lorry garages was always open and so it was, on this evening, within seconds, we touched these garages for the first time. We walked around them looking for an easy to open door and found a wooden frame. Martin got the crowbar out and started working on it. It was a lot harder than we thought but before almost giving up the door gave. The garage was very dark but when our eyes became accustomed to it all we could see were some civilian vehicles and one MOD van. It was the wrong garage.

Again we checked the doors, even trying the big bay doors at the front as this is how the 'Seeds of Hope' women entered their hangar. At last we found one, amazingly, open. In this garage all the lights were on. We listened to hear if there was anyone inside, which seemed unlikely after all our crowbar noise, but still we needed to know. Then we entered. There was a staircase up to some offices and a hallway with a door at the end of it. Behind this door we found the convoy we were looking for.

Still cautious, first we did the silent things like hanging up our banners and laying out our leaflets and books that we had brought. Then we couldn't delay the hammering any more. It wasn't easy to give that first hammer blow and make holes in Britain's nuclear weapons programme, but after that first strike, it got easier. We expected soldiers to come running in after every resounding blow, but nothing happened. After hammering on every bit that wasn't dangerous to hammer on, I placed folded cranes on the

Susan der Hijden

[Sketches by Peter Lanyon]

lorry and in the cab. We scattered seeds and ashes around. At this point all fear had left me, we had managed to do what we had come for, things could only get better. We sang: 'Servite Domino in Laetitia', a canon meaning 'Serve the Lord with happiness'. Then we sat down for a bit to discuss our next step. We went to look at the office and used the phone to call our supporters and tell them the good news. We destroyed the memory card of the mobile phone for security reasons. We then opened one of the big baydoors of the garage and stepped out to admire our dismantling job, which looked beautiful with all the banners. Again we said a prayer thanking God and remembered the people we did this for – the poor and oppressed in the third world and in England and Europe.

Now we were ready to get arrested and went to the guard-house, which was just around the corner. We knocked on the window and after a while a sleepy looking young soldier with shoes in his hands opened the door. We introduced ourselves and offered him flowers and fair-trade chocolate, which he accepted with a 'Thanks' followed by 'Well would you like to go now?' That baffled us a bit. We told him first to look at our dismantling work. That seemed to wake him up a bit. A colleague of his went out to the garage while he called the police. Within minutes a lot of MOD vans appeared. They brought dogs to search for more activists. The flowers were no longer a nice gift but 'evidence' and were handed in to the police. All this took some time so that our nice soldier brought us tea while we waited. Finally we were thought arrest-worthy and were handcuffed and put in a police van together. Now my knees started shaking a bit and I was glad to be together with Martin. We had time to pray some more, to wish each other good luck for the coming months of prison. The sun was just coming up over the horizon, and a new day had started.

It is now more than four months ago but the memory of that day makes me feel intensely happy, satisfied and proud.

We are still in prison waiting for trial. Prison is a good place to be. I know many places I would rather be but I have also learned a lot and met people I would otherwise never have befriended. I have learned that there are very few 'bad' people in prison. I cannot name even one woman in here who is truly evil. I have learned that there is not much justice happening in court; so many prisoners get unfair treatment. I have learned what it is like to be looked upon as a 'criminal', not worthy to be treated like 'normal' people and I've felt the love and compassion that lives in drug addicts, prostitutes and shoplifters. Being in prison has changed my views of the world and strengthened my conviction to resist injustice and violence.

Going to trial is still frightening me. So much seems to depend on what I will say there and people expect so much of it. I haven't found the 'all is well and all will be well' trust I had for the actual disarming and worry a lot over my ability to say the right things at the right time. My decision to defend myself does not make things easier. It does however fit our action. We had never done this kind of thing before, had no experienced people in our group during the preparation. It is a do-it-yourself disarmament that will hopefully inspire other people, who like ourselves do not understand all the laws and politics but do burn with a longing for peace and justice, to do something. If we can do it, anyone can.

The Brown Envelope

by George Farebrother, *Dialogue and Negotiation Affinity Group*

My mother used to insist that I must wash my ears out every day, otherwise cauliflowers would grow out of them. After a rigorous university education I began to question this. Aged about 45, and really grown-up now, I began to doubt her warning about little bits of cork swelling up inside you. These folk beliefs are oddly comforting and curiously difficult to dislodge.

It's been like that with nuclear deterrence. I never exactly believed in it; but I didn't question it either. Nuclear weapons were just there and the government must be right because, well, it's the government. Realisation dawned soon after I understood about the corks.

So when I was invited to be part of the Trident Ploughshares Dialogue and Negotiating team I felt that I had passed the age of gullibility.

Not so. There was still one myth to put aside. It was pretty obvious to me that Trident is illegal. But I always suspected that somewhere in Whitehall there was a brown envelope. Inside was the knockdown argument, which showed that our deterrent could, after all, be used lawfully. Sometimes people like the Queen or the Lord Chancellor were allowed to look at it. Perhaps members of Trident Ploughshares Dialogue and Negotiation would be given a peek as well if we presented reasoned arguments.

So time and again we wrote to the Prime Minister, who must, after all, know about the brown envelope. We also sent letters to the Queen, various secretaries of state, distinguished naval persons and legal officers.

The Queen's reply was gracious but uninformative. The others were simply depressing. It's so obvious that Trident is outrageously wrong and must be illegal. You don't need to prove that jumping out of 50 storey buildings is bad for you. But we're told that the government is 'confident that the United Kingdom's minimum nuclear deterrent is consistent with international law' with absolutely no supporting argument; and that it depends on the circumstances in which you use it; and that there's no point in making hypothetical speculations about these.

But the correspondence is not a waste of time. Little weaknesses are exposed, tiny admissions are made, and we learn a little more each time. We can also hope that some civil servant, somewhere, can be encouraged to think a little instead of repeating the tired old reach-me-down phrases.

One feature in government replies stands out: the refusal to meet, talk or reveal. Responses to the request: 'open the brown envelope and show us that Trident could be used lawfully' presuppose the answer that Trident is lawful. Thus, 'direct encouragement of service personnel to refuse to carry out their legal duties is totally unacceptable', and 'unless Trident Ploughshares 2000 is prepared to confine itself to legitimate methods of protest... it will not be possible to arrange the meeting'.

Meanwhile we have been given no evidence whatsoever that the use of Trident would never result in totally unacceptable casualties to non-combatants, violation of neutral rights, irreparable harm to the environment, and severe damage to our genetic inheritance.

However, we can relax: 'Legal advice would be available to

Ministers if circumstances were extreme enough for the Government ever to have to consider the use of nuclear weapons ...'. The idea of lawyers in bunkers is a comfort.

It's hard to imagine that the various officials who write to us, all well educated and rather bright, actually believe their own words.

Which leads me to an unworthy suspicion which I hardly dare utter. The government knows that Trident is illegal; and it's saying that it doesn't really matter. We're not going to use it anyway; and if we did, the law wouldn't come into it. We would be living in a world in which law has no meaning.

Unfair? Well, in a strange way, it's the mirror image of Trident Ploughshares' lawful excuse defence. Something normally illegal is allowed if you were driven to it by necessity. That is why the government seized on the World Court's pronouncement that, because it lacked information from the nuclear states, it couldn't decide whether use of nuclear weapons might or might not just about be lawful 'if the very survival of a state was at stake' (conveniently ignoring the court's unanimous finding that, even in such dire circumstances, the use of nuclear weapons had to comply with international humanitarian law – which Trident never can). Some of the legal arguments defending the Kosovo intervention were a bit like this; and there were hints in the UK and US submissions to the World Court that sometimes the law could be put aside.

George Farebrother (on left) with some of the boxes containing 3.8 million Declarations of Public Conscience which were presented to the World Court in 1996. Each signatory declared their belief that nuclear weapons are immoral and should be brought before the World Court.

Trident Ploughshares is playing by the rules. Every action, great or small, is based on upholding the law and preventing nuclear crime. But what if the government is not playing by its own rules? Is it prepared, knowingly, to ride roughshod over every principle of law in a crisis, putting its responsible leaders, and the Trident submarine crews, in the position of Nuremberg criminals?

The core of the problem for both the government and judges is this. If Trident were ever used in earnest, the law and its infrastructure could become a casualty of nuclear war. So, if the British judicial system, with its massive reputation and glittering history and traditions, fails to condemn the continuing threat from nuclear weapons, it could be assenting to its own murder.

So now I'm having to abandon another comforting myth. There might be a brown envelope somewhere. But all that's inside is another brown envelope.

CHAPTER TWO

The Legal Battle at Greenock

WE SPENT FOUR MONTHS on remand at Cornton Vale Prison near Stirling and a further month in prison travelling backwards and forwards to Greenock where our 19 day trial took place before Sheriff Gimblett and a jury of 15 men and women. Ellen and Ulla found lawyers to represent them and I defended myself. Our indictment itself was quite an eyeful:

Angela Christine Zelter (dob 5.6.51), Bodil Ulla Roder (dob 24.8.54) and Ellen Moxley (dob 12.3.35), all prisoners in HM Prison Cornton Vale, Stirling

You are indicted at the instance of The Right Honourable THE LORD HARDIE, Her Majesty's Advocate, and the charges against you are that

(1) on 8 June 1999 on board the vessel 'Maytime' then moored in the waters of Loch Goil, near Lochgoilhead, Argyll, you Angela Christina Zelter, you Bodil Ulla Roder and you Ellen Moxley did wilfully and maliciously damage said vessel and did score two windows on board said vessel with a glass cutter or other similar object and did attempt to drill a hole in one of said windows;

(2) on date and at place above libelled you Angela Christina Zelter, you Bodil Ulla Roder and you Ellen Moxley did attempt to steal two inflatable liferafts from said vessel and did remove said liferafts from their mountings on said vessel and deploy said liferafts in the waters of Loch Goil aforesaid;

(3) on date and at place above libelled you Angela Christina Zelter, you Bodil Ulla Roder and you Ellen Moxley did maliciously and wilfully damage equipment, fixtures and fittings on board said vessel 'Maytime' and in particular did cut a hole in a metal wire fence in the laboratory of said vessel, did smash the contents of electronic equipment cabinet and rip out electrical cables in said cabinet, did cut off the main control switch for the winch on said vessel, did damage a padlock on the door to the control room of said vessel by attempting to saw through same with a hacksaw and thereafter covering said padlock in glue or a similar substance rendering said padlock inoperative, did pour glue or a similar

substance onto the wires and controls of a crane on the upper deck of said vessel, on the controls of the winch aforesaid and onto the cleats securing the hatch on said vessel, did place a chain around the crane on the upper deck of said vessel thereby preventing said crane from operating, and did smash a computer monitor on said vessel, did damage a wall clock in the laboratory of said vessel and did damage a cabinet containing a power supply to an adjacent platform, by forcing said cabinet open and damaging same;

(4) on date and at place above libelled you Angela Christina Zelter, you Bodil Ulla Roder and you Ellen Moxley did maliciously and wilfully damage a quantity of computer equipment, electrical and office equipment, acoustic equipment and amplifier, recording equipment, fax machines, telephone, tools, documents, records, electronic components, a briefcase, radio equipment, range finder, books and a case and contents, and did deposit said items in the waters of Loch Goil, whereby said items became waterlogged, useless and inoperable;

OR ALTERNATIVELY

date and place above libelled you Angela Christina Zelter, you Bodil Ulla Roder and you Ellen Moxley did steal said quantity of computer equipment, electrical and office equipment, acoustic equipment and amplifier, recording equipment, fax machines, telephone, tools, documents, records, electronic components, a briefcase, radio equipment, range finder, books and a case and contents, and did remove said items from said vessel and did deposit said items in the waters of Loch Goil and did thus steal same;

BY AUTHORITY OF HER MAJESTY'S ADVOCATE

At no time did we deny the damage caused to the equipment on *Maytime* that was listed in the indictment. At all times we consistently maintained that our acts were justified because we were trying to prevent preparations for indiscriminate attack and that we were upholding international and Scots law. Our defence was that we were engaged in crime prevention through the disarmament of illegal and criminal weapons of mass destruction and that we were acting out of absolute necessity.

The prosecutor spent two weeks itemising all the damage and showing a video of starfish draped artistically over computers 61 metres below the laboratory. He put forward a very simple case proving what we had never denied in the first place – that we were on *Maytime* and had done all the damage itemised. The two advocates, John Mayer and John McLaughlin representing Ulla and Ellen, and I representing myself, then spent two weeks calling a brilliant array of five international experts to testify on our behalf.

Our defence was that we were engaged in crime prevention through the disarmament of illegal and criminal weapons of mass destruction and that we were acting out of absolute necessity

Francis Boyle, International Law Professor at Illinois Univer-sity in the USA gave evidence that international law applies everywhere, and that, due to its destructive power, Trident could not be used in any manner that was lawful. Judge Ulf Panzer from Hamburg, Germany, gave evidence of the legitimacy of nonviolent action to uphold the law. He described how he had blockaded the Mutlangen nuclear base along with 20 other judges because they had learned from the Nazi era the high cost of remaining silent when the government acted unlawfully. Professor Paul Rogers from Bradford University, England, gave evidence on the composition and capabilities of the Trident system, the danger of nuclear war and nuclear accidents. Professor Jack Boag, from Edinburgh, Scotland, testified on the imminence of the nuclear weapon danger. And finally, Rebecca Johnson from the Acronym Institute, Geneva, Switzerland, explained the consequences of the failure of successive UK governments to fulfil their obligations under the Nuclear Non-Proliferation Treaty and how the present administration continues to block negotiations. She described how *Maytime* is an essential link in the Trident nuclear weapon system, and how other states perceive Britain's deployment of Trident as a threat.

After Ellen, Ulla and I had all taken turns in the witness box, the advocates and I put our detailed legal arguments. The Sheriff was very fair, allowing all parties ample opportunity to present their case and being very patient with the language difficulties – Ulla had everything translated into Danish.

We had a team of Trident Ploughshares supporters who gave up weeks of their time to help prepare our papers and look after the witnesses, deal with press enquiries, and give us much needed moral support. They also kept vigil outside and inside the court, reminding everyone present in the proceedings that this trial was not merely the trial of three women but a trial against Trident, that the outcome was important to them too.

The Sheriff began her ruling and soon the tears were streaming down our faces as, to the obvious delight of the jury and of our supporters, she directed the jury to acquit us. The tension of the last few weeks was wiped away in a flood of joy and excitement.

We were acquitted on the grounds that our view was a reasonable one and arguable in a court of law and that there was no criminal intent in our action because it was based on a sincere belief, backed up by objective evidence, that we were acting against a continuing criminal conspiracy to contravene international humanitarian law, or in the words of Sheriff Gimblett:

20 October 1999 – Greenock Court Room, Sheriff Gimblett's Ruling.

> The three accused took the view that if it was illegal, and given the horrendous nature of nuclear weapons, that they had an obligation in terms of international law, never mind morally to do the little they could to stop ... the deployment and use of nuclear weapons in a situation which could be construed as a threat. They were not objecting to the possession *per se*. It follows I think that if I consider that Ms Zelter, Ms Roder and Ms Moxley were justified in the first leg of their defence, namely the international law defence, and had given that as their principal reason for their actions that the Crown had a duty to rebut that defence. They have not done so and accordingly I uphold the three defence submissions.

She had directed the jury to acquit us by saying, 'I have heard nothing which would make it seem to me that the accused acted with ... criminal intent'.

These words vindicated our campaign entirely. At last we had found a judge who saw beyond the damage to property that we openly admitted to and who recognised we had a humane and justifiable reason for doing it.

The media had a field day.

Trident Three released outside court

Credit: David MacKenzie

'Outcry as Sheriff rules nuclear weapons illegal' [*The Scotsman* – 22/10/99]

'Saboteurs cleared as 'Trident is illegal' [*The Times* – 22/10/99]

'Trident case set to test Holyrood' [*Sunday Herald* – 24/10/99]

'A Sheriff made legal history and caused a political storm after ruling that the Government's deployment of nuclear weapons was illegal under international law ... It is the first time a country's law courts have declared its nuclear defence system illegal and the political fall-out from Sheriff Gimblett's decision will be felt by other nuclear powers.' [*The Herald* – 22/10/99]

The one I like best, although I wish it were really true, was

'How Four Middle-Aged Ladies Sank UK Defence' [*Daily Record* – 22/10/ 99]

– the fourth lady referred to was, of course, the Sheriff herself.

The furore continued, with right-wing MPs horrified that we were not locked up again in prison and asking for an immediate appeal while on the other side there was widespread support which led to resolutions and notices in the Scottish parliament, the Welsh assembly, Westminster and the European parliament, acclaiming our acquittal as a ray of hope for the just implementation of international humanitarian law.

Citizens Inspect Aldermaston

by Marguerite Finn, *Woodwoses Affinity Group*

Come with us, gentle reader, on a Woodwose action at Aldermaston. It is 12 November 2000.

Word went rapidly around the animal kingdom, spread by the Green Finches who had been the first to spot them: 'they have been eating Rachel's Organic Yoghurt for 24 hours now – something must be going to happen soon. Get ready'

Meanwhile, back at the abbey, the Woodwoses are preparing to go into action. They are going to carry out a citizen's inspection at Atomic Weapons Establishment (AWE) Aldermaston and the team members are making their final plans.

09.30am The team sets off dressed in white anti-radiation suits and safety helmets. As they drive through the country lanes towards their chosen point of entry, the countryside seems incredibly beautiful, with the beech trees resplendent in their glorious autumnal colours. The sky is blue and clear and there is no sign of the rain that deluged the camp the previous day. The omens are good.

09.45am As they approach their destination they see to their dismay, a police transit van parked in the exact spot where they want to climb over the fence on to AWE land.

09.47am They quickly reverse up the lane – hoping that they had not been spotted – and drive down another lane out of sight of the police van. There is a magical quality in the air – a rabbit comes out to look as they pass, a squirrel runs up a tree to get a better view, and a small deer suddenly appears to escort them down the road. Nature is on their side. The pollution from the AWE site is ruining their environment too.

09.49am The Woodwose Citizen Inspectors leave the van, cross the road, bent double and moving swiftly, they enter the wood, carefully keeping out of sight of the road. The bracken is tall and awkward to negotiate.

09.55am They reach a clump of trees and pause for breath – a 'photo opportunity' – and a chance to introduce the Woodwose Citizen Inspectors to you: they are (from left to right) Barbara Sunderland, Peter Lanyon, Davida Higgin, Simone Chimowitz (Marguerite Finn is the photographer).

71

The Woodwose Citizen Inspectors in their white suits
Credit: Marguerite Finn

They forge on through the thick bracken. The guard dogs at the AWE sense something is afoot and start barking.

10.15am The perimeter fence looms into view. The Woodwoses crouch in the bushes to don the last of their anti-radiation gear – white boots and masks. They stand up to move towards the fence. Suddenly a patrol van appears, driving down on the inside of the fence. The four intrepid 'cutters' together with their legal observer, Allen, and their photographer, Marguerite, dive for cover and drop to the ground (ouch!). The van passes. Had the driver spotted them? They wait patiently to see if the van would return. Nothing. They move forward again and start cutting a hole in the fence. Without warning an unmarked brown van appears, driving at speed on the inside of the fence. The Citizen Inspectors keep their nerve and continue cutting. How long have they got before the police would be on to them?

10.20am Peter is the first in through the hole in the fence, followed closely by Davida, then Simone and finally Barbara. They all cross immediately to the inner weld-mesh fence and commence cutting. Peter and Davida are on their stomachs on the ground using their bolt-cutters on the fence, working from the ground upwards, trying to avoid touching the sensor wire. They are making progress. But how much time is left? Will they succeed in cutting through the weld-mesh?

'Go for it!' urge Allen and Marguerite.

10.23am A police van appears in the distance racing towards them on the inside of the fence with blue lights flashing. It screeches to a halt and two police officers jump out shouting at the Citizen Inspectors to stop what they are doing. As the weld mesh fence was separating the police from the cutters, they could only stand and shout!

10.24am Peter and Davida calmly continue cutting. A second police transit van arrives, a policewoman gets out. Peter and Davida are arrested for alleged criminal damage. Peter continues cutting the fence. Davida stands up, and the policewoman helps her out of her anti-radiation suit, and 'frisks' her thoroughly.

Barbara and Simone are not yet arrested – which is causing them some anxiety!

The policewoman and the second van depart as quickly as they had come, leaving a single policeman called Simon (no.1133) with the Citizen Inspectors.

Peter is still on the ground cutting away at the weld-mesh, ignoring all orders to stop.

10.25am Another transit van arrives – this time on the same side of the fence as the Citizen Inspectors, two policemen jump out. At the same time, a policeman and a policewoman arrive on foot, agitated and out of breath from running.

10.30am Peter stops cutting and gets to his feet. He holds out his hand to the arresting officer who shakes it and subsequently calls him a 'gentleman'. Peter, much chuffed, shouts this out to Alan and Marguerite. Simone is arrested then – and, finally, Barbara is arrested too. (Whew!) 'Frisking' all round.

Two dog handlers arrive on the outside of the perimeter fence – just as a policeman and policewoman emerge from the wood behind Allen and Marguerite. The dog handlers are told to stay there and guard the hole in the fence.

10.35am Peter, Davida, Barbara and Simone are bundled into a transit van and driven off.

10.40am The two police officers turn their attention on Allen and Marguerite still calmly observing and photographing – their Rachel's Organic Yoghurt (Maple Syrup Flavour) – levels still running high. Would they be arrested too?

'Good morning' say Allen and Marguerite, 'it's a lovely day for a stroll in the woods' and with that start walking slowly back towards the woods. 'Hey', says the policeman, 'There's an easier way out than that' 'Er?' says Allen. 'Just walk along by the fence and you will come to the road'.

'Oh, er thanks very much', say Allen and Marguerite, and set off along the fence, still followed by the two police officers.

When last heard of the four were still walking – around and around the Aldermaston site.

A single question hovered on everyone's lips at Aldermaston on the weekend of 10-12 November 2000:

Question: What is caked with mud, seasoned with wood smoke, and runs on Rachel's Organic Yoghurt?
Answer: A Woodwose.

There was a very serious purpose to this action and this is what the Citizen Inspectors had to say, when they were taken into police custody:

Remembrance Day 2000

AWE Aldermaston Citizen Inspection

We believe that AWE Aldermaston is a key part of the Trident weapons system and that this system constitutes a crime in international law. Therefore, we need to undertake a Citizen's Inspection especially of 'A' area, in order to establish the nature of the work going on there – particularly the development of new forms of Trident warheads – and to underline for the public what illegal, life-threatening work is being done there. We intend to conduct our inspections with all necessary regard for safety of all concerned, including site personnel, people living in the area, ourselves and the environment.

We are doing this inspection on Remembrance Day because the existence of AWE Aldermaston makes a mockery of the mourning for all those killed in wars and the hopes for peace being expressed everywhere today. Every action at Aldermaston provides valuable intelligence to the Trident Ploughshares

Movement and enables us to plan future actions with greater accuracy. This place is a blot on the conscience of mankind and must be closed down for good.

With a Little Help from our Friends
by Alison Crane, *Midlands Affinity Group*

Before signing the Pledge to Prevent Nuclear Crime, all potential Pledgers take part in a two-day workshop. The content is put together by the Quaker 'Turning the Tide' programme for the use of active nonviolence to achieve positive social change, and most of the trainers are Quakers and part of this programme.

The workshop includes sessions on personal hopes and fears, as well as group processes and nonviolence. Working in groups is considered to be an important way of ensuring that actions remain nonviolent, and that the campaign in general keeps the nonviolence principles at the heart of everything we do. The sessions about working in groups include considering what makes a good group work well and effectively together, the different roles within groups, practising consensus decision-making, and using role-plays and trust exercises.

Since I became part of Trident Ploughshares, it seemed that there was a role for me in 'Turning the Tide' as well, helping with training and making sure that new Pledgers workshops and the mini-camp and pre-action sessions happen. Trident Ploughshares really gives you a chance to try things you never thought you could do before – in all sorts of ways.

I am part of the Midlands Affinity Group. The profile of this group is – age range 45 upwards, several Quakers, a wide range of financial circumstances and more women than men. Members are from an area roughly corresponding with the English Midlands, but actually stretching from Manchester to Stroud.

So how does theory compare with reality in this affinity group? I can easily think of roles each of us has taken, as for example drivers, photographer, meeting facilitator, dealing with practicalities such as arranging meetings, people willing to be arrested, media link, support people, mobile phone owner, caterer, font of knowledge, swimmers, people with court experience, court and prison supporters. However, although we have excellent skills and experience using bolt-cutters, none of us can climb a fence (without ladders anyway).

In my experience, trust and commitment to the peace group grows as we work together – planning actions, living together at camp, doing actions together, preparing evidence for trial, going to court.

What are the highlights for me over the last couple of years?

Four of us sharing food in the middle of a warm July night outside the nuclear bomb factory at Aldermaston, before cutting through the fence.

Or walking across the moors between Garelochead and Coulport, the glorious landscape contrasting with the evil prospect ahead. First the lookout towers come into view, then the fence, the lights and the cameras, and finally the nuclear warhead loading bay on the loch below. The silence we shared there, as in Quaker worship, was a profound experience. I keep the photo by my desk at work to remind me of what is important.

But best of all was the moment when Sylvia and River were

Some of the Midlands Affinity Group meeting above the loading bay at Coulport, August 2000. Top right to bottom – Alison Crane, River, Marlene Yeo, Sylvia Boyes.
Credit: Roger Franklin

acquitted by the jury at their conspiracy trial at Manchester Crown Court.

The different members of the affinity group didn't know each other before Trident Ploughshares started. All of us in our various ways were used to working as individuals, or with different groups. In these circumstances, especially with the physical distances involved, building a new group can be quite a challenge. What made progress smoother was that the Quakers among us are used to consensus decision-making – I'm sure that has made it easier to make decisions that we are all happy with. Also, each of us seems happy, if one of us wishes to take responsibility for fulfilling a particular role or doing things in a particular way, to let them get on with it.

Perhaps the things we have succeeded less well at, as a group, have been connected with our strengths in working as individuals, such as generally making sure that each of us feels supported by the others. For instance we were slow to arrange support when Sylvia and River were remanded in custody. However, one of the main points of conflict seems to be how strong to make the tea – we aren't going to reach consensus on that one!

Although we have only known each other since the start of the campaign, at the risk of appearing sentimental, I know that whatever happens to Trident or Trident Ploughshares, I have friends for life. And if the time comes for me to become a grandparent, I need look no further than my affinity group for excellent role models.

The Art that Art Conceals

Profile of Judith Pritchard, *Midlands Affinity Group*
by David Mackenzie, *Local Heroes Affinity Group*

At the Peaton Wood campsite there is a buzz of activity. On the grassy bank there is a small group in a training session. At the far end of the marquee the cooks and their helpers are chopping and dicing. A group of three activists at this end of the tent are poring over the Ordnance Survey map of the area, planning their next action. Just outside the tent a young man is honing his fence cutting skills on a piece of weld-mesh and from the caravan there is the hum of voices talking to the media or the police. An exception

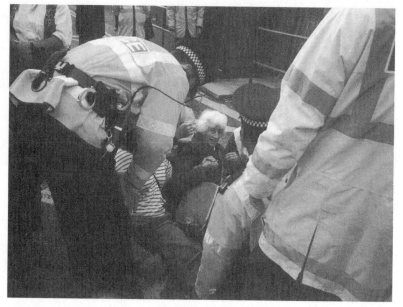

Judith Pritchard

to this industry is a group of people seated round the campfire, apparently just lounging and gossiping, among them three or four older women. Appearances can be deceptive – work is going on here too. The younger group of activists who have just returned from the police cells after an action are going through a de-briefing process, telling the story and perhaps feeling raw and uncertain after what they have done and gone through. At the heart of the older group is Judith, bringing her experience of life to bear in reassuring the activists and restoring their confidence, deploying her alert mind and consummate interpersonal skills to play midwife to their thoughts and aspirations. This does not fit readily into the usual campaign work headings and is almost invisible but we just cannot do without it.

CHAPTER THREE

The Lord Advocate's 4 Questions

IN VIEW OF ALL the controversy the government were forced to set in motion a very rare legal process in Scotland called a Lord Advocate's Reference (LAR). This was because the state could not appeal against our acquittal but needed to step in to challenge it, by the back door, to try to stop any other judges giving similar acquittals. The validity of citizens acting to prevent international crime in Scotland as well as the content of international law was therefore now opened to the highest legal scrutiny – something the peace movement had been trying to do for a very long time.

We were sent a Petition from the Lord Advocate which set out a summary of the Greenock case and the four legal questions which the High Court were to answer. Each of us (now called Respondents) would be allowed to put our point of view as would the Lord Advocate. We were all expected to be legally represented as the questions were considered to be highly technical.

January 2000 – Lord Advocate's Reference, High Court of Justiciary, Petition of the Right Honourable The Lord Hardie, Her Majesty's Advocate.

- In a trial under Scottish criminal procedure, is it competent to lead evidence as to the content of customary international law as it applies to the United Kingdom?

- Does any rule of customary international law justify a private individual in Scotland in damaging or destroying in pursuit of his or her objection to the United Kingdom's possession of nuclear weapons, its action in placing such weapons at locations within Scotland or its policies in relation to such weapons?

- Does the belief of an accused person that his or her actions are justified in law constitute a defence to a charge of malicious mischief or theft?

- Is it a general defence to a criminal charge that the offence was committed in order to prevent or bring to an end the commission of an offence by another person?

The four questions were designed to be answered in the negative in order to prevent Trident Ploughshares putting forward any legal defences in the future and to prevent any other Sheriff from acquitting in similar circumstances. However, I believed that if these questions were answered in the negative then the whole moral basis and thus legitimacy of the Scottish judiciary would be undermined and any respect for the law as an independent arbiter of justice would be shattered.

I decided to represent myself, as I had done at Greenock. I felt it was too important to leave to the experts. I wanted to know that I had done all I could to say directly and firmly to the judges that Trident was a weapon system of mass murder and mass murder was criminal. I did not want the basic argument to get lost in legal technicalities.

Ulla and Ellen opted to be represented again. This was essential. None of us were lawyers and we needed the very best lawyers we could get to enable the very best legal arguments to be put to the judges. We wanted both an ordinary everyday perspective put by a 'global citizen' who would put the legal arguments into ordinary language, understandable by all – one of the people's disarmers – and we also wanted the legal arguments put in a manner and language that could be acceptable to the judges and to which they would have to give a professional response. This was a chance we knew we would never have again. Many groups and individuals in the peace movement had been asking for a full judicial inquiry into the legality of British nuclear weapons systems and policies over many years but this had always been denied. We were scared and enthralled by the opportunity to do the best we could to enable the Scottish judiciary to back up the rule of international humanitarian law and to put an end to our state threatening to use weapons of mass destruction. What a responsibility, what an honour. There were times when I just wanted to run away from it all.

Our problems began when we called for a joint meeting of Ellen, Ulla and their solicitors and counsel and myself and Jane, who came as my 'Mackenzie Friend'. A Mackenzie Friend is someone who an unrepresented person can have in court to help them with notes and support, although they are not allowed to address the court in person. We had previously worked quite well with the solicitors and junior counsel in the original Greenock trial but had not met the two senior counsel.

We wanted to agree that we would all work as a co-operative

team and get advice from other international lawyers around the world who would be willing to help and share their thoughts and knowledge with us. We wanted to know what their opinions on international law and its incorporation into Scots law were and expected to get into a detailed debate about our legal strategy. Most of all we wanted to know if they backed us, if they believed that we had a right in law to do what we had done and if they also believed that Trident was criminal. We wanted to be represented by lawyers that cared about the world's future in the same way as we did.

The meeting was a disaster, a terrible shock. We were told in no uncertain terms that it did not matter what they thought about the rights and wrongs of our disarmament action, the lawyers were in charge, that it was not possible to work in a team, that each lawyer had only one client and had to put her interests above all the others, that it was not professional to tell us what they really thought, that whether a client was innocent or guilty, a murderer or thief, they would always act professionally and do their best. The most senior lawyer said he was the one in charge and it was obvious that he did not appreciate the offers of help from other sympathetic lawyers around the world. They could not understand why this upset us – why we wanted to know what they actually thought and felt, why we wanted to know them as people rather than purely as professional lawyers, why we wanted to be able to consult openly and fully with each other. They could not take on board that the three of us worked together and always worked by consensus. They had also done no work for this meeting, not expecting more than platitudes I suppose, and so we could not begin to talk about the real, important issues that we had prepared for.

By the end of the meeting I was in tears but I was also angry. This was just too important for egotistical, patriarchal, power games, masquerading under cover of 'professional rules'. We certainly did not feel that they were acting in any of our best interests. It was an interesting lesson in the clash of cultures. This clash continues as Trident Ploughshare Pledgers confront their lawyers, sometimes having to confront them in court because they refuse to consult properly or do not prepare thoroughly enough.

One of the senior counsel dropped out and it took months to sort out the composition of the legal representation for the LAR and it was only a few weeks before it started that we knew for certain who would be representing Ellen and Ulla. In the event their lawyers submitted good arguments but it would have been much better if we had all been able to work openly together from the start. The junior counsel – John Mayer and John McLaughlin – who had helped us win the case at Greenock, did back us, but their hands were tied by the outdated rules of their profession.

Luckily, there were lawyers in other countries who recognised the importance of the LAR and to whom I was able to send my draft submissions for much needed advice and useful criticism. Above all they gave me confidence to say in court what I felt needed to be said by a 'global citizen'. Nevertheless, I was sorely disappointed that no top Scots lawyer searched the foundations of Scots law to marshal the best legal arguments against the threat to use nuclear weapons. I would have liked to have seen such arguments put expertly, confidently and with passion.

The first procedural hearing was on 4 April 2000 and it was made clear that we would be stopped from trying to engage the judiciary in an impartial discussion of the real public interest issue of whether the UK Trident system is actually illegal and criminal. I was told the question of whether Trident is criminal in international law would not be looked at by the court. I was also told to stop making a speech after having spoken for less than a minute, that a full transcript of the original trial would not be ordered; that permission for a recording or transcript to be made of the Reference was refused, and that only five days were reserved for the Reference.

More importantly the most senior of the three Scottish judges sitting on the bench, who was directing the proceedings, was the Lord Justice General of Scotland, Lord Rodger – the very same man who, as Lord Advocate in 1992, refused to institute an inquiry into the nuclear preparations being made because he was 'satisfied as to the legality of the activities at Faslane and Coulport'.

The second legal battle had begun.

I commenced my attack with a sustained and reasoned barrage of letters, addressed mainly to the Principal Clerk of the Scottish judiciary, which assertively demanded my right to represent and speak for myself and which asked for clarity and justice in the proceedings. The letters were put up on our Trident Ploughshares website as they were written and replied to and the record shows that between February and October over 40 letters were exchanged. I formally asked for the resignation of Lord Rodger from the proceedings of the LAR on the grounds of lack of impartiality, it being essential in any democracy that the judicial system is willing and able to impartially examine the legality of all official government policies. I also asked that the major legal question that had arisen in the Greenock trial, that of the illegality of Trident itself, be examined impartially.

Through these letters and the various preliminary hearings we were finally presented with a bench of judges headed by Lord Prosser along with Lord Penrose and Lord Kirkwood. The murky process of the LAR and how it differs from an appeal process was never really settled. No one really seemed to know what was going on or what the rules of the LAR game were supposed to be. I found myself thinking I was in a strange Alice in Wonderland world where everyone appears to know what they are doing and why until you question them, when all certainty and rationality seem to float away – a world of bluff and counter bluff.

However, I managed at the second preliminary hearing on 12 September 2000 to get the judges to agree that the amicus curiae (literally a 'friend of the court', this is a lawyer brought in to make sure that the legal arguments in the interests of an unrepresented person are put before the court), Jerry Moynihan QC, should not be allowed to contradict any of my legal arguments but should only back them up. I also got permission for him to consult with me in order to know what my arguments were so that he would know what he was not to contradict. This meant that we had a fine legal mind who would only be allowed to make submissions on our behalf. This proved very useful as he brilliantly dissected the Advisory Opinion by explaining that the ICJ, on the instigation of the nuclear weapon states, had taken into account the possibility of small, so-called clean or discriminating nuclear weapons despite the absence of evidence that any such weapon existed. He argued that this possible reservation to the general illegality of nuclear weapons however, did not apply to Trident because Trident was not a small scale, discriminating weapon nor did the UK possess such a discriminating nuclear weapon.

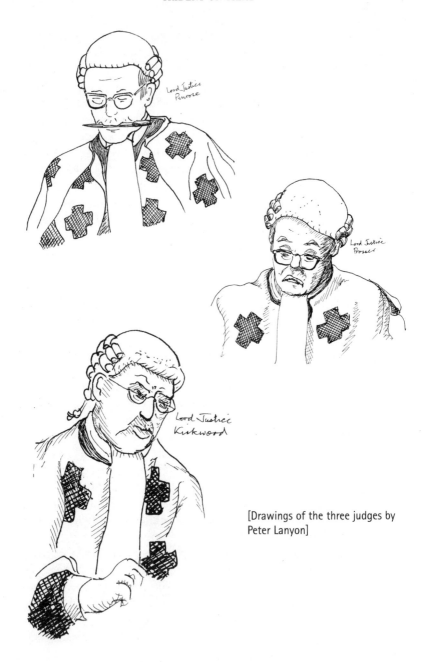

Lord Justice Penrose

Lord Justice Prosser

Lord Justice Kirkwood

[Drawings of the three judges by Peter Lanyon]

Commotion

by Sheila MacKay, *Gareloch Horticulturalists Affinity Group*

Trident Ploughshares 2000 is bringing the Trident weapons system to where it should be on the public agenda and it has revived my energy to protest about it. Bit by bit the public seem to be grasping the enormity of what Trident means. We are paying billions of pounds for the mistaken idea that we are defended by a huge deterrent weapon system which will never be used. The reality is that we don't control when and if it will be used. It is constantly ready to be used and there have been some very close shaves already. If it is ever used it will destroy the democracy that people think they are defending by having it – and at the same time destroy much of the planet. We have created a terrible legacy for future generations

When I think about Trident I either adopt the ostrich position or else the terrier emerges and I have to get out and do something about it.

The early 1980s were turbulent and amazing years for me. At the age of 33 I had three ground shaking revelations. I guess everyone has to get there in their own time!

The first was when I saw a very aggressive confrontation between protesters and the police at Faslane naval base and realised that if CND was taken seriously the state might use strong-arm tactics to squash the movement and I would need nonviolence training. The next was when, as a community worker, I was confronted for the first time with the reality of violence against women and began to understand what the term 'patriarchy' meant and that it actually affected me. And the third and most amazing of all, was that I discovered I was a lesbian and fell in love with Margaret who is still my partner.

The first two of these revelations have provided much of my energy and direction since then as well as plenty of anger, and feelings of powerlessness. The third has been my sustenance and joy.

Margaret and I met at a nonviolence training session and went on to be part of the Gareloch Horticulturalists nonviolent direct action group. This group has been the context of all my anti-nuclear and anti-Trident protest since 1983. We have cut the fence

Sheila MacKay (2nd from left) practising with 'Commotion'

and decorated it; gardened on MOD land and trespassed on it. We leafleted the workers and held vigils as Coulport grew from the holiday village of my childhood to the hollowed out hill filled with death that it is today. We took our message to the shoppers in Glasgow, to the Ministry of Defence in London, to the baffled people and tourists of Edinburgh and Aberdeen. We sang and we prayed, wove webs and planted bulbs. The group is a support and an inspiration. It has even filled the gap in my spiritual life from when I left the church. We make up our own liturgies to praise the beauty of the Scottish hills and the planet earth. We have mourned at Coulport, raged at Faslane and done penance countless times in the cold and rain.

When Trident sailed up the Clyde I could only sit in my canoe and weep. I remember some of the American anti-Trident protesters who had come over to join the protest saying 'you just have to keep protesting till they get rid of it'. I was overwhelmed with a sense of failure and futility and couldn't take it in. My campaigning for Trident shifted dangerously towards the ostrich position. It was only loyalty to the Horties and their support that kept me involved until Trident Ploughshares came along. It felt a bit strange to us at first. We had always kept in contact with Faslane Peace Camp and Scottish CND. In our different styles we had all been protesting about Trident for years, chipping away at it constantly but only rarely making a national impact. Suddenly there was a huge surge of energy and the possibility of major change.

Before Trident Ploughshares, during the 1990s, my energy had shifted to the struggle against violence against women. The impact of rape and abuse on women and the prevalence of both are frightening. Every second woman in our country has had experience of some form of abuse from a man. Violence against women is used to ensure the dominance of men in society just as Trident is used to try and maintain dominance over other nations in the world.

I find it totally compatible to campaign against violence against women and to campaign against Trident. And one of the most satisfying ways to do both is to drum with the Edinburgh women's drumming band Commotion on protest marches or at the gates of bases. We are part of a new tradition of women's Brazilian drumming groups. The tunes are loud, powerful, up-beat and great for dancing. They make a stirring sound without being in the least bit militaristic. It is empowering to play with a group of women. You know for sure you will be heard!

The institutions and traditions of male dominance make sure that the global violence of Trident and the worldwide violence of men against women and children are both carried on. Individuals choose to commit these acts of violence but they do not do so in a vacuum. I don't think there is any point in replacing the men at the top with others (women or men) who will be sucked into the power structures. The structures themselves must change and the individuals within them must find the will, the courage and the means to do it.

Nonviolence is about empowerment for the ordinary person including myself. It is about confronting the fear that makes us comply with unjust authority, powerless and voiceless. It is about developing the strategies for achieving change and demonstrating how the world could be. If we make mutual respect instead of dominance the new basis for our relationships and if we accept nothing less, it will be a revolutionary beginning both to the end of violence against women and to the decommissioning of Trident. Watching three women dismantling the floating Trident laboratory on Loch Goil one glorious summer evening was a powerful lesson in nonviolent action.

Since 1999 I have worked in the Scottish Centre for Nonviolence where my main area of work is training with community groups. I've learned a lot about how nonviolence opens up a different way of relating, a different set of assumptions, and ways of organising that draw on the best of our human instincts instead of the basest.

Drumming on the March against Violence against Women and drumming at the gates of Faslane during a Trident Ploughshares action are ways of reclaiming my faith in the possibility of change and my optimism. It is a way of shouting to the rooftops that we will not put up with violence in silence.

Wheelchairs and Websites
by Mark Leach, *Ceilidh Creatures Affinity Group*

It is Monday afternoon, 12 February 2001 – the day of the Big Blockade. I am in a cell at Greenock police station. I don't know what the time is but the sunshine is bursting through the tiny sky-lights. I'm on my own in a bare, vaguely warm, cream painted cell, complete with a stainless steel toilet pan. It feels like being locked into a large (reasonably clean) public loo!

My mind is buzzing. Most of mine and my friends' activity during the last few weeks has been leading up to this (unjust but expected) incarceration. Earlier today we were lifted from the roadway leading to the north gate of HM naval base Clyde at Faslane. Faslane is where Britain's Trident submarines are based. We did not want to get arrested, really we wanted Strathclyde police to arrest those people making the preparations to use Trident.

We were part of a magnificent display of resistance to Trident and all its implications. A blockade jointly organised between Scottish CND and Trident Ploughshares. Over a thousand brilliant people attending from all over the UK, Europe and the world –

men and women – elderly and young – of different ethnicities – with money and without – from all religions and none – from varying political viewpoints – from colourfully costumed to those in suits. All coming together to celebrate life, hope and to reject the machinery of death and war.

Ten of us under arrest were driven in the police minibus to Greenock police station – males and females were already separated. We were a real mix of people: there was Mark, a student from Germany studying in Glasgow; Ciaron, a veteran ploughshares activist from Australia who has spent jail terms in the US for anti-nuclear disarmament work; John, a Scottish CND worker; Billy, the ex-Scottish National Party Vice-President, and several 'first-timers' including Micah, a friend of mine from Edinburgh.

Our own action thankfully worked as planned. Twelve of us walked up the road with our silver 'totally 'armless' spaceship and positioned ourselves in front of the north gate. The blockaders wanted to stop workers driving into the base during their morning shift change at 7am. It was to disrupt the ongoing threat of the Trident nuclear weapons system.

Pipes within the spaceship allowed for lock-ons – where people attach their wrists to another through a pipe using webbing and clips. This makes it harder for the police to separate and lift us. My partner, in addition to having her arm locked into the spaceship made use of her wheelchair. She had a tube positioned within the frame of her chair to enable a lock-on between a further two folk. All this meant that we were there two hours holding up base work. Sadly, the spaceship was cut up by the police moving us – it had been hastily completed only the day before, having been a fun task for lots of us – both children and grown-up children!

Last week, half of us ran our third annual fund-raising ceilidh in Edinburgh. It was a lively and enjoyable night that raised awareness about Trident Ploughshares and nuclear weapon issues generally.

The Trident Ploughshares website which I run from home is part display board too, and upkeep of the site can keep me occupied for hours! Running the site is one of the many supportive roles in Trident Ploughshares. The web site acts as a central point for the latest news, information and press releases. It forms an on-line magazine, library, back catalogue with index and notice board

Roz being processed at Faslane, August 1 2000. Roz Bullen in the centre and Grace Nichol on the right.

all in one, providing information for journalists and the public. The *Tri-Denting It Handbook* is on-line, as are legal documents, correspondence and articles relating to Trident. This has saved a small fortune in photocopying and postage costs, and provides an in-depth resource for activists. It also shows our open and accountable nature by giving an up-to-date list of all the Pledgers.

My involvement began because of my partner. After 17 years of wanting to do more about resisting nuclear weapons than merely letter writing to MPs, Roz took part in her first Trident Ploughshares action as soon as she was well enough to travel to Faslane. The action was with Morag, who had been active in Trident Ploughshares from its outset, and also used a wheelchair and so gave Roz confidence to take part. As Roz's enabler, before I was prepared to risk arrest myself, I was going to actions to drive Roz there, and to pick her up hours later from Clydebank police station!

Since then I've reviewed my over-compliant nature with certain powerful sectors of our society, and realised the necessity to do something instead of just talking about it. I decided to accept some responsibility to do something about the presence of these weapons. We formed an affinity group of five people and undertook a two-day nonviolence and safety training. It was only then that I decided I too was prepared to risk arrest. With practical help from others in Trident Ploughshares and friends, Roz and I have been able to take part in actions on an equal footing with the rest of our group. Help ranges from dog-sitting, to Una who puts up with our rushed overnight stops at her home not far from Faslane, to people helping Roz in and out the wheelchair, and legal support from Jane. Through actively taking part, I've gained in self-confidence and self-esteem by making a commitment to something that I feel good about and believe in.

Today I've had two hot meals brought to me in my cell. Just as I hope to be released, two more blockaders join me in my cell, and I get to hear news about how well the blockade has been going. The base was blocked for hours, and over 360 arrests were made they tell me, including church ministers, an MP, MSP, MEP, even a QC! – I am ecstatic! Good news coverage too, they tell me. Not long afterwards I get finger-printed, DNA-tested, photographed and released at 9.30 in the evening – my cell mates won't be out of Greenock for another seven hours. It's great to finally get out, so I can find out if Roz and the others in our group are still locked up in a cell somewhere.

Melangell

by Kath McNulty, *Melangell Affinity Group*

Ange, Sid and I met at a nonviolence training session for Trident Ploughshares Pledgers at Sylvia's house in Birmingham. Ange and I had worked a lot together in Bangor trying to stop a luxury housing development on a green field site. Sid was an ideal partner as not only was he on a similar wavelength to us, but he was also from Wales. Soon we were joined by Sarah who lives not far from Sid. Thus the only Welsh Trident Ploughshares affinity group was formed.

We chose Melangell as our name. She is the Celtic patron saint of small animals and protector of the weak. This seemed appropriate against such an object as Trident. Now I must say a few words about Welsh pronunciation, because poor old Melangell must turn in her grave when she hears her name pronounced. It is not Mel-angel. To make the 'll' sound, put your tongue where it would be for 'l' and breathe out. Now try the whole word again. Say it with conviction. MELANGELL. See, it's easy really. Don't worry, Sid is still practising his 'll'.

Our first action together was to hand ourselves in at Brecon police station. After an hour the poor confused police officer phoned the CID duty officer who decided that although we sounded serious about conspiring to commit criminal damage she did not really want to arrest us.

We all felt that Scotland was a long way away and that we were not very familiar with the Scottish judicial system and so we decided to act locally. Approximately the same distance from Builth Wells (Sarah and Sid) and from Bangor (Ange and myself) lies Criggion, near Welshpool. This is home to one of the two VLF (Very Low Frequency) systems managed by British Telecom and used to communicate with submarines under water. VLF is used when a submarine is at about 30 feet below the surface; this would probably be the system used to order it to fire. Sid arranged a meeting with the manager. We were served tea and invited into the conference room to speak with him and a colleague from BT's policy branch. After about an hour and a half, the manager practically agreed with us about Trident (much to his colleague's consternation). He asked us if we would kindly go and target the other VLF system instead.

Our visit to Criggion made us realise that an action against the VLF system would be extremely dangerous as the current used was in excess of 14,000 volts. Apparently in some areas of the station your hair would stand up on end.

Time went by, we visited Faslane a few times. Sid was struck by the nonviolence practice of all the Trident Pledgers and the amazingly good relationship with the Scottish police. As a Christian he felt it was akin to the gospel reading to love one's enemies.

One day my local friendly CID officer came to visit (this is a semi-regular event; I think he likes the organic tea). As we were sipping, he suddenly announced that one of the masts at Criggion

Kath McNulty. August 1st 2000 Blockade at Faslane.
Credit: Andrew McColl

had fallen over and asked if Melangell had had any involvement. My face must have said it all! That night I said a little prayer for the pixies. Great work little people! BT has since announced that they will be shutting Criggion down. Unfortunately it will be succeeded by an American controlled satellite system.

Once the new Welsh assembly was formed, Sid and Sarah successfully lobbied their assembly member Kirsty Williams who tabled two statements of opinion (the Welsh equivalent to an Early Day Motion): to have a legal audit of Trident and to endorse Wales' historic Nuclear Free Status. So far these have been signed up to by approximately 20 assembly members.

In May 2000, the Trident issue grabbed the attention of the Welsh assembly. Angie Zelter, Professor Paul Rogers and Professor Nick Grief spoke about Trident Ploughshares, international law and the UK nuclear weapon system.

Nonviolent activism and anti-nuclear campaigning are certainly not new to Wales. In the late '70s the government was looking for underground dumping locations for nuclear waste. A myriad of anti-nuclear groups formed across Wales and lobbied their councils to declare nuclear free status. On 23 February 1982, Clwyd was the last council to sign up, making Wales the first self-declared nuclear-free country in the world. In August 1981, there was a protest walk from Cardiff to Greenham to object to the arrival of NATO nuclear missiles.

Melangell would like to grow. We are too few and too dispersed. We would like to see Trident Ploughshare groups all over Wales; in the north, the south and the middle. Would you like to join us?

Trashing Trident
by Rachel Wenham, *Aldermaston Trash Trident Affinity Group*

HMS *Vengeance*, the last of the British government's Vanguard class Trident submarines to be built, was in a dockyard in Cumbria undergoing final tests. According to people living around Barrow the sub was due to sail within weeks, around the end of February, to start its sea trials – testing the radio signals, radar, sonar etc. Then after crossing the Atlantic (traversing merchant shipping routes) *Vengeance* was to be provided with borrowed US missiles at Kings Bay Georgia. The real 'owner' of the Trident fleet is of course the USA. The US is responsible for the targeting of the submarines with the UK being given the right to veto its subs from being used to bomb any particular place. Needless to say, we rested assured that the UK government will carry on supporting the US in any sphere to aid it in its quest for 'Full Spectrum Dominance' (USDOD Vision for 2020). *Vengeance* would return from the US to be armed in Scotland and to resume polluting the environment (terrestrial and space) by firing tonnes of chemicals, fuel and non-recyclable metals into the sky.

At this time the US (idea) and UK (100% support) had stepped up its constant bombing of Iraq to wide-scale heavy bombing especially of Baghdad – including the people trying to live there in peace. Operation Desert Fox had been launched, veiled threats had been made by US *Rubin* that any use of force could not be ruled out in the event of an attack on the US by Iraq. HMS *Vanguard* was stationed at Gibraltar ready to move quickly into

Training exercise in the Lake District, January 1999.
From left to right: Rosie James, Rachel Wenham
Credit: Aldermaston Women's Trash Trident Affinity Group

firing range of the one of many civilian targets that had 'military value'.

On 30 January 1999 Rosie and I swam into the dockyard of Barrow-in-Furness, Cumbria, intending to damage the submarine so it could not go out for its sea trials, when it would constitute even more danger and threat to the global population than it already did in dock. With a badly designed nuclear reactor aboard and within metres of people's houses it constitutes a major hazard.

From subsequent court cases we have learnt that safety procedure at the dockyards are in line with the rest of the UK's civil defence. From the evidence of the security personnel and police, it seems that Marconi Vickers and the Ministry of Defence's safety policy is to cross their fingers and hope nothing will happen, whilst making police and security believe that in the event of a radioactive leak a mythical 'someone high up' will magically appear to tell them what to do.

We were dropped off by members of our fantastic Aldermaston Women's Trash Trident Affinity Group at the road that runs parallel to the dockside walk at about 2am and made our way to the bridge where we discarded our clothing (we already had wetsuits on).

There was a full moon, clear sky and no wind, so the dock was like a reflective mill-pond. The sub was brightly floodlit and had workers walking around on board and on the dockside. It took us approximately 1 1/2 hours to slowly make our way bobbing to the sub by pulling ourselves along the chains around the dock water-line. The water was filthy and polluted and we later both suffered stomach upset and extreme thirst in the police holding cells. Apparently there is toxic blue algae in the water but none of the usual warning signs were in evidence. Pulling ourselves out of the water under the gangplank leading from dock to sub we tug o' warred our wetsuit gloves off outside the security cabin, then unseen and unhindered strolled onto the submarine.

Plan A, to get into the sub and break whatever we could get to was abandoned because there were blokes in the sub hatches, so on to Plan B, spraying the subs conning tower with words truly descriptive of its nature. 'DEATH MACHINE', 'ILLEGAL INTERNATIONAL COURT OF JUSTICE 1996', 'NO MORE HIROSHIMAS'. Photographic evidence of this has never appeared in court. It was wiped off before it caught any passerby's eye and confirmed a breach of security, but we were charged £5 criminal damage for the cleaning fluid. We were subsequently acquitted of the charge by a High Court jury.

Plan C was quickly identified as climbing the ladder to the 'howdah' – a temporary platform around the conning tower. Here we found the box of high tech tricks that we are still (at time of writing, two trials on) charged with damaging. We opened and hammered on this, then climbed into the top hatch down into the submarine, passed a bloke, said hello to him, and disappeared into the machinations of the sub. The alarm had been raised by when we hung a WOMEN WANT PEACE banner from the howdah. Deciding to get it over with we climbed out of the sub and walked off past the milling aghast blokes and into the security cabin to our arrest.

Two years on we are looking forward to our next trial date, or hopefully looking forward to the charges being dropped by the Crime Prosecution Service in light of Sylvia and River's acquittal in Manchester in January 2001.

The Trident programme really is one of the crudest displays of a patriarchal system of control by threat, the most-followed male strategy of getting what they want i.e. by violence and the threat of violence.

Simplified Patriarchs Strategy

1 Anyone who objects, does something different to what they're told or simply doesn't agree with the over-balance of appropriated power held by the 'individual' (/US) gets threatened with a punch (/bomb).

2 If dissent & self-determination carries on they get the punch/bomb.

3 If dissenter is not cowed to absolute fear and subjugation, go to –

4 Dissenter gets punched into hospital/bombed until infrastructure is decimated, food and water sources rendered unfit for consumption, long term damage is inflicted to the environment caused by toxic weapons and the bombing of oil wells, chemical plants, nuclear power stations etc. etc.

5 Powerful one justifies action, denies they did anything wrong (i.e. not within their own grasp of human conduct/military strategy) and maintains it was in everyone's best interests, not least the assaulted as they'll come round to acknowledge their wrongdoing in provoking the attack in the first place.

The Trident programme is the epitome of threat and a constant reminder of the ruthlessness of Britain and the United States. Billions of pounds are thrown at the military at the expense of public health, welfare and education. It is anti-woman in the way that women get the mouse's share of the nation's financial resources. At the time of the multi-million dollar Desert Fox, cuts in single parent and disability benefit were being proposed in parliament. All wars affect women who are invariably left to pick up the pieces of their children and their living space after the men have taught them a lesson. It forces women as tax payers to pay for the bombing of people and hence keeping other women in a state of fear and insecurity in their name. How sickening is this.

So direct action against the military is vital, as it is the best way to delay, annoy, and expose the military's obvious desire to dominate, threaten and control.

CHAPTER FOUR

Setting the Legal Context

10 October, 2000 – High Court of Justiciary, Edinburgh, submission of Angie Zelter, 1st Respondent in the Lord Advocate's Reference, No.1. 2000.

'Had we been preventing an ordinary, everyday kind of murder it is very unlikely that such proceedings would have been instituted. Hidden under the guise of official and legitimate self-defence and bolstered by people's very understandable fears are preparations for the mass murder of innocents. Until Sheriff Gimblett's ruling we had wondered if this truth could ever be seen clearly by a judge, so many of them appeared to be seduced by the 'deterrence myth' that they seemed to have lost touch with ordinary human values. If a judge could not discern that mass murder was wrong what did that mean for our society?

Our act of lawful disarmament did not occur in a vacuum. It occurred in the context of 772 arrests of Trident Ploughshares Pledgers, a back-log of cases before the lower Scottish courts, and a commitment on our behalf to continue with our attempts to prevent nuclear crime. They occur in a wider context where citizens in all of the eight nuclear weapons states are engaged in resistance to the nuclear crime in one way or another and many of whom are facing various judicial proceedings. They occur in the international context of 114 states continuing condemnation of the nuclear weapons states' refusal to honour their commitments under the Non-Proliferation-Treaty and to immediately disarm their nuclear weapons.

Thus there is a political context to this LAR of which the court should be aware. I say this advisedly in the light of the specific questions chosen for the court to discuss and the deliberate refusal, by the Crown, to ask the court to look at the most serious of the questions raised by the Greenock acquittal – the question of the legality of Trident itself and why Scotland is allowing 100 kiloton nuclear warheads to be based, serviced and deployed from bases in Scotland in clear contravention of the basic human rights of the earth's peoples. If this question could be examined impartially by the court then people's disarmament would probably be unnecessary. I have asked on numerous occasions for this question to be raised at this hearing but to no avail. I have been told that it is for the Lord Advocate alone to determine which questions are asked of the court.

I was heartened to see in the Sheriff's Report that she also considers it 'right and proper that all matters raised by this trial ... should be considered'. She specifically included 'the question of what is meant by the threat and use and deployment' of nuclear weapons.

I think it is relevant, at this point, to remind the court that the Lord Advocate is a political appointee and a member of the executive of a major nuclear weapon state. The official policy of the UK is one of possession, deployment and threat to use the 100 kiloton nuclear warheads on Trident. If our argument is correct that Trident is criminal then everyone within the executive and military is actually aiding and abetting the preparation for the commission of major crimes against humanity and war crimes.'

> **Scotland is allowing 100 kiloton nuclear warheads to be based, serviced and deployed from bases in Scotland in clear contravention of the basic human rights of the earth's peoples**

Right from the start of my submissions I made it clear that the people engaging in people's disarmament are not the criminals – the government and military are. My role, as a non lawyer, as a woman and mother, as a responsible global citizen, was to state in plain language that murder is murder and is inexcusable. But this was going to prove to be a difficult job.

The first few days of the LAR were very uncomfortable and tense. I was surrounded by men in black gowns and wigs, none of them prepared to look me in the eye. They really did not like what they regarded as an upstart in their midst, who

> **My role was to state in plain language that murder is murder and is inexcusable**

couldn't speak Latin, had an English accent, did not know the rules and etiquette and who expected to be treated like an equal.

I had done my best not to be too different – I dressed smartly – and tried to tread that narrow line of respect for others' conventions without compromising my own integrity. By the fifth day we were all much more relaxed with each other. At the end of the nine days most of the lawyers, including those representing the Lord Advocate, were admitting that it had been a very interesting case, that they had all learnt a great deal about international law. There was even an impression that some of them might be sympathetic to our view that if nuclear weapons were lawful then the law was an ass.

The court did not allow an official transcript of the LAR but after an international appeal we raised the money to employ court transcribers and most of the proceedings are now on our web site. Many of the submissions were detailed technical legal arguments and there will no doubt be many academics and lawyers who will analyse them.

As our campaign is about ordinary people's disarmament, I have only included an edited version of my own submissions written after consultation with other concerned people, sympathetic international lawyers and friends. It will give a flavour of our arguments and concerns.

The first issue in my submissions to the High Court was to try to redress the partial and one-sided interpretation of our actions that came through in the wording of the questions and in the Lord Advocate's presentation of the facts of the case. They did not reflect our actions, nor our intentions or motivation nor did they match the facts as they had emerged in the evidence given in the trial at Greenock. Basically the Lord Advocate wanted to portray our act of disarmament and international crime prevention as one of purely opposition to and protest against nuclear weapons. He did not want to get into any kind of legal analysis of the possible criminality of Trident.

However, the LAR became a direct challenge to the legitimacy of the UK nuclear defence policies as well as a direct challenge to the Scottish judiciary.

10 October, 2000 – High Court of Justiciary, Edinburgh, opening remarks to the first submission of Angie Zelter, 1st Respondent in the Lord Advocate's Reference, No.1. 2000.

These proceedings, however cloaked in technical legal language, relate to whether there is a right for ordinary citizens to try to prevent innocent people from being murdered. More precisely, they will determine whether the Scottish legal system allows ordinary people in Scotland to try to prevent the 'most serious crimes of concern to the international community as a whole that is –

crimes against humanity and war crimes. What we will witness in this court is whether the Scottish judiciary have taken to heart the lessons from the horrific experiences of 'total war' in the Second World War and the necessity of ensuring that state practices are kept within the spirit and rule of international humanitarian law. We will learn whether Scottish law can accommodate what is known as the Nuremberg Obligation, i.e. the obligation placed upon individuals by the 1st Nuremberg Principle.

I then explained that my position in the LAR was that the threat or use of the nuclear warheads on the UK Trident weapon system is criminal under international law and that the UK's reliance on Trident in its military posture is a criminal conspiracy to carry out future war crimes and crimes against humanity in contravention of international humanitarian law. Asking the court to appreciate that the common theme underlying all the Lord Advocate's questions was the legal status of Trident, it was then time to lay out the legal arguments for the criminality of Trident.

10th and 11th October, 2000 – High Court of Justiciary, Edinburgh, submission of Angie Zelter, 1st Respondent in the Lord Advocate's Reference, No.1. 2000.

International Law and Nuclear Weapons

The 8 July 1996 Advisory Opinion of the ICJ outlines the sources of international law as they relate to nuclear weapons and is an authoritative articulation of customary international law on the legality of the use or threatened use of nuclear weapons. It is thus of exceptional relevance to this court providing guidance on whether and in what circumstances the 100 kiloton nuclear warheads on Trident are in breach of international law.

In my opinion the Advisory Opinion of 8 July 1996 makes it quite clear that nuclear weapons would generally breach all of the following:

The Declaration of St. Petersburg, 1868 because unnecessary suffering would be caused.

The Martens Clause, 1899 because humanity would not remain under the protection and authority of the principles of international law derived from established custom, from the principles of humanity and from the dictates of public conscience.

The Hague Conventions, 1907 because unnecessary suffering would be caused and there would be no guarantee of the inviolability of neutral nations.

The UN Charter, 1945 because such a use of force would not be proportionate.

The Universal Declaration of Human Rights, 1948 because long-lasting radioactive contamination would interfere with innocent people's inherent right to life and health.

The Geneva Conventions, 1949 (which has been brought directly into UK law through the 1957 Geneva Conventions Act) because protection of the wounded, sick, the infirm, expectant mothers, civilian hospitals and health workers would not be ensured.

The Protocols Additional to the Geneva Conventions, 1977 (which have also been directly brought into UK law through the 1995 Geneva Conventions (Amendments) Act) because there would be massive incidental losses of civilian lives and widespread, long-term and severe damage to the environment.

Serious violations of these treaties and declarations are defined as criminal acts under the Nuremberg Principles, 1946 in that Principle VI defines crimes against peace, war crimes and crimes against humanity. Specifically, Nuremberg Principle VI (a) defines crimes against peace as 'Planning, preparation, initiation or waging of ... a war in violation of international treaties, agreements or assurances ... Participation in a common plan or conspiracy for the accomplishment of any of the acts mentioned'. Nuremberg Principle VI (b) defines war crimes as 'violations of the laws or customs of war' and Nuremberg Principle VI (c) defines crimes against humanity as 'murder, extermination ... and other inhuman acts done against any civilian population ... when ... carried on in execution of, or in connection with any crime against peace or any war crime'.

In addition the Non-Proliferation Treaty (NPT), 1968 is being violated now because the United Kingdom is not fulfilling its obligation to negotiate nuclear disarmament.

The various rules of international law applicable to a consideration of whether Trident is in breach of international law can be summarised thus:

Rule of Proportionality: 'The Rule of Proportionality... prohibits the use of a weapon if its probable effects on combatant or non combatant persons or objects would likely be disproportionate to the value of the anticipated military objective.'

Rule of Necessity: 'The Rule of Necessity provides that, in conducting a military operation, a State may use only such a level of force as is 'necessary' or 'imperatively necessary' to achieve its military objective and that any additional level of force is prohibited as unlawful. The State must have an explicit military objective justifying each particular use of force in armed conflict and there must be a reasonable connection between the objective and the use of the particular force in question. If a military operation cannot satisfy this requirement, the State must use a lower level of force or refrain from the operation altogether.'

Rule of Moderation: 'The law of war recognises a general principle of moderation, expressed in the Hague Regulations by the maxim that 'the right of belligerents to adopt means of injuring the enemy is not unlimited' (Article 22). This principle is a basis of and generally overlaps with the principles of necessity and proportionality.'

Rule of Discrimination: 'The Rule of Discrimination prohibits the use of a weapon that cannot discriminate in its effects between military and civilian targets. The law recognises that the use of a particular weapon against a military target may cause unintended collateral or incidental damage to civilian persons and objects and permits such damage, subject to compliance with the other applicable rules of law, including the principle of proportionality. However, the weapon must have been intended for – and capable of being controlled and directed against – a military target, and the civilian damage must have been unintended and collateral or incidental.'

Also, 'On the question of the controllability of nuclear weapons, the issue becomes central as to whether the controllability element of the discrimination rule requires only that the attacking State be capable of delivering the weapons accurately to a particular military target, or whether it also requires that the State be able to control the weapon's effects, including radiation, upon delivery.'

Rule of Civilian Immunity: 'Occupying much the same ground as the Rules of Discrimination and Proportionality is the Rule of Civilian Immunity. The law of armed conflict prohibits 'the directing of attacks against civilians, making them immune from such attack.'

An analysis of these fundamental principles of international law and the ICJ Advisory Opinion clearly shows that Trident, as a high yield nuclear weapon system, is in breach of all of these rules. Moreover, Trident is also in breach of the two cardinal principles of international law that the ICJ details as being contained in the above 'fabric of humanitarian law'. It explains that

'The first is aimed at the protection of the civilian population and civilian objects and establishes the distinction between combatants and non combatants. States must never make civilians the object of attack and must consequently never use weapons that are incapable of distinguishing between civilian and military targets. According to the second principle, it is prohibited to cause unnecessary suffering to combatants: it is accordingly prohibited to use weapons causing them such harm or uselessly aggravating their suffering. In application of that second principle, states do not have unlimited freedom of choice of means in the weapons they use'.

Trident, as a high yield nuclear weapon system, is in breach of all of these rules

The United Kingdom confirmed these fundamental, intransgressible rules as customary laws at the Nuremberg International Military Tribunal and the Tokyo Tribunals, and supported them in the United Nations Security Council creation of the International Criminal Tribunal for the former Yugoslavia and in the International Criminal Tribunal for Rwanda.

In other words the international humanitarian principles used to assess the legality of nuclear weapons are well established in the international legal order. These customary rules are binding on all states at all times. Moreover many of these customary law principles have now been brought directly into UK Statute Law through the Geneva Conventions Act 1957 and the Geneva Conventions (Amendments) Act 1995.

Possible lawful use?

The only possible loophole that may have been left by the ICJ was when the Court stated, 'However, in view of the current state of international law, and of the elements of fact at its disposal, the court cannot conclude definitively whether the threat or use of nuclear weapons would be lawful or unlawful in an extreme circumstance of self-defence, in which the very survival of a State would be at stake'.

However, it is clear that this possible exception cannot apply to the British Trident 100 kiloton nuclear warheads. If a nuclear weapon existed that was of low yield and where its effects could be confined to a particular military target then it might be that its use would not be unlawful under this exception of self- defence.

The point is well put by Judge Shahabuddeen who says, 'An 'extreme circumstance of self-defence, in which the very survival of a State would be at stake' ... is the main circumstance in which the proponents of legality advance a claim to a right to use nuclear weapons. This is so for the reason that, assuming that the use of nuclear weapons is lawful, the nature of the weapons, combined with the limitations imposed by the requirements of necessity and proportionality which condition the exercise of the right of self-defence, will serve to confine their lawful right to that 'extreme circumstance'. It follows that to hold that humanitarian law does not apply to the use of nuclear weapons in the main circumstances in which a claim of a right of use is advanced is to uphold the substance of a thesis that humanitarian law does not apply at all to the use of nuclear weapons. That view has long been discarded; as the Court itself recalls, the NWS [Nuclear Weapons States] themselves do not advocate it. I am not persuaded that a disfavoured thesis can be brought back to an exception based on self-defence.'

What is beyond doubt is that Trident could never be justified in an 'extreme circumstance of self-defence' because 100 kiloton warheads would always fail the test of proportionality, necessity, controllability, discrimination, and civilian immunity. Most important of all it breaches the cardinal, or intransgressible, rule of humanitarian law in its inability to discriminate between military and civilian targets.

100 kiloton warheads would always fail the test of proportionality, necessity, controllability, discrimination, and civilian immunity

Judge Bedjaoui, President of the ICJ, stated very clearly, 'I cannot sufficiently emphasize that the Court's inability to go beyond this statement of the situation can in no way be interpreted to mean that it is leaving the door ajar to recognition of the legality of the threat or use of nuclear weapons'. He also stated that 'at no time did the Court lose sight of the fact that nuclear weapons constitute a potential means of destruction of all mankind ... By its very nature the nuclear weapon, a blind weapon, therefore has a destabilizing effect on humanitarian law, the law of discrimination which regulates discernment in the use of weapons'.

Illegality of the United Kingdom's nuclear weapons

The ICJ was asked to consider a general question. However, if we apply the principles and rules of international law confirmed by the ICJ to the Trident system and place this within the context of the destructive capacity of the warheads and their likely targets then it is quite clear that Trident is unlawful.

As we established at Greenock through the expert witnesses, British Trident nuclear warheads are 100 to 120 kilotons each – that is around 8 to 10 times larger than the ones used at Hiroshima and Nagasaki – and have military targets assigned to them in and around Moscow. Such use of these nuclear weapons could not distinguish between civilian and military. Indeed it is nonsense to suggest that a nuclear bomb eight times larger than the Hiroshima bomb could possibly do so. The reason nuclear weapons are targeted in this way is to try to deter war by threatening mass destruction. The tragic flaw in this logic being that if nuclear deterrence fails and the United Kingdom's bluff is called, the threat of mass destruction must be carried out. It follows that the purpose of Trident is to terrorise and to create 'incalculable and unacceptable' risks, just as the NATO Strategic Concept Document specifies. Whilst politicians and others fudge the issue, the very point of 'nuclear deterrence' is to threaten mass destruction.

the sword of Damocles remains perilously over our heads

It was submitted at Greenock that the British Trident system is an immediate and ongoing danger to life on Earth, a threat to international peace and specifically unlawful as a breach of the intransgressible rules of humanitarian law as expressed by the ICJ. I continue to submit that we are still in imminent danger of extinction. As our expert witness, Professor Jack Boag, so graphically explained at Greenock, the sword of Damocles remains perilously over our heads.

Self-Defence

The ICJ held that 'a use of force that is proportionate under the law of self-defence must, in order to be lawful, also meet the requirements of the law applicable in armed conflict which comprise the principles and rules of humanitarian law'.

The main stumbling block for the United Kingdom can be found by examining the oral presentation given by Sir Nicholas Lyell to the ICJ on 15 November 1995. After admitting that 'there is no doubt that the customary law of war does prohibit some uses of nuclear weapons, just as it prohibits some uses of all types of weapons', he then undermines this by elaborating a situation in which states are faced with invasion by overwhelming enemy forces: 'If all other means at their disposal are insufficient, then how can it be said that the use of a nuclear weapon must be disproportionate? Unless it is being suggested that there comes a point when the victim of aggression is no longer permitted to defend itself because of the degree of suffering which defensive measures will inflict'.

Yet this is the point of international humanitarian law. It is intended to limit the terrible effects of war and to ensure that there is a world left after a conflict ends. This means self restraint even in justified self-defence.

international humanitarian law is intended to limit the terrible effects of war and to ensure that there is a world left after a conflict ends

According to the President of the Court, Judge Bedjaoui, 'self-defence – if exercised in extreme circumstances in which the very survival of a State is in question – cannot engender a situation in which a State would exonerate itself from compliance with 'intransgressible' norms of international humanitarian law. ... The fact remains that the use of nuclear weapons by a State in circumstances in which its survival is at stake risks in its turn endangering the survival of all mankind, precisely because of the inextricable link between terror and escalation in the use of such weapons. It would thus be quite foolhardy unhesitatingly to set the survival of a State above all other considerations, in particular above the survival of mankind itself'.

As Professor Christopher Greenwood QC who represented the United Kingdom at the hearings before the ICJ observed, 'To allow the necessities of self-defence to override the principles of humanitarian law would put at risk all the progress in that law which has been made over the last hundred years or so'.

The International Committee of the Red Cross has stated, 'The basic rule of protection and distinction ... is the foundation on which the codification of the laws and customs of war rests: the civilian population and civilian objects must be respected and protected in armed conflict, and for this purpose they must be distinguished from combatants and military objectives. The entire system established in the Hague in 1899 and 1907 and in Geneva from 1864-1977 is founded on this rule of customary law.'

The significance of the humanitarian rule for the deployment of British Trident nuclear weapons is not that all nuclear weapons are prohibited as such, though they will generally be contrary to international law; nor, necessarily, that there can be no use of smaller, low yield, tactical nuclear weapons yet to be invented; or that there could be no policy of some kinds of nuclear deterrence; or no reservation for use in an extreme circumstance of self-defence in which the very survival of the state would be at stake. The point is that the humanitarian rule governs any such weapons or uses. Any low yield weapon, or deterrence/self-defence policy must comply with the humanitarian rule; any weapon which cannot comply is unlawful.

Taking into account the blast, heat and radioactive effects of the detonation of a 100 kiloton nuclear warhead, especially since radioactive effects cannot be contained, the use of even a single British Trident warhead in any circumstance would inevitably violate the prohibitions on the infliction of unnecessary suffering and indiscriminate harm as well as the rule of proportionality. Further, since the UK deploys its nuclear forces in a state of readiness for use pursuant to a declared policy contemplating use of nuclear weapons in a variety of circumstances, including first use, the deployment of Trident warheads is a threat in violation of humanitarian and other international law.

Many citizens and organisations have asked for examples of what the government considers a lawful use of Trident nuclear weapons. They have never been given a straight answer. This is not surprising since, simply put, each Trident warhead is a potential holocaust. Instead, the government states that 'Maintaining a degree of uncertainty about our precise capabilities is a key element of a credible minimum deterrent. It is precisely to retain this degree of uncertainty and so sustain our minimum deterrent that secrecy must be maintained in this area.' But hiding behind this veil of secrecy allows the fudging and crooked thinking to continue.

The fact remains that Trident nuclear weapons are being used to frighten and intimidate and to threaten mass destruction. This is unlawful.

Present policy statements show that the United Kingdom does not limit its use of nuclear threats to 'extreme circumstances of self-defence'. The government clearly recognises that the United Kingdom is not in danger of a threat to its 'very survival'.

hiding behind this veil of secrecy allows the fudging and crooked thinking to continue

The Strategic Defence Review conducted by the government states 'The end of the Cold War has transformed our security environment. The world does not live in the shadow of World War. There is no longer a direct threat to Western Europe or the United Kingdom as we used to know it and we face no significant threat to our Overseas Territories'.

Given that the survival of the United Kingdom is not in question, the deployment of Trident nuclear submarines is an unlawful threat even if the government vouches that there is only one nuclear warhead of below one kiloton deployed, let alone the 144 warheads of up to 120 kilotons each that could be deployed [on the three Trident submarines currently in service].

Defence Of Vital Interests

It is clear that the United Kingdom's nuclear weapon deployment and policy are not purely concerned with self-defence or even with retaliation against a nuclear attack from another nuclear weapons state, but are also 'to defend our vital interests to the utmost' as expressed in the Rifkind Doctrine.

The Strategic Defence Review specifically sees military power as 'a coercive instrument to support political objectives' which the rest of the report explicitly identifies as economic and oil-related. The government says in the Review that Trident must perform a 'sub-strategic role' stating that the 'credibility of deterrence also depends on retaining an option for a limited strike that would not automatically lead to a full-scale nuclear exchange'. There has been a great deal of confusion and a certain amount of scepticism about what Trident's sub-strategic role might look like in practice. The Secretary of State for Defence for the previous Conservative Government, Malcolm Rifkind, referred to a 'warning shot' or 'shot across the bows'. More recently, British officials have described a sub-strategic strike as 'the limited and highly selective use of nuclear weapons in a manner that fell demonstrably short of a strategic strike, but with a sufficient level of violence to convince an aggressor who had already mis-calculated our resolve and attacked us that he should halt his aggression and withdraw or face the prospect of a devastating strategic strike'.

For a sub-strategic role there has been speculation that some of the 100 kiloton MIRVed warheads would be replaced with single 1 kiloton or 5 or even 10 kiloton warheads, or that commanders could choose to detonate only the unboosted primary, resulting in an explosion with a yield of just a few kilotons.

There are three core problems with the concept of a warning shot to deter further aggression:

i) it cannot be used against non-nuclear parties to the Non-Proliferation Treaty without violating Britain's security assurances, most recently enshrined in the UN Security Council Resolution 984 (1995);

ii) it is not clear where such a warning shot could be fired so that civilians are not endangered; and

iii) it is not apparent how, in the uncertain context of a hotting-up conflict, Britain would ensure that the adversary interpreted such a nuclear shot from Trident as a warning rather than a nuclear attack. Since pre-emption requires fast decision-making, it would be likely that a sub-strategic nuclear use would cause nuclear retaliation and possibly all-out nuclear war. British planners tend to duck the questions rather than address the dilemma, leaving the impression that they hope the bridge will never have to be faced, never mind crossed.

> **British planners tend to duck the questions rather than address the dilemma, leaving the impression that they hope the bridge will never have to be faced, never mind crossed**

As Lord Murray (a former Lord Advocate of Scotland) pointed out, even a one kiloton bomb 'would flatten all buildings within

0.5 km with up to 50 per cent fatalities up to 1 km. A prevailing wind could carry fallout as far as 25 km downwind'. As Professor Paul Rogers agreed, in his testimony at Greenock, 'the lowest British nuclear bomb is a weapon of mass destruction'.

The deployment of nuclear weapons is perceived as an imminent ever-present threat by most states in the world, which in times of crisis is specifically backed up by verbal threats. This view is corroborated by Judge Schwebel in his reply to testimony from Ambassador Ekeus in the Senate Hearings on the Global Proliferation of Weapons of Mass Destruction which shows that Iraq perceived that there was an active threat to use nuclear weapons against it in 1990. In Schwebel's section headed 'Desert Storm', he starts, 'The most recent and effective threat of the use of nuclear weapons took place on the eve of Desert Storm' and continues to describe how the threat was communicated.

In the February 1998 Iraq crisis there was also talk of the possible use of nuclear weapons against Iraq. Any such use would have been unlawful because neither the United Kingdom nor the United States were under threat of obliteration by Iraq. It is worth remembering that the only possible window of legality left undecided by the ICJ was 'an extreme circumstance of self-defence, in which its very survival would be at stake'.

And yet in the Commons Debate of 17 February 1998, Foreign Secretary Robin Cook said of Saddam Hussein: 'As in 1991, he should be in no doubt that if he were to do so [use chemical weapons against joint British-US air strikes] there would be a proportionate response'.

Interviewed on BBC Radio 4 on 18 February 1998, Defence Secretary George Robertson was given an opportunity to deny the nuclear option and did not do so. These were signals suggesting that nuclear weapons would be considered.

The whole purpose of nuclear deterrence is to create uncertainty about intentions. This means that the British government has to persuade its 'enemies' that it might be willing to break international law without actually saying it this clearly. For instance, in the 1991 NATO Strategic Concept Document, Article

38 asserted that nuclear weapons are essential and permanent because they 'make a unique contribution in rendering the risks of any aggression incalculable and unacceptable'.

If the effect of a nuclear weapon is incalculable and unacceptable then it also follows that it is unlawful. Nuclear weapons are useful only in so far as they can be used to make threats that are themselves in breach of international law. Nuclear deterrence may be official British policy but that does not make it lawful.

To stress the words used in the ICJ, given that nuclear weapons are generally illegal, there is only one situation when the use of nuclear weapons might be conceivable, and that is 'in an extreme circumstance of self-defence, in which the very survival of a State would be at stake'.

That does not include protecting cheap oil supplies overseas or ensuring the survival of its troops in a foreign land.

War Crimes

Any individual who ordered the use of the United Kingdom's nuclear weapons which are currently deployed on Trident submarines would have committed a war crime as determined by the International Criminal Court Statute. This Statute sets forth offences under which individuals would be prosecuted once that court is in operation. Its substantive provisions were explicitly negotiated on the basis that they would reflect the present state of law binding on all states. While the Statute is not yet in effect, as the required number of states (60) has not yet ratified the instrument (the UK are preparing to ratify it in this new parliamentary session), the Statute stands as a consensus-based statement of presently binding law defining war crimes.

Article 8 (2) (b) parts (iv) and (v) of the International Criminal Court Statute state, 'War crimes means... serious violations of the laws and customs applicable in international armed conflict, within the established framework of international law, namely, any of the following acts; ... (iv) Intentional launching an attack in the knowledge that such an attack will cause incidental loss of life or injury to civilians or damage to civilian objects or widespread, long term and severe damage to the natural environment which would clearly be excessive in relation to the concrete and direct overall military advantage anticipated, (v) Attacking or bombarding, by whatever means, towns, villages, dwellings or buildings which are undefended and which are not military objectives'.

Article 25 of the Rome Statute contemplates criminal responsibility not only in the case of those who personally commit offences, but also in the case of those who order them. Article 28 has far-reaching provisions on the responsibility of commanders and other superiors who may be liable in some situations for not giving appropriate orders.

In relation to this responsibility it is important to note that the British government has always refused to answer our question of how the crew of Trident can take personal responsibility for their actions when their targets are coded and they do not know where their nuclear warheads will explode? The Law of Armed Conflict states, 'Military personnel are required to obey lawful commands. There is no defence of 'superior orders'. If a soldier carries out an illegal order, both he and the person giving that order are responsible.' The Nuremberg principle is binding. If Trident crews do not know what the targets of their weapons are, how can they know if they are legal targets or not? Trident crews fire blind. This is a criminal procedure.

> **The British government has aways refused to answer our question of how the crew of Trident can take personal responsibility for their actions when their targets are coded and they do not know where their nuclear warheads will explode?**

The 100 kiloton warheads on Trident are each eight times more powerful than the bomb used against Hiroshima. The Hiroshima bomb had killed approximately 140-150,000 people by the end of 1945, and devastated an entire city.

Moreover, in Hiroshima this March I met survivors of that bomb who told me of the continuing suffering. A book I was given there states, 'The damage caused by the A bomb failed to heal normally with the passage of time. Over the decades, the horrors of radiation grew more conspicuous. Research into radiation effects, strictly suppressed during the occupation [by the US] proceeded rapidly when Japan was once again independent. This research gradually brought radiation after-effects and the plight of the survivors into the open'. That destruction in Hiroshima was ruled a war crime in the Shimoda Case where it was stated that the 'act of dropping such a cruel bomb is contrary to the fundamental principles of the laws of war that unnecessary pain not be given'.

According to the ICJ threat or use of nuclear weapons must 'be compatible with the requirements of the international law applicable in armed conflict'. It was confirmed that 'States must never make civilians the object of attack and must consequently never use weapons that are incapable of distinguishing between civilian and military targets ... states do not have unlimited freedom of choice of means in the weapons they use'.

The threat to target civilians with nuclear weapons, whether as an unprovoked attack or as a reprisal, is therefore unlawful. In the oral statement that the United Kingdom gave to the ICJ on 15 November 1995, Sir Nicholas Lyell admitted that '... even a military target must not be attacked if to do so would cause collateral civilian casualties or damage to civilian property which is excessive in relation to the concrete and direct military advantage anticipated from the attack'.

> The destructive power of nuclear weapons cannot be contained in either space or time. They have the potential to destroy all civilisation and the entire ecosystems of the planet

However, as the ICJ points out 'By its very nature ... nuclear weapons as they exist today, release(s) not only immense quantities of heat and energy, but also powerful and prolonged radiation ... These characteristics render the nuclear weapon potentially catastrophic. The destructive power of nuclear weapons cannot be contained in either space or time. They have the potential to destroy all civilisation and the entire ecosystems of the planet'. This general statement about nuclear weapons is equally true when applied to British nuclear weapons.

Faslane in Scotland is the primary base used by the United Kingdom's four nuclear-armed Trident submarines. There is at least one Trident submarine on 24-hour patrol at all times. Each Trident submarine has 48 warheads of 100 to 120 kilotons each. A 100 kiloton warhead is too powerful to distinguish between civilian and military targets and its long lasting effects cannot be contained within space or time and therefore violates international law.

Today the scale of Britain's nuclear capability and the way it is deployed suggest that it remains oriented principally against Russia. An attack using the warheads on one submarine against likely targets in the Moscow area would result in over 3 million deaths and there would also be massive nuclear fallout over urban areas. Thousands of people would die over a 4 to 12 week period from this fallout.

Other potential targets are Russian northern fleet submarine bases. In the United Kingdom there are towns and villages close to every key submarine facility – Faslane is near the civilian population in Glasgow. There are also civilian populations close to Russian bases near Murmansk. Trident warheads exploding above these bases would cause devastation over a wide area and in each case would result in thousands of civilian casualties in urban areas. The areas affected would also be dangerous to rescue and medical staff and civilians who would want to use the area in future.

Preparations for War Crimes

The preparation for war crimes is itself a war crime, as made most explicit in the International Criminal Court Statute Article 25 (3). 'In accordance with this Statute, a person shall be criminally responsible and liable for punishment for a crime within the jurisdiction of the Court if that person: ...(c) For the purpose of facilitating the commission of such a crime, aids, abets or otherwise assists in its commission or its attempted commission, including providing the means for its commission'.

This is a culmination of various precedents such as the last paragraph of Article 6 of the Charter of the International Military Tribunal at Nuremberg on 'instigators and accomplices participating in the formulation ... of a common plan or conspiracy'.

The Prime Minister and other officers of the state are engaged in planning and preparation for use of nuclear weapons, in that they are actively deploying nuclear weapons of such a size that they could never be used lawfully. These are activities that incur individual criminal responsibility in international law. Any use of current British nuclear weapons would be manifestly unlawful and thus policy makers, state employees, researchers and technicians are engaged in the planning and preparation of gross violations of humanitarian law, itself a crime under international law.

Nuclear Policy

Just as the use of British nuclear weapons would be illegal and criminal so is the threat to use them. If we look at the statement given to the ICJ by Japanese lawyers in 1995 it states, 'The world's citizens are being threatened at this very moment'. They explained, 'Since Hiroshima and Nagasaki the nuclear powers have always hinted at the possibility that they might use nuclear weapons and have continued saying that it is legal. Nobody on earth can live their lives while putting their trust in this 'humanity' of the nuclear powers. This is because resigning oneself to a condition of servility, in which one's very existence as a human being is controlled by the intentions of a handful of nuclear-armed states, goes against the nature of human beings, and jeopardises our supreme and inalienable right to life, which is universally affirmed in the Universal Declaration of Human Rights and the International Covenant on Human Rights. This state of nuclear servitude also jeopardises our enjoyment of other human rights and basic freedoms, and therefore means that 'human dignity' is violated.'

The ICJ argues that a credible deterrent is a threat. I quote, 'Possession of nuclear weapons may indeed justify an inference of preparedness to use them. In order to be effective, the policy of deterrence ... necessitates that the intention to use nuclear weapons be credible. Whether this is a 'threat' contrary to Article 2, paragraph 4, [of the UN Charter] depends upon whether the particular use of force ... would necessarily violate the principles of necessity and proportionality. In any of these circumstances the use of force, and the threat to use it would be unlawful under the law of the Charter.'

Even US Judge Schwebel explains that states have threatened to use their nuclear weapons 'by the hard facts and inexorable implications of the possession and deployment of nuclear weapons; by a posture of readiness to launch nuclear weapons 365 days a year, 24 hours of every day; by the military plans, strategic and tactical, developed and sometimes publicly revealed by them; and, in a very few international crises, by threatening the use of nuclear weapons. In the very doctrine and practice of deterrence, the threat of the possible use of nuclear weapons inheres'. He re-iterates the point, 'If a threat of possible use did not inhere in deterrence, deterrence would not deter'.

UK government policy is that Britain has a 'credible nuclear deterrent'. This means far more than possession. A credible deterrent requires the other side to be convinced that the weapons would be used. So to have a credible deterrent means that preparations have been made to use the weapons and there is an intention to use them in some circumstances. One strand of strategic thinking is 'existential deterrence'. This approach says that the possession of nuclear arms is in itself sufficient to constitute a deterrent. Existential deterrence is not currently practised by any of the main nuclear weapons states.

The former Permanent Under Secretary at the MOD, Michael Quinlan, has dismissed this approach. He said of existential deterrence, 'We cannot however infer from this that our own armoury will be durably effective in contributing to deterrence, especially in times of pressure when it is most needed, if there are no realistic concepts for its use or if we have a settled resolve never to use it. ... Deterrence and use in logic can be distinguished, but not wholly disconnected. We cannot say that nuclear weapons are for deterrence and never for use, however remote we judge the latter possibility to be. Weapons deter by the possibility of their use, and by no other route; the distinction sometimes attempted between deterrent capabilities and war-fighting capabilities has in a strict sense no meaningful basis ... The concept of deterrence accordingly cannot exist solely in the present – it inevitably contains a reference forward to future action, however contingent. The reference need not entail auto-maticity, or even a firm intention linked to defined hypotheses; it need entail no more than a refusal to rule out all possibility of use; but it cannot entail less'.

In fact the UK goes much further than this. According to one of the more detailed assessments of the range of options for sub-strategic Trident warheads, David Miller, for the International Defence Review in 1994, outlined four different uses, in the third one of which he says, 'they could be used in a demonstrative role: i.e. aimed at a non-critical uninhabited area, with the message that if the country concerned continued on its present course of action, nuclear weapons would be aimed at a high-priority target.' This is backed up by a recent letter of 28/9/2000 received from the Ministry of Defence which talks of sending a 'signal' and which also leaves open the possibil-ity of firing 'all the nuclear weapons at its dis-posal'. However, even a limited warning shot would not be lawful because its purpose would be to warn that much worse will come and that worse would be an indisputably illegal high-yield bomb and therefore the warning shot itself would be an illegal threat. I come back once more to the simple underlying purpose of the British nuclear deterrent – to threaten awful destruction. It is that awful destruction that we three women were trying to prevent by our action.

the warning shot itself would be an illegal threat

The Advisory Opinion makes it clear that it is illegal to threaten to do an act if the act itself is illegal, 'If the envisaged use of force is itself unlawful, the stated readiness to use it would be a threat prohibited under Article 2, paragraph 4' of the UN Charter. The United Kingdom possesses nuclear weapons, of a size that can-not be used discriminately, which are constantly deployed on submarines, ready to be used, and has made statements of con-ditional willingness to use them in British policy documents. This 'stated readiness to use' its nuclear weapons is exactly the kind of threat that is prohibited under Article 2(4) of the UN Charter.

British nuclear warheads of 100 kilotons could never be used in conformity with the principles of necessity and proportionality and the requirements of international law. Therefore continuous active deployment combined with a stated readiness to use them constitutes an illegal threat to use nuclear weapons and as such is illegal.

Refusal to Negotiate under Article VI of the NPT

The ICJ appreciated 'the full importance of the recognition by Article VI of the Treaty on the Non-Proliferation of Nuclear Weapons of an obligation to negotiate in good faith a nuclear disarmament'. It ruled unanimously, 'There exists an obligation to pursue in good faith and bring to a conclusion negotiations leading to nuclear disarmament in all its aspects under strict and effective international control'. It stated, 'The legal import of that obligation goes beyond that of a mere obligation of conduct; the obligation involved here is an obligation to achieve a precise result, nuclear disarmament in all its aspects, by adopting a particular course of conduct, namely, the pursuit of negotiations on the matter in good faith.'

British nuclear warheads of 100 kilotons could never be used in conformity with the principles of necessity and proportionality and the requirements of international law. Therefore continuous active deployment combined with a stated readiness to use them constitutes an illegal threat to use nuclear weapons and as such is illegal

The United Kingdom has made clear it has no immediate intention of eliminating its Trident system. The Strategic Defence Review specifies plans for upgrading Trident in the medium term and keeping options open for a replacement in the long term. Recent press revelations and a report by Alan Simpson MP present evidence of the new refurbishment programme at the Atomic Weapons Establishment at Aldermaston costing one hundred and fifty million pounds sterling and of a linkage with the US 'son of Trident' programme to upgrade nuclear warheads. There is also proof of increased scientific collaboration between the United Kingdom, France and the US. Simpson's report concludes, 'there is strong evidence that Britain is currently involved in the development of prototype designs to replace the current Trident nuclear warhead'.

Nor has the United Kingdom been working in good faith within the UN for nuclear disarmament resolutions. For instance, in 1998 the United Kingdom voted against the resolution, 'Towards a Nuclear Weapon-Free World: The Need for a New Agenda'. Ian Soutar, the British ambassador to the UN, said that the resolution contained measures that were 'inconsistent with the maintenance of a credible minimum deterrent'. The United Kingdom also voted, for the third consecutive year, against the 1999 UN Resolution on 'Follow-up to the ICJ Advisory Opinion'.

The United Kingdom's refusal to stop deploying Trident and to start its practical disarmament of Trident flouts Article VI of the Non-Proliferation Treaty

The United Kingdom's refusal to stop deploying Trident and to start its practical disarmament of Trident flouts Article VI of the Non-Proliferation Treaty as interpreted by the ICJ in paras.99 and 105(2F) of the Advisory Opinion. The continuing development of new nuclear weapons is also a breach of Article VI and constitutes a violation of international law. At the recent Review Conference of the Non-Proliferation Treaty in New York in May 2000, although the United Kingdom joined in the consensus 'unequivocal undertaking by the nuclear weapon states to accomplish the total elimination of their nuclear arsenals', nevertheless, they have not done anything practical to put this into effect. The original Non-Proliferation Treaty promises by the nuclear weapons states were not fulfilled. The United Kingdom continues to fund research into new nuclear weapon systems, continues to deploy armed nuclear missiles and continues to state that it relies upon nuclear deterrence. In this context it is not surprising that ordinary citizens have felt the necessity to begin the disarmament themselves.

Conclusion

The government has frequently been asked but has never explained to the ICJ or to the British public how it could possibly use its nuclear weapons legally. It has not even been able to outline one hypothetical example. The government has, in fact, been very careful to say that it could never foresee the precise circumstances and could therefore not determine the legality until the time came to use them. It is hard to see how, with no criteria apparently available as guidance, any responsible commander could make a decision to unleash Trident missiles within the probable fifteen minutes time frame that would be available. It is clear that the British government has to date been unable and unwilling to open itself to independent legal scrutiny.

The government has frequently been asked but has never explained to the ICJ or to the British public how it could possibly use its nuclear weapons legally. It has not even been able to outline one hypothetical example

The form of words the government usually uses is: 'the legality or otherwise of any specific use of any nuclear weapons ... can only be determined in the light of all the circumstances applying at the time such use is being considered. It is impossible to anticipate in advance with any confidence the exact circumstances which might arise, and to speculate on particular hypothetical cases would serve no purpose'.

It is absurd to think that had such legal scrutiny and exercises not taken place before, any thorough legal scrutiny of an actual use of nuclear weapons could take place in the heat of a war of self-defence in which the very survival of the United Kingdom was at stake. The fact that the British government cannot identify a single hypothetical case that could be presented into the public domain for independent legal scrutiny suggests there are none.

Finally, with the permission of the court, I would like to share some extra information from the classic corpus of post World War Two war crimes trials, which directly counter the impression that nothing can be illegal so long as it assists the UK in a situation it defines as one of extreme necessity.

In the Hostages Case the Nuremberg Tribunal clearly stated that 'the rules of international law must be followed even if it results in the loss of a battle or even a war. Expediency or necessity cannot warrant their violation'. This passage was prominently cited by the Commission in the concluding Digest of Law and Cases as well as being followed in the German High Command Trial where the Tribunal explicitly repudiated as 'a denial of all laws' the theory that 'the laws of war lose their binding force in case of extreme necessity, which was said to arise when the violation of the laws of war offers other means of escape from extreme danger, or the realisation of the purpose of war – namely, the overpowering of the enemy.'

> the rules of international law must be followed even if it results in the loss of a battle or even a war. Expediency or necessity cannot warrant their violation

In the same case the Tribunal placed use of poisoned arms in a category of conventional and customary rules that 'do not lose their binding force even if the breach would effect an escape from extreme danger or the realization of the purpose of law'.

And it also went on to quote the key sentence in the judgement of the Tribunal in the Krupp trial:

'However, quite apart from this consideration, the contention that the rules and customs of warfare can be violated if either party is hard pressed in any way must be rejected on other grounds. War is by definition a risky and hazardous business. That is one of the reasons that the outcome of war, once started, is unforeseeable and that, therefore, war is a basically unrational means of 'settling' conflicts – why right-thinking people all over the world repudiate and abhor aggressive war. It is an essence of war that one or the other side must lose and the experienced generals and statesmen knew this when they drafted the rules and customs of land warfare. In short these rules and customs of warfare are designed specifically for all phases of war. They comprise the law for such an emergency. To claim that they can be wantonly – and at the sole discretion of any one belligerent – disregarded when he considers his own situation to be critical, means nothing more or less than to abrogate the laws and customs of war entirely.'

The implication of all this is that British government officials involved in the Trident programme, from the Prime Minister down, including all members of the executive and the Lord Advocate, and the military personnel involved, are all international criminals subject to trial before an international panel similar to the Nuremberg or Tokyo Tribunal or the current tribunals dealing with the atrocities in Rwanda and the former Yugoslavia.

So far no court of law or tribunal has upheld my view (which is shared by millions of other people around the world) because no court has been allowed to look directly and thus to rule on the issue of the legal status of the UK's Trident system. This is not for want of trying.

In fact, many citizens, over the last 20 years, have put motions and petitions before the Lord Advocate and Attorney General asking that the UK nuclear forces be ruled unlawful under the Geneva Conventions Act or that the issues are at least examined impartially in a public inquiry. Many citizens have asked for legal permission at numerous magistrates courts around England and Wales to institute private prosecutions against ministers and military leaders, indicting them for conspiracy and incitement to violate the most fundamental principles of international and United Kingdom law – but to no avail – so far.

These attempts still continue. In answer to a written question put by Tony Benn MP in December last year, the Solicitor General admitted that, 'A request for a private prosecution under the Geneva Conventions Act 1957 was received last year. However, the law officers take the view that the application of the government's nuclear deterrence policy does not involve an infringement of either domestic or international law, and accordingly permission was not given.' Many citizens have also approached the police to ask them to investigate the crime and take legal proceedings in the public interest. But to no effect. The rule of law is still being thwarted. This is a serious failure and indictment of the judicial system in both Scotland and England.

The rule of law is still being thwarted

In view of the general failure of the executive to allow remedies to be taken by ordinary citizens against crimes being committed by the state, it is not surprising that ordinary people, like us three women, have felt the absolute necessity to try to work with others to prevent this crime ourselves.

I hope that this court will now help to remedy this situation which is one of the utmost seriousness, involving as it does the right of ordinary people to protect themselves and others and their planet from utter destruction. I hope also that this court, although it has not allowed the addition of a question to look at the legality of Trident, will nevertheless see the wisdom of at least recommending, in the final ruling, that there be an immediate independent judicial enquiry into the legal status of Trident.

It is just not good enough for the Crown to lamely repeat the official government line that Trident is lawful. At Greenock we brought evidence to show that Trident is not only unlawful but also criminal. This decision should not be undermined in any way unless and until a full, independent, publicly accountable inquiry into Trident and present British policy is set up with opportunities for all concerned citizens to present full evidence backed up by testimony from expert witnesses.

Confronting Fears
by Sue Davis, *Muriel Lester Affinity Group*

I'm a late starter. At Greenham I was on many blockades, often moved by the police, but never arrested. Blockades and years later, August 2000, it was time. The whole issue of the illegality of nuclear weapons, with the ICJ Advisory Opinion, and the Greenock acquittals, followed now by the Manchester acquittals, has made the law (upholding it, breaking it?) a seriously possible mainstream route to the final abolition of nuclear weapons. And I had become a Trident Ploughshares Pledger, which tested my true commitment!

So there I was again sitting in the road outside Faslane Trident submarine base, and at last – refusing to move when politely asked by the policeman. I had no idea what to expect or how I would react. The rest of the day was like a game. At Clydebank police station we joined a number of women waiting to be processed. The policemen (all men) guarding us joined our game, stooping down obediently under the web made by one of us with a ball of wool, in order to cross the room. Each of them showed true pleasure – wonder even – when given a paper crane, which two Buddhist nuns were busily making. We could make mugs of tea, courtesy of Her Majesty. As we left for the cells the policemen all shook hands with us. It seemed clear to me then that they were 'on our side'. The removal of possessions, including watches, was no hardship since there were three of us in the cell, so plenty of chat, and time passed easily enough. We tried playing 'I spy', but soon ran out of things to spy! We could ask to go to the toilet privately, escorted there by a friendly policewoman. There was a choice of three dishes on the menu for lunch and supper, and in between I rang the bell and asked if it was time for a cuppa. 'Oh yes of course. Milk and sugar?' And along came three mugs of tea.

So it all felt like a game. Even the fingerprinting was pointless and friendly – and interesting to a first-timer – ritual: since we were first 'offenders' we knew it was likely we would hear no more, and our prints would be destroyed. We were out by midnight, and the nice policeman at the desk kindly phoned for a taxi, as the transport arranged by the organisers had been snowed under by the number of those arrested.

But my second arrest, 12 February 2001, was painfully different, not a game any more. Of course I knew that I would be free by the end of the day, and that fact distinguished me instantly from the thousands who fill our police cells daily, rightly or wrongly arrested for 'real crimes'. I also had the comfort – even the self-congratulation – of knowing that I was acting out of high-falutin' principles, that I had taken the moral high ground, that I had chosen to be in that cell for a day, and that if ever I am brave enough to do a serious disarmament action I have international law on my side.

However, none of this vanity compensated for the reality of that cell. I was alone, 'in solitary' for a day, and spent some time trying to reflect on the thousands of brave people throughout the world who spend years in solitary confinement as a result of their principled stand. I tried reciting poetry, but the only piece I could remember fully was 'To be or not to be', not exactly calculated to raise my spirits! I found, to my shame, that I was devoid of the inner resources to enable me to use that time creatively. So what was it, this time, that made me face the reality of prison, and, later, seriously to reflect on whether I could cope, if indeed I ever did anything 'worthy' of a prison sentence?

I think the answer to that question is the total loss of autonomy.

I have been single, living alone, all my life, in charge, coping reasonably adequately with whatever life chucks at me. And suddenly I am alone and powerless, nakedly vulnerable to the whim of whatever 'they' may choose to do. I was not going to be tortured – I did know that! Yet I reacted as if to torture when the two young policewomen (who we guessed were in training, and so doing everything by the book), having marched me to the 'medical room' (shades of Soviet gulags!) holding me by both wrists, forcibly took the combs and elastic from my hair, and then lifted my jersey to feel between my breasts. I lost it completely, crying hysterically and trying to stop them – and then bitterly ashamed of reacting so pathetically, humiliated both by them and – even worse – by myself! So this time there was no question whether the police people were on our side: we had disobeyed the police and were to be treated with contempt, just like everyone else arrested for whatever reason. Of course I should have been proud of that, proud to share the experience of generally disadvantaged folk in our prisons, who don't have the luxury of choosing whether or not to be arrested.

Never was I more glad to see anyone than the brother from Scottish CND who greeted us when we were discharged at about 6pm, with transport back to the warmth of friends at Friends Meeting House where we were staying, and literal warmth. For I had been very, very cold in that cell: they had refused me permission to put on the extra jersey I had brought, which was taken from me, along with everything else, on arrival at the police station; and my jacket and boots were also removed. So the literal and metaphorical use of 'cold' and 'warm' have taken on new significance for me.

It is apparently unlikely that we shall hear any more from the Procurator Fiscal this time. But I now have to make a decision about whether I have the guts to do it again, and more importantly, can I seriously try to disarm Trident – as I believe I am pledged to do – and risk prison?

Prison Thoughts 1

by Marcus Armstrong, *Waterbabies Affinity Group*

It's kind of strange to be writing this about my first stay in prison. Just over 18 months ago I was at the August 1999 camp at Coulport doing media work and convincing myself that I would not ever consider arrest and the consequences, while people were getting arrested all around.

When I handed myself in at court for my unpaid fines they seemed a bit confused and didn't know what to do. They went away, came back and said that they couldn't help me because they didn't have the paperwork! They said to call the office later and sort it out with them. So I called and they were almost apologetic explaining that the paperwork had become lost when I appealed. They said they would send it to Helensburgh that day, and could I please hand myself in again 2 days later by which time it should be there. I found myself thanking them and it was only later I began to realise how crazy and absurd it all was.

One of the first things I remember on the way to prison was the other prisoners' conversation. You know how you chat over supper with family or friends about things like your day, food, the news etc? Well, these guys were talking in the same matter of fact tones (not really macho or heavy) but about their crimes and lives. The guy I was handcuffed to said 'Well I used to be a football hooligan, but the travelling got too dear so now I sell drugs in Glasgow'. Others were talking about 'doing' people and 'jobs' they'd done. It was all very surreal.

I was a little scared to open my mouth because of my English accent, but almost everyone I saw wanted to know if I had any smokes or drugs (up my bum) and what I had done and how long I was in for. When I told them and they realised I was 'with' Tommy Sheridan (the parliamentarian who had been in prison recently for Ploughshares actions) it was all pats on the back and 'Gud on ya!' which was a great relief.

Prison wasn't really hard in itself, worse is the stigma surrounding breaking the law and being a convicted criminal with a record. It has been much harder for my three young daughters than it has for me. It did grind me down a bit – though not nearly as much as being in a police cell for long periods without a window. One of my strongest images was the boredom of it all – a bit like being in Butlins as a child when the weather is bad – stuck inside being fed three strange meals a day and my brain slowly turning to mush from too much daytime TV.

Some of the guards were cool and okay, but some of them just seemed to like shouting (often very loudly) to get things done – which felt like one of the more upsetting things going on. I was left wondering if the prison service just attracted these conventional angry men, or if they employed them purposefully. Seeing the lovely sweet smelling nurse for my medical was like heaven.

As I write this I'm travelling south from Glasgow on the train and it is so beautiful outside. Mountains and fields snowbound, white and shimmering, radiant in a misty winter sun. If I needed a reminder of why I went to prison, this is it.

One of the hardest things inside was being ignored a lot and treated a bit like I was a scumbag and unclean. I asked for a pencil and paper a dozen times but never got them. They wouldn't let me have the clean pants and socks I'd brought, saying 'You're only in for a few days'. Then some poor guy had a fit outside my cell and they used my towel for his head, which was fine. But they tried to give it back to me afterwards. When I said I wanted a clean one because it had been on the floor and the guy had salivated on it they said the towel was okay. I had to fight to get a clean one which felt quite depressing at the time. My breakfast was placed on the floor outside my cell, not on a plate or tray. I wonder if the guards would drink tea made from bags that had been left on a dirty floor?

I had a window though, which was such a joy! I could tell roughly what time it was by the light and could see the sky and the clouds rolling by and people wandering about their business. It was like a lifeline to the outside world. Being in windowless police cells for days and nights at last August's camp had been very distressing.

My life is very fragmented these days. It's a real exercise to juggle it all. The children and old friends down south, my community and various part-time jobs near Milton Keynes and the peace work in Scotland, but it's wonderful and exciting too. I never thought it would be easy. And paradoxically, doing this work and realising that my comfort and happiness are not really so important in the grand scheme has brought me more happiness and peace of mind than I've known.

I was never happy or at ease living a 'normal' life, whatever that is. It always felt a bit nightmarish to me. So to have stepped out of that feels perfectly natural although alienating at times. I wouldn't change a thing though. For the first time I'm living reasonably honestly and feel my life may actually make a difference. A few days prison has made me appreciate my liberty like never before, and seems such a small price to pay considering what is at stake and what people sacrifice for war.

Marcus Armstrong by the Loch at Peaton Wood, August 2000
Credit: Val Purcell

Prison Thoughts 2
by Helen Harris, *Aldermaston Trash Trident Affinity Group*

I have been to prison six or seven times over the last ten years, most recently for refusing to pay fines for Trident Ploughshares actions. All my sentences have been short, from five to twenty one days, but prison has affected my life both before and after the sentence itself.

Between conviction and sentencing lies a long gap filled with low level anxiety. When will the fine be transferred to my local court? How many times will the bailiffs call, and will they be known to my partner, who works in housing? Can I negotiate a court date with the warrant officer, and should I try to be sent down before a job interview, or after? Have I got enough holiday left if the magistrates give me 14 days? Will I make it to my parent's wedding anniversary?

So the actual sentencing comes as a relief – all uncertainty is over and the process takes over. Handcuffs, and the tiny cells in the prison van. I can look out of the darkened window directly into someone's face, but they can't see me at all. This invisibility continues while in custody. In my privileged life out of prison, I'm used to being greeted politely, to having my opinions sought. In custody, I walk in a room and am ignored, or told to sit, stand, wait.

On arrival at prison, there are showers and a stripsearch. Most new women are surprised to find the search is not an 'intimate' or internal search. But it is still a powerful symbol of entry into prison, and can arouse strong emotions. The only time I've lost control in prison and screamed and kicked at the door was when I was locked into a cubicle listening to the frightened wailing of a woman with learning difficulties being forcibly strip-searched.

Helen Harris on left decorating the fence at Aldermaston

Finally I am processed: photographed, recorded, ticked off by the surprised doctor as not requiring medication for drugs withdrawal. I am left to a set number of days of minor irritation and discomfort – sleeping with the light on, not being able to have a cup of tea when I fancy one. Missing my partner and not being able to phone because the queue is too big or the allocated time is not today. Queuing up like a child at school to be fed food I didn't choose or prepare. The constant din, tension and cigarette smoke.

The most enduring impact of prison has been meeting the other women. I've shared a cell with a woman who talked all night of her five children left behind, the youngest a tiny baby. I've given my flowers to a woman whose 'boyfriend' makes her work as a prostitute and never bothers to send her flowers inside. I've taught card games to some sixteen year old inside for stealing teddies from a toyshop. I've listened to some stories of violence suffered by the women which have literally kept me awake at night.

Why go to prison? The answer is collective: our time mounts up and causes the authorities expense – a good nonviolent tactic. More importantly, we show that as a community of activists, the deterrent of prison won't work. On a personal level I confront some of my fears. I'd still be nervous about a long sentence, but I now know it's not the worst that could happen.

CHAPTER FIVE

Answering the Lord Advocate

HAVING SET OUT THE legal context for the LAR by explaining why Trident is criminal, I then presented my answers to the four questions.

Answer to Question 1

10th and 11th October, 2000 – High Court of Justiciary, Edinburgh, submission of Angie Zelter, 1st Respondent in the Lord Advocate's Reference, No.1. 2000.

In the foregoing circumstances the questions of law should be answered as follows:

Question 1 asks **'In a trial under Scottish criminal procedure, is it competent to lead evidence as to the content of customary international law as it applies to the United Kingdom?'**

My short answer is – Yes, if an issue of customary international law is properly raised.

An issue of customary international law was integral to our defence and having been properly presented in the case and appropriate evidence on it tendered to the Court the first question of law should not be answered in the negative.

It is not obvious why leading evidence on the content of customary international law should not be competent in Scottish criminal proceedings where an issue of international law arises. An expert international lawyer properly testifies to the content of international law but not to its application within domestic jurisdiction which is, of course, a matter for the court.

Customary international law is part of the common law of England and Scotland.

Sir Hartley Shawcross, the UK prosecutor at Nuremberg, said, 'In England and the United States our Courts have invariably acted on the view that the accepted customary rules of the Law of Nations are binding upon the subject and the citizen, and the position is essentially the same in most countries.'

The Nuremberg Principles, which were adopted in 1950 state 'the fact that internal law does not impose a penalty for an act which constitutes a crime under international law does not relieve that person who committed the act from responsibility under international law.'

I also hold that war crimes and crimes against humanity are subject to universal jurisdiction under customary international law and may be prosecuted by any state. Dixon states, 'Under International Law, there are certain crimes which are regarded as so destructive of the international order that any state may exercise jurisdiction in respect of them. This is a jurisdiction that exists irrespective of where the act constituting the crime takes place and the nationality of the person committing it'. He goes on to say, 'it remains the case that ... war crimes and crimes against humanity ... are crimes susceptible to universal jurisdiction under customary international law and may be prosecuted by any state'.

As I said, customary international law is part of the common law of England. Lord Lloyd of Berwick stated in the Pinochet case 'the common law incorporates the rules of customary international law... 'The application of international law as part of the law of the land means that, subject to the overriding effect of statute law, rights and duties flowing from the rules of customary international law will be recognised and given effect by English courts without the need for any specific Act adopting those rules into English law.'

Lord Lloyd, in the same case, said, 'the requirements of customary international law ... are observed and enforced by our courts as part of the common law' and referred to 'well-established principles of customary international law, which principles form part of the common law of England'.

The same must be true in Scotland. Although Scotland has a distinct legal system, it is part of the UK. Since the UK is 'the State' for the purposes of public international law, the domestic effect of international law should not differ according to which part of the UK is involved. Just as a treaty to which the UK is party is enforceable throughout the UK if it has been incorporated into domestic law by statute, so rules of customary international law have the same internal effect throughout the UK. This is acknowledged in Oppenheim's 'International Law' where it says, 'As regards the United Kingdom all such rules of customary international law as are either universally recognised or have at any rate received the assent of this country are per se part of the law of the land.'

The question then is: what is the relevant rule of customary international law? How is the court to ascertain it?

Rosalyn Higgins QC, now the UK Judge on the ICJ has stated, 'international law ... is not a foreign, unknown law... All [the municipal court] has to do, with the assistance of counsel before it, is to examine the sources of international law on the topic to hand.'

However, where the existence of a rule of customary international law is at issue before a national court, correctly determining its existence and content is critical. It would be foolish to proceed on the false notion that all members of the legal professions in Scotland, or elsewhere, have the knowledge and training to deal with international law when it arises in their courts. A visit to Argyll and Bute District Court would be a salutary lesson in the state of knowledge and respect for international law! The Procurator Fiscal, Mr. Donnelly, has continually claimed that 'international law is not real law and does not apply in Scotland'. It is in the context of such an ignorant and biased view of international law that expert testimony is essential.

Even in more informed courts expert assistance is sometimes required. In Compania Naviera Vascongado v. S.S. Cristina, Lord Macmillan said: 'it is a recognized prerequisite of the adoption in our municipal law of a doctrine of public international law that it shall have attained the position of general acceptance by civilized nations as a rule of international conduct, evidenced by international treaties and conventions, authoritative text-books, practice and judicial decisions. It is manifestly of the highest importance that the courts of this country before they give the force of law within this realm to any doctrine of international law should be satisfied that it has the hallmarks of general assent and reciprocity.'

The fact that customary international law is part of the law of the land and therefore, unlike foreign law, does not have to be proved as a fact should not mean that expert evidence cannot be admitted in order to establish the existence or content of particular rules.

In the Trendtex case, Lord Denning referred to the need for the courts to determine the rules of international law 'seeking guidance from the decisions of the courts of other countries, from the jurists who have studied the problem, from treaties and conventions'

There are several domestic cases in which the opinions of international law text-book writers have been relied on. See, for example, the Piracy Jure Gentium case where the Judicial Committee of the Privy Council relied extensively on such opinions in order to determine whether actual robbery was an essential ingredient of the crime. It states, 'In considering such a question, the Board is permitted to consult and act upon a wider range of authority than that which it examines when the question for determination is one of municipal law only. The sources from which international law is derived include treaties between various States, State papers, municipal Acts of Parliament and the decisions of municipal Courts and last, but not least, opinions of juriconsults or text-book writers.' The helping hand of testimony of 'juriconsults' must be useful in at least some cases, of which our case at Greenock was a good example. It may, indeed, provide the best way to get the points before a busy trial judge.

Extensive reference to the writings of learned authors was also made in the Pinochet case. There was clearly no need for expert evidence as to the content of international law in that case since, as Lord Goff observed, three of the fourteen counsel who appeared for the appellants and their supporters were 'distinguished Professors of International Law'.

In the absence of any clear legal authority on the matter in Scotland (or elsewhere in the UK for that matter) and whatever the technical position, a court dealing with the possible application of customary international law plainly requires expert professional guidance upon it from qualified international lawyers. This is apparent from the confusion, doubt and ill-informed comments on international law that are being heard from both lawyers and magistrates in the lower District Courts, where most of the disarming citizens are appearing and attempting to have their international law arguments accepted. If customary international law forms an integral part of Scots Law, as I have argued it does, but most Scottish Courts are unfamiliar with it, the interests of justice demand that they should be able to call on experts to assist them with the content and interpretation of international law.

It is not uncommon in other jurisdictions to introduce such evidence. For instance, the American Law Institute's highly authoritative Restatement of the Foreign Relations Law of the United States states that 'courts may in their discretion consider any relevant material or source, including expert testimony, in resolving questions of international law.' It also says, 'Some judges have adopted the practice of receiving evidence, including expert testimony, on questions of international law. No rule precludes that practice and the courts tend to reject challenges to it based on the argument that international law must be treated like domestic laws for this purpose.'

The Canadian courts, also, do not seem to have any problem with the introduction of evidence as to international law. See R.v. Bonadie, where it states that 'Two experts in the field of international law and consular immunity testified on this application. They held widely divergent views on vital issues'.

In German and Austrian law of procedure, fundamental principles of 'oral proceedings' and of 'directness' are interpreted to mean that the parties are entitled to have their experts, including experts of the law, testify directly and orally to the Court.

My argument is not that expert testimony on international law is always competent. There may be some crystal clear cases where there is no room for it. My argument is that there are some cases (like at Greenock) where such testimony is not only competent, but crucial to an understanding of the defence. The trial judge must have some discretion in the matter and his or her discretion should not be overturned without evidence of a very clear error.

In our case, the content of international law was pivotal to showing that an international crime was being committed by the possession and deployment of Trident – it was the very crime we were trying to prevent. There could not have been a fair trial without the examination of international law as it applied to the UK. It was crucial to an understanding of the defence. Because such law is complex and the courts are relatively unfamiliar with it they sometimes need experts to help them.

I also think it is important to acknowledge the Sheriff's own reasoning for allowing our expert witness, Professor Boyle, to lead evidence on the content of customary international law as it applies to the UK. She says in her Report, 'it was clear that ... the defence was not simply going to be based on reasonable belief plucked out of the air, or simple necessity'. She also said that she 'was not entirely sure how much she could rely on Mr. Mayer and Mr. McLaughlin to address me on the international law should this really be at issue.' She went on to say that 'in principle I could not see why an expert in international law could not address me especially if the law was the underlying reasonable excuse in the mind of these women'. She therefore 'allowed evidence so far as the defence of necessity at the time of the offence was concerned and also, the law by an expert to assist me in reaching a decision.' At the end of her Report she re-iterates, 'it was absolutely necessary for expert evidence to be led from an expert in international law, and whether or not it has ever been done in Scotland before seemed not to matter if I considered it essential. It did not seem appropriate that counsel, not necessarily skilled in international law should address me on such a vital part of the defence.'

In any case involving international law, therefore, the domestic court should be permitted to decide whether to allow an expert to be called. The overall objective must be to ensure a fair trial with equality of arms. Article 6(1) of the European Convention on Human Rights guarantees the right to a fair trial. And Article 6 (3) (d) guarantees a person charged with a criminal offence the right to 'obtain the attendance and examination of witnesses on [her] behalf'. The Sheriff was therefore entitled to conclude that unless expert evidence as to customary international law was admitted, the defendants would not have had a fair trial because customary international law was an essential part of their defence.

The High Court of Justiciary should not answer this question to the effect that it is never competent to lead the evidence of an expert international lawyer as a witness in Scottish criminal proceedings as to customary international law. It would be unwise to leave the courts in a position where they are unable to get advice from experts on subjects outside their knowledge and expertise.

An Iona Perspective

by Norman Shanks, *Dialogue and Negotiation Affinity Group*

My involvement in Trident Ploughshares – and my arrest at Faslane this year and last is part of both my personal journey and a logical progression. After 15 years in the Scottish Office, working between Edinburgh and London, I went back to university in 1979 to train for the Church of Scotland ministry. I had had long links with Iona and at that point also joined the Iona Community with its commitment to action for peace and justice and in particular to campaigning for nuclear disarmament.

I well remember taking our whole family, while still young, to join in 'Arms across Scotland' in the 1980s. As a member then convenor of the Church and Nation Committee I became more involved and better informed through the period when the Church

Norman Shanks (4th from left) standing with other church ministers in the blockade line at Faslane, February 2000.

of Scotland took an increasingly strong stance against nuclear weapons, Trident especially. I'm now totally convinced that Trident is theologically and morally indefensible, strategically irrelevant, illegal in terms of international law, and a colossal waste of resources that could be creatively used for the common good, both in Britain and overseas. And I recognise the need not only to speak out but also to stand up and 'put our bodies on the line' for the sake of what we believe to be right and true. 'The Big Blockade', especially with, for many of us, its Christian dimension – an act of witness expressed in the context of worship, was truly, as one of the ministers described it, a 'Festival of Peace'!

Answer to Question 2

Question 2 asks 'Does any rule of customary international law justify a private individual in Scotland in damaging or destroying property in pursuit of his or her objection to the United Kingdom's possession of nuclear weapons, its action in placing

such weapons at locations within Scotland or its policies in relation to such weapons?'
This question is not appropriate in the circumstances of this case and should not be answered.
This second question of law as stated is premised on the view that our intent in doing what we did amounted in law to no more than a demonstrative protest at the UK's possession of nuclear weapons and its policies and actions in relation to them. This misrepresents and wholly underestimates our declared intent. Further, our plea of justification – in effect upheld by the Sheriff – does not depend on our objections to the policies and weapons, but on the alleged criminality of the UK's nuclear weapons posture. The question is thus inept and does not advance matters. The Court should decline to answer it.
If the Court nevertheless does intend to answer this question then I must point out several matters.

i) With respect to the way the question asks whether there is any rule to justify individuals carrying out specific actions it must be pointed out that this is beside the point. I could just as easily say that there are no specific rules preventing such action. It progresses us no further. One would not expect international law which relates to very general and wide-ranging principles and rules to specify how criminal actions carried out by a specific State, like the UK, can be stopped by its own citizens in Scotland.

I hold that it is an integral part of any civilised judicial system that there is a right to prevent crimes, especially those as serious as the conditional intention to use weapons of indiscriminate mass murder. Certainly there is an undisputed right for individuals within the UK as a whole to use reasonable force to prevent the commission of serious crimes.

In the same way as the ICJ clarified that although there is no specific authorisation of the threat or use of nuclear weapons in international law, there is also no universal prohibition and then went on to apply the principles and rules to the question of the use or threat to use nuclear weapons in general, so should we here now look at the principles of law and apply them impartially and with wisdom to the issues before the Court today.

I think this Court must face squarely the psychological processes that are taking place underneath the whole of this Lord Advocate's Reference process including this hearing. We are not in a vacuum. We are all part of a society that has been traumatised and corrupted by the actions of our State over the last hundred years, which has, step by step, led from the brutal excesses of our colonial past, to the concentration camps of the Boer War, to the aerial bombardment of German city centres, to the ongoing bombarding of civilian infrastructure in Iraq that is continuing at this very moment by the RAF, to our present descent into official weapons of indiscriminate mass murder. Moreover, neither the UK, nor the other Allied States, has ever been confronted by the world community in a War Crimes Tribunal, nor unlike Germany and Japan, ever had to apologise, pay compensation and come to terms with its own wrong-doing in World War II.

We are all part of a society that has been traumatised and corrupted by the actions of our State

This terrible legacy from the past means that it is very difficult for many people, including some in this Court, to look at British nuclear weapons, at Trident, at what is going on at Faslane and Coulport, in any objective and rational manner. There is a fear of what implications this may have on past crimes and present policies and a desire to try to keep these crimes closed in the cupboard rather than face the consequences, which would undoubtedly affect our view of the United Kingdom's place in the world. It is easier to think in terms of strict good and evil, perfect friends and monstrous enemies, final solutions – rather than face the complexity of the real world and to see Trident for what it really is and face up to the necessity for global justice and the rule of law in order to encourage our own and others' long-term security.

For in fact, the nuclear weapons on board Trident are anathema to law. To accept the legality of Trident – is to accept the legality of mass murder – is to bring the law into contempt. The very basis of law is to protect innocents but the very basis of nuclear weapons is to threaten mass destruction. Clever lawyers may attempt to distort the law and prove that somehow if the State authorizes weapons of mass destruction then the matter is closed because the State can choose whatever means it likes to 'defend' itself but this is a corruption of the law and any State that does this ultimately loses legitimacy. The law cannot survive such corruption. Our society cannot survive such mendacity, as we can see if we care to look at the crumbling morality around us.

The UK Prosecutor, Sir Hartley Shawcross, in his final speech at Nuremberg, in 1946, said, 'There is no rule of International Law which provides immunity for those who obey orders which – whether legal or not in the country where they are issued – are manifestly contrary to the very law of nature from which international law has grown. If international law is to be applied at all, it must be superior to State Law in this respect, that it must consider the legality of what is done by International and not by State law tests.'

He went on to say, 'It is true that the lawyers and the statesmen who, at the Hague and elsewhere in days gone by, built up the code of rules and the established customs by which the world has sought to mitigate the brutality of war and to protect from its most extreme harshness those who were passive non-combatants, never dreamed of such wholesale and widespread slaughter. But murder does not cease to be murder merely because the victims are multiplied ten million-fold. Crimes do not cease to be criminal because they have a political motive.'

Crimes do not cease to be criminal because they have a political motive

Judge Bedjaoui, the President of the ICJ, said in the recent Advisory Opinion, in 1996, in respect of nuclear weapons, 'By its very nature the nuclear weapon, a blind weapon ... has a destabilising effect on humanitarian law, the law of discrimination which regulates discernment in the use of weapons used. Nuclear weapons, the ultimate evil, destabilize humanitarian law which is the law of the lesser evil. The existence of nuclear weapons is therefore a major challenge to the very existence of humanitarian law, not to mention their long-term harmful effects on the human environment, in respect to which the right to life may be exercised. Until scientists are able to develop a 'clean' nuclear weapon which would distinguish between combatants and non-combatants, nuclear weapons will clearly have indiscriminate effects and constitute an absolute challenge to humanitarian law. Atomic warfare and humanitarian law therefore appear to be mutually exclusive; the existence of the one automatically implying the non-existence of the other.'

Judge Weeramantry, also in the ICJ Advisory Opinion Hearings, stated, 'all the postulates of law presuppose that they contribute to and function within the premise of the continued existence of the community served by that law. Without the assumption of that continued existence, no rule of law and no legal system can have any claim to validity, however attractive the juristic reasoning on which it is based.'

ii) Now I would like to unpack a little the word 'justify'. This question we are looking at arises out of the Greenock Trial and this context is of the utmost importance because a different answer could be given depending on what the specifics of the case may be. In other words, generalities are likely to be misleading and dangerous. It is therefore imperative to continually link the question to the specifics of the Greenock Trial. Underlying the question, there is an implication that there was no justification for damaging and destroying Trident related equipment.

I refute this. I hold that there is justification in UK and in Scots law for private individuals to damage or destroy if they need to do this to prevent a terrible catastrophe or injury or loss of life or stop the commissioning of major crime – especially if the law enforcement agencies refuse to stop it for you. Most legal systems have similar legal justifications.

For instance, if someone took a loaded machine gun from a man in a crowded underground where he was threatening people with it and threw it under the train where it was destroyed – that destruction would be considered as justifiable.

The Trident context is more controversial because it involves state complicity – which is where impartial common sense must come in along with a good moral sense and a global perspective. Maybe it is easier psychologically to place the justifiable acts of property destruction into a proper perspective if we put them into another context – far enough away to be more balanced. For instance, I am sure that no-one in the Court would say that an Iraqi citizen would not have been justified in attempting to destroy an essential part of the chemical weapon system that was used to gas the village of Halabja, in order to prevent that terrible crime taking place, or to suggest that such an act would have been criminal.

> It would be a nonsensical legal system that could punish the perpetrators of such a horrendous crime after it had taken place but not allow people to prevent the crime in the first place

And to take another example, during the Nuremberg trials various industrialists who had manufactured the Zyklon B gas used to exterminate victims in the Nazi concentration camps were convicted and hanged as criminals and I am sure that no-one here would suggest that any citizens would be criminal if they had tried to stop that Zyklon gas from reaching the concentration camp in the first place by destroying any of the equipment used. It would be a nonsensensical legal system that could punish the perpetrators of such a horrendous crime after it had taken place but not allow people to prevent the crime in the first place.

A similar case can be made out to justify the disarmament of *Maytime*. It is important to remind you of the arguments I made earlier about the specific illegality and criminality of Trident. May I also stress that we were acting to prevent crimes that came out of the specific British Trident nuclear weapons system and not acting against nuclear weapons 'in general'. It is also important to remind everyone that we used reasonable force in the circumstances. We did not blow up the nuclear submarine base or set fire to the research lab. We carefully, nonviolently and safely threw the equipment from *Maytime* into a deep loch so that it could not be used again to help Trident in its criminal activities.

iii) The question asks us to look at the rules of customary international law but in fact we have to look at the inter-relationship between international and domestic law. For instance Article 38 of the Statute of the ICJ sets forth the sources of international law and states that one of the sources is what is known as 'the general principles of law recognised by civilised nations'. One of these general principles of law recognised by all civilised nations is the duty to act to prevent the commission of a crime. And so, under international law, as a general principle of law, there is a duty to act to prevent the commission of threatened war crimes, crimes against peace, and crimes against humanity. As a matter of common law there is also a common law right to take steps necessary to inhibit this type of activity.

In other words we can look to both international and to national law to give authority to the disarmament of *Maytime*. This could be a source of confusion so I would like to try to unravel it a bit.

In some international law contexts there may well be a problem of deciding which jurisdiction – Scots or International Law – applies, because it is conceivable for an act to be technically lawful within one jurisdiction but not the other.

Nevertheless, as the US Prosecutor, Dodd, said at Nuremberg, 'The Tribunal will give a warning ... mankind will know: that no crime will go unpunished because it was committed in the name of a political party or of a State, that no crime will be passed by because it is too big; that no criminals will avoid punishment because they are too many.'

I hold that since Nuremberg any of the Nuremberg Crimes i.e. Crimes against Peace, War Crimes and Crimes against Humanity, can never technically be lawful within any domestic jurisdiction – there is absolute adherence to these Nuremberg Principles and they take precedence over all other legal systems.

Moreover, within our context here, I hold that under international law there is a right, which in certain circumstances, for instance if you are a Commander in the field, even becomes a duty, for anyone to prevent the commission of the Nuremberg crimes wherever they are taking place, regardless of the state of the domestic law in that individual's country.

The right to prevent the commission of a crime against humanity can be derived from the principles of humanity coupled with that of individual responsibility.

The Martens Clause (as contained in the Additional Protocol 1 of 1977) refers to the 'principles of humanity'. It states 'In cases not covered by this Protocol or by other international agreements, civilians and combatants remain under the protection and authority of the principles of international law derived from established custom, from the principles of humanity, and from the dictates of the public conscience.'

the dictates of the public conscience

The ICJ explained that the Martens Clause was 'an effective means of addressing the rapid evolution of military technology' and applied to nuclear weapons. As Judge Weeramantry concludes 'The attempt to place nuclear weapons beyond the reach of these principles lacks the support not only of the considerations of humanity but also of the considerations of logic'.

an acquiescent and supine public leads to power abuses by governments

The ICJ referred to 'the overriding consideration of humanity'. See also the Corfu Channel Case, 1949, where the ICJ held that Albania's obligations were based on 'elementary considerations of humanity, even more exacting in peace than in war'.

Surely the principle of humanity does not only bind States? In *Oppenheim's International Law* concerning the evolution of the principle that States have the right to punish foreign nationals for crimes against humanity, the authors refer to 'recognition of the supremacy of the law of humanity over the law of the sovereign state when enacted or applied in violation of elementary human rights in a manner which may justly be held to shock the conscience of mankind.'

The supreme law of humanity must bind individuals as well as States and involve responsibilities as well as rights. As the Nuremberg Tribunal held, the essence of the Nuremberg Charter is that individuals have international duties which transcend the national obligations of obedience imposed by the State. It is but a short step from the Nuremberg Tribunal's conclusions about individual responsibility to the position advocated by Trident Ploughshares. As Edmund Burke once said, 'The only thing necessary for the triumph of evil is for good [people] to do nothing.' We none of us ever know the ultimate consequences of what we do. We may never know how effective our acts of disarmament and civil resistance are. But we certainly know that an acquiescent and supine public leads to power abuses by governments. One of the reasons nuclear weapons have never yet been used on purpose since Hiroshima and Nagasaki is because of the sheer weight of public condemnation and concern and the stigma that would attach to any State that did use them. Such public pressure has to be continually shown in order to be effective. It is a responsibility that is terrifying in its necessity. And, of course, such public pressure alone is not enough, it cannot protect us from accidents for instance.

iv) The question talks about 'private individual' – international law traditionally operated at the level of States and was not seen as attaching to heads of State or national leaders. State sovereignty protected individuals. However, the horrendous violations of basic human dignity in World War II decisively changed the situation. Had Hitler or Mussolini survived they would have been tried as war criminals. So strong was the feeling regarding war crimes that even the direct orders of such heads of State afforded no protection to officials implementing them. The Nuremberg Tribunal held that the imposition of duties and liabilities upon individuals had long been recognised.

'Crimes against International law', observed the Tribunal, 'are committed by men, not by abstract entities, and only by punishing individuals who counsel such crimes can the provisions of international law be enforced'. It went on to state 'the very essence of the [Nuremberg] Charter is that individuals have international duties which transcend the national obligations of obedience imposed by the individual State. He who violates the laws of war cannot obtain immunity while acting in pursuance of the authority of the State if the State in authorizing action moves outside its competence under International law'.

The concept of individual responsibility was confirmed by the British Lord Chancellor in 1963 when he stated in Parliament that the UK looked upon the Nuremberg Principles as 'generally accepted among States and have the status of customary International law.' Individual responsibility is not only well-recognised, but is a concept of growing importance in international law.

The Lord Advocate's question carefully talks about private individuals to perhaps give the impression that whilst these Nuremberg principles of individual responsibility do apply to individual members of the armed forces or governments, they do not apply to individual private citizens. However, the trials of various industrialists heard at the British Military Court at Hamburg in 1946 clearly show the application of individual responsibility to private citizens as well.

individuals have international duties which transcend the national obligations of obedience imposed by the State

One example that I used in my original legal submissions at Greenock is of the case of Bruno Tesch, who was the owner of a firm that supplied the prussic acid gas, known as Zyklon B, to the Nazi concentration camps, where it was used to kill four and a half million people in Auschwitz/Birkenau alone. He and other private individuals were charged with a war crime as accessories before the fact and were eventually found guilty and put to death. The British Jurisdiction was based on 'the general doctrine called Universality of Jurisdiction over War Crimes, under which every independent State has an International law jurisdiction to punish ... war criminals.' The decision of this British Military Court is a clear example of the application of the rule that the provisions of the laws and customs of war are addressed not only to combatants and to members of the state and other public authorities, but to anybody who is in a position to assist in their violation

At the risk of appearing tedious I wish to point out once again that not only does individual responsibility apply to violations of international law but also to prevention of crime.

v) There could be some debate about whether the term 'property' can be used to describe objects that are used for unlawful purposes and certainly I object to the tone of the word conferring some kind of respectability and normality on objects which I consider as more accurately described as mass killing equipment. It would be better to qualify the word 'property' with the phrase 'which is being used for criminal purposes'.

vi) The use of the word 'objection' in the question is also misleading. We are not talking about objections here but our legal rights – the right to live without fear of nuclear annihilation and the right to prevent the commission of crimes. One does not 'object' to the threatened destruction of the planet – it is a matter of life or death. We are all in imminent danger. None of us know when nuclear weapons will be used – by design or accident – but we know that sooner or later they will be, if we do not disarm them, and meanwhile our planet is becoming more and more contaminated with long-lasting nuclear contamination as accidents and wastes proliferate.

'Objection' implies a matter of opinion or a political view, a state of mind, rather than action to protect the very possibility of life. We are talking here about a fundamental and deep-rooted instinct for self-preservation – the right to life itself.

It would be more accurate to put into the question that we were trying to prevent a terrible crime. After all that is what the evidence at Greenock shows.

The way this question is phrased at the moment is premised on the view that our intent in doing what we did amounted in law to no more than a demonstrative protest at the UK's possession of nuclear weapons and its policies and actions in relation to them. This misrepresents and wholly underestimates our declared intent. Our plea of justification – in effect upheld by the Sheriff – does not depend on our objections to the policies and weapons, but on the alleged criminality of the UK's nuclear weapons posture. The question is thus inept and does not advance matters.

vii) And finally the question talks about 'possession' – however, the facts in the original case made it clear that we were not talking merely about possession of nuclear weapons. The context of our disarmament action was one of active deployment of 100 kiloton nuclear warheads. The warheads were and are still being deployed.

There is always at least one Trident at sea armed with tens of warheads of 100 kilotons each plus the deterrence policies and plans to use them. Trident submariners are willing and able to press the nuclear buttons and regularly practise such launches on exercises. Expert evidence was led and accepted without rebuttal on the issue of current deployment and threat to use. I was cross questioned by the Procurator Fiscal on the issue of possession and what the ICJ had said about possession but in response said, 'We are not talking about pure possession, but about deployment.' I made it quite clear in my answer that the ICJ Advisory Opinion was not asked to rule on the possession of nuclear weapons but on the threat or use of nuclear weapons. I did not get the opportunity to expand on my views on possession in the witness box but certainly did not concede that possession was lawful, only that possession *per se* was not an issue when looking at the British Trident system. I still do not concede that possession of 100 kiloton nuclear warheads could ever be lawful because I cannot see how they could ever be used lawfully and to this extent I would argue that the Helen John Appeal came to the wrong conclusion because there was not an informed argument put on both sides. However, we do not need to go into this here.

I would like to emphasise that Sheriff Gimblett also accepted that we were not acting against 'possession *per se*' but against the deployment of Trident. Her Report states, 'this trial was not concerned with the possession of nuclear weapons... What was at issue in this trial was the active deployment and the moving them that was seen as a threat'.

I had also quoted in my evidence from the witness box that part of the ICJ Advisory Opinion which says that possession and deployment of a weapon with the stated conditional intention to use it would constitute an illegal threat if the purpose of its use would inevitably violate the principles of necessity and proportionality. It stated that even a proportionate response to a threat or attack would still have to meet the requirements of humanitarian law. This would have to require discrimination.

The use in the phraseology of the question of the euphemism 'placing such weapons at locations within Scotland' is a continuation of this misleading idea of pure possession. It suggests that what the UK does is simply place its weapons in some hidden corner as some never to be used ultimate deterrent that will be so effective it will never be used. However, the reality is quite different and we made that clear at Greenock. These weapons are not just placed in Scotland, they are operationally based at Faslane with many hundreds of workers, tons of equipment and millions of pounds worth of resources, keeping them at a moment's notice to fire off indiscriminate weapons of mass destruction. The spare nuclear warheads are stored a few miles away at Coulport and Tridents regularly visit Coulport to exchange their warheads for checking and maintenance. Tridents are regularly going up and down the Clyde on the way out to patrol. The Trident *Vengeance*, just last month, test-fired its missiles in the USA. They patrol the oceans and occasionally allow themselves to surface and be seen in areas of conflict. They are a continuing threat. The reality is that Trident is always on a war footing. Crises can appear very quickly and no submariner ever knows if he will be the one to start off a nuclear holocaust.

no submariner ever knows if he will be the one to start off a nuclear holocaust

And finally, the question, being so general, does not talk about the very specific circumstances at the time of our disarmament action. We gave evidence through the joint statement that we had left on *Maytime*, from the witness box and through our expert witnesses, which was not rebutted, to the effect that June 8th was a time of special crisis and concern. We were at war in Iraq and in Kosova. As the Sheriff said in her Report it was a 'time of great international unrest'.

A fairer wording for Question 2 would have been: 'Does international law and/or Scots law justify an individual in Scotland in damaging or destroying property which is being used for criminal purposes, in order to prevent those criminal actions being carried out by the United Kingdom – namely the United Kingdom's deployment, within and without Scotland, of Trident nuclear warheads and its threat to use such warheads in accordance with HM Government's current defence policy.'

And my answer to such a fairly formulated question would have been an unequivocal yes – both international and domestic law justify individuals in damaging and destroying the Trident system.

However, if the question remains as it stands then my answer is that this question is not appropriate in the circumstances of this case and should not be answered.

We're all in the Same Boat

by Jane Tallents, *Local Heroes Affinity Group*

It's not as simple as good and bad, right and wrong, moral and immoral. It's how to recognise the humanity in all of us, our hope in the future, our desire for a better world. Living in Helensburgh, with Navy and base workers at every turn, I know we share so much. When I work alongside an MOD policeman to collect food for an aid convoy to Bosnia, when I teach Cubs to swim alongside a Trident submariner, when I campaign to improve the local park alongside a Navy wife, it's the things that we agree on that matter not those that we don't.

22 December 2000. Jane Tallents doing prison support with Tommy Sheridan MSP outside Greenock jail on Tommy's release after five days in jail for non payment of his fine for taking part in the blockade the previous February.

Credit: David MacKenzie

But there among the many conversations comes Trident, the unfinished business of the last century. And gradually all the long patient explanations, the passionate speeches from the dock in Helensburgh District Court, the hours standing in the rain with a banner start to pay. At the gates of Faslane on 12 February when one police officer was asked to move in and arrest people, he looked at them, and said, 'I'm sorry, I can't do this', and walked away.

Answer to Question 3

Question 3 asks 'Does the belief of an accused person that his or her actions are justified in law constitute a defence to a charge of malicious mischief or theft?'

This question also is not appropriate in the circumstances of this case and should not be answered.

This question misses the point entirely. Belief can be a vague, undefined feeling – a personal understanding that does not necessarily have any wider significance. Belief is an imprecise term that is not the same as 'objective knowledge'. The issue in the case was not whether we 'believed' Trident to be unlawful, but that we knew in fact that it is unlawful, and that we reasonably believed our actions would help terminate its existence. The basis of our disarmament action was, in other words, stronger than belief. It was a conviction based on fact and legal argument provided by the world's highest judicial authority. The defence presented evidence that was not rebutted by the Crown. By using the 'belief' phraseology, the Crown takes for granted that the threat or use, or even deployment, of Trident would not be illegal.

Neither I, nor Greenock Court, relied on 'belief' to sustain our defence but on well reasoned argument and evidence. This is not the same as belief. As the Sheriff said in her report, 'The trial related to their understanding of international law based ... on an in-depth study of international law, customary law *ad bellum* and *in bellum* ... and had formed an unchallenged, sincere, unshakeable view not just of the illegality of the use of nuclear weapons ... but of the ... ongoing threat of use of nuclear weapons'.

This third question of law focuses solely on an accused's belief that actions are justified in law without regard to any wider factors including the grounds of such belief and its reasonableness in the circumstances. This oversimplification renders it inept. Mere belief that actions are justified in law could not of itself found a successful plea of justification in law. But that does not mean that there is no room for the doctrine of justification in an appropriate context in Scots law. The court should decline to answer this question also.

Question 3 is linked to Question 1 in that we need to lead evidence as to the content of international law in order to demonstrate that our belief is not just a belief but is a reasonable belief – a fact even – and can be shown to be such. If it is just assumed that we have no knowledge of 'legal justification of our actions', that we just hold a belief, and the Court comes to this opinion because of its own ignorance of international law, and does not allow evidence as to the content of international law to be led, then a grave injustice is done to the accused.

Belgian Nights – Koen Moens, Titanic Trident! Affinity Group

by David Mackenzie, *Local Heroes Affinity Group*

He is a nocturnal creature, is Koen, with eyes that glitter more intensely in the wee small hours when other legal supporters are leaning back on the caravan cushions and thinking of their sleeping bags. Keep him plied with tea and he just motors on, marshalling the lists of those arrested and drawing the duty officers in the police stations into that delicate engagement that is balanced between rigorous attention to the interests of the folk in the cells and good, respectful communication. His deep continental timbre

Koen Moens

Credit: David Mackenzie

in itself carries weight, but much more comes from how he is so obviously on the ball and from his considerable knowledge of the law in Scotland. You wonder what it feels like for the police desk people, phoning up the number from the bust cards and getting this brisk, warm, business-like voice at 4am in the morning. I think you would be pleased that there was a good chance of getting this job done with the minimum of fuss and for the benefit of all. You would also know immediately that you would not get away with any nonsense. You would be quite impressed with this outfit. Koen is, of course, not truly nocturnal and will want to be excavated from his tent to go to whatever bizarre venue the district court have found for those held over to appear before the JP. Then the workers in the caravan may get some extra amusement from his ablutions in the Peaton burn, conducted with a good deal less privacy than he imagines.

Answer to Question 4

Question 4 asks 'Is it a general defence to a criminal charge that the offence was committed in order to prevent or bring to an end the commission of an offence by another person?'

This question as it is presently phrased should be answered to the effect that, depending on the particular circumstances of the case, it may or may not be a defence to a criminal charge that the alleged offence was not criminal but an attempt to prevent or bring to an end the criminal conduct of another or others.

However, this fourth question of law raises an issue of principle – whether Scots law admits a defence to a charge that what was done was directed to preventing or ending another's criminal actions. It can reasonably be submitted that in appropriate circumstances such a defence could and should be allowed. It would turn crucially on the particular facts and circumstances. In this sense it could hardly be categorised as a general defence. Appropriately qualified this question could be answered in the affirmative.

The question is badly written in that it makes out that if we had reasonable grounds for our action it would still be an 'offence'. At the very least the question should have worded it as an 'alleged offence'. We were not saying that we committed an offence and had a general defence (e.g. unsound mind) but that we did not commit an offence in the first place. In the case of malicious mischief, to have committed this offence, we would have had to have had deliberate disregard for the rights of others. But we were arguing that these rights did not exist in the first place, because the whole operation was unlawful and so no offence was committed to start off with.

Perhaps a better wording for this question would have been, 'Is it a defence to a criminal charge to show that the conduct alleged to constitute an offence was the only means available to the accused person to prevent HM Government committing one of the most serious international crimes, or that it was undertaken in the reasonable belief that it was the only available means of preventing the commission of such a crime?'

The Sheriff, in her Report stated, 'I was not able to find that what these three women did was done with any criminal intent, but only in an attempt to prevent what they honestly believed to be a much greater crime. That honest belief in itself was based on informed opinion, given directly to them, and more particularly their actions were carried out at a time when all three considered that they and everyone else was in imminent danger from nuclear weapons ... I considered that their defence had been well made out, remained uncontradicted and unchallenged, and that further there was no *mens rea* ... I also had in mind that if one believes the police when giving evidence in trials involving knives and weapons one of the most common excuses given by an accused – not accepted by the court is – 'I only had it for my protection'. Even if the knife is carried for protection that is not considered a good reason even if there was some understandable reason for the person having the knife which might go to mitigation'.

By necessity is meant the assertion that conduct promotes some value higher than the value of literal compliance with the law

At Greenock the Procurator Fiscal tried again and again to cast our actions as those of vandals or thieves. He refused to look at the bigger picture. But the bigger picture is essential.

In the 1986 case of State of Vermont v. McCann we can see another global citizen acting to prevent crime. Harold McCann tried to stop US munitions from going to Central America where such munitions were regularly used 'in random air attacks on civilian populations in ... El Salvador.' His crime prevention was presented as being justified by the principle of necessity. The case defines this through Glanville Williams' words, 'By necessity is meant the assertion that conduct promotes some value higher than the value of literal compliance with the law' and goes on to state, 'Where a person has acted meritoriously [justification] he has no need for forgiveness [excuse] ... Historically, there are relatively few recorded cases in which the concept appears. This is true because in most instances such cases are not prosecuted in the first place.'

I think this is a very important point and explains why, although the principle of individuals preventing crime seems to be clear, yet it is difficult to find cases to illustrate it in practice. If our action had been one of nonviolently disarming the equipment essential to the mad plans of a local drugs dealer who was threatening to blow up a whole street of innocent families where his rival lived, we would probably not have been brought to trial.

The Vermont case is also useful because it cites the Yamashita case to uphold the view that 'International law may, under appropriate circumstances, create 'an affirmative duty to take such measures as [are] within [an individual's] power and appropriate in the circumstances' to prevent criminal violations of international law'. The case then goes on to explain the common-law privilege which allows one to prevent the commission of a crime by stating that, 'An individual other than a government official is justified in using reasonable force to prevent or to terminate what he reasonably believes to be the commission of a crime.'

I would like to remind you of my testimony concerning the frequent complaints about the illegality and criminality of Trident that I formally made to the police, courts, Attorney General, Lord Advocate etc. If you refer to the Sheriff's Report she refers to these, 'She outlined all that she had done by way of peaceful legal means to bring an end to nuclear weapons. She explained how she had tried to get the police to take up her cause of what she perceived was the illegality of nuclear weapons and how she herself had tried to raise action through the courts in England but on each occasion had been denied access to that remedy. She had been given different excuses by different magistrates being either that it was not in the public interest or that it was frivolous or vexatious, or the Crown would take over the proceedings she had already raised but then drop them on the basis that it was not worth proceeding with them. She had tried a direct approach to the Attorney General but was told it was the job of the police to make enquiries about her claim. So she went to the Norfolk police and wrote to the Chief Constable ...' etc etc. As a responsible citizen reporting a major crime that if not stopped could cause millions of deaths, what am I expected to do if I cannot get relief from the Executive, Legislature or Courts? If nothing comes out of this Lord Advocate's Reference that finally rids us of the threat from Trident I will have to make further disarmament attempts.

The lack of adequate redress from the authorities is not only negligent and culpable in itself but is clearly in breach of our international rights to have our grievances properly dealt with. There is a right of effective remedy in Article 8 of the Universal Declaration of Human Rights which states that 'Everyone has the right to an effective remedy by the competent national tribunals for acts violating the fundamental rights granted him by the constitution or by law.' This is echoed in the International Covenant on Civil and Political Rights in Article 2(3) where the undertakings of all State Parties (which includes the UK) are set down as being '(a) To ensure that any person whose rights or freedoms as herein are violated shall have an effective remedy, notwithstanding that the violation has been committed by persons acting in an official capacity; (b) To ensure that any person claiming such a remedy shall have his right thereto determined by competent judicial, administrative or legislative authorities, or by any other competent authority provided for by the legal system of the State, and to develop the possibilities of judicial remedy; (c) To ensure that the competent authorities shall enforce such remedies when granted.'

Our appeals to the authorities have not led to an effective remedy. Trident and the UK Government nuclear deterrence policies have still not been examined directly and impartially and we still all live in daily terror of a catastrophic accident or purposeful use of the UK nuclear weapons that are still based here in Scotland. This is inexcusable. It is clearly unsatisfactory that ordinary women like Ulla, Ellen and myself should have to try to disarm these criminal weapons of mass destruction ourselves and yet we have no alternative at present. I am hoping that this Court at least will tackle the root issue and enable an effective remedy to be found to our distress and to secure for us relief from the horrifying threat to our ultimate right to life.

The legal systems of most civilised countries allow and encourage citizens to report and prevent crime, particularly serious offences. Most people understand that any legal system that does not act upon reports of major criminal activity or bring criminals to justice is undermining the very basis of legal conflict resolution and encouraging civil conflict. This basic civic responsibility has been deliberately obstructed by UK courts which either declare themselves incompetent to enforce international law or listen wearily to such argument before ruling it irrelevant. Such evasion of the law is a wilful violation of the legal principles held to be binding at Nuremberg, and of the many international commitments made by British governments.

As I have previously pointed out, the International Military Tribunal at Nuremberg observed that, 'the very essence of the [Nuremberg] Charter is that individuals have international duties which transcend the national obligations of obedience imposed by the individual state.' Under the Nuremberg principle of individual responsibility, regardless of a superior's orders or national law, all persons, military and civilian, whatever their rank or position, are obligated to terminate their commission of, or complicity with, acts connected to the use of a nuclear weapon in violation of humanitarian and other law proscribing international crimes. This is only a statement of the principle's minimal consequences in the context of nuclear weapons. In the present context of the threat of global catastrophe posed by the Trident system, the principle of individual responsibility supports reasonable, nonviolent acts by citizens and taxpayers of nuclear-armed states, not personally otherwise involved in deployment or use of nuclear weapons, directly to confront and oppose the potential commission of atrocities by use of those weapons.

> In the present context of the threat of global catastrophe posed by the Trident system, the principle of individual responsibility supports reasonable, nonviolent acts by citizens

This extension of the Nuremberg principle of individual responsibility is consistent with human rights law. Relevant provisions are found in the Universal Declaration of Human Rights. The Universal Declaration is widely accepted as an authoritative interpretation of the human rights clauses of the United Nations Charter, a treaty to which the UK is a party, and additionally evidences customary international law.

Preambular Paragraph 3 states: '[It] is essential, if man is not to be compelled to have recourse, as a last resort, to rebellion against tyranny and oppression, that human rights should be protected by the rule of law'.

Preambular Paragraph 8 states: '[Every] individual and every organ of society, keeping this Declaration constantly in mind, shall strive by teaching and education to promote respect for these rights and freedoms and by progressive measures, national and international, to secure their universal and effective recognition and observance, both among the peoples of Member States themselves and among the people of territories under their jurisdiction.'

Article 28 states: 'Everyone is entitled to a social and international order in which the rights and freedoms set forth in this Declaration can be fully realized.'

Together with other human rights as well as the UN Charter, Article 28 of the Universal Declaration articulates a right to peace. Article 3 sets forth the right to life. The ICJ at paragraph 25 held that the right to life, recognized in Article 6(1) of the International Covenant on Civil and Political Rights, a treaty to which the UK is a party, must be respected in time of war, and that in that context humanitarian and other law governing the conduct of warfare determines whether deprivation of the right to life is arbitrary in violation of Article 6(1).

The above-mentioned provisions of the Universal Declaration and International Covenant on Civil and Political Rights support a right of nonviolent resistance to threatened violations of the right to life and the right to peace. Harm to civilian populations is inconsistent with the principle that 'human rights should be protected by the rule of law' and the 'right to life'.

Nonviolent prevention of threatened harm vindicates the rule of law while avoiding 'recourse, as a last resort, to rebellion against tyranny and oppression'. Nonviolent crime prevention also fulfils the responsibility to strive for the 'recognition and observance' of human rights including the right to life and promotes the attainment of a 'social and international order in which rights and freedoms set forth in this declaration can be fully realised'.

In this fourth question put by the Lord Advocate, it may need emphasising once again that 'the other person' whose criminal activities we are trying to prevent is her Majesty's Government. In this regard I would like to refer you to the compelling dissent by Judge Brandeis in Olmstead v. United States where he says, 'Decency, security and liberty alike demand that government officials shall be subjected to the same rules of conduct that are commands to the citizen. In a government of laws, the existence of the government will be imperiled if it fails to observe the laws scrupulously. Our government is the potent, the omnipresent teacher. For good or ill, it teaches the whole people by its example. Crime is contagious. If the government becomes a lawbreaker, it breeds contempt for the law; it invites every man to become a law unto himself; it invites anarchy. To declare that in the administration of the criminal law the end justifies the means … would bring terrible retribution. Against that pernicious doctrine this court should resolutely set its face.'

Finally, in respect of this question it is also important to note here that if it is a defence then in order to run this defence it is essential that evidence is allowed to show that there was indeed an offence committed by another person. In other words, it gives added weight to the answer to Question 1, that in the context of the Greenock case, it was appropriate and competent that experts were allowed to testify on the factual and objective basis necessary to prove the illegality and criminality of Trident.

My answer to this last question is that depending on the particular circumstances of the case, it may or may not be a defence to a criminal charge that the alleged offence was not criminal but an attempt to prevent or bring to an end the criminal conduct of another or others and that in the particular circumstances of the Greenock acquittal it was certainly a defence.

Sentenced to a Comfy Chair

Joan Meredith, *Northumbria Affinity Group*

'Alnwick magistrates excused Joan Meredith, 70, an anti-nuclear protester from Rock Moor, near Alnwick, a £100 fine and the alternative of a week in prison for a peace protest at Faslane naval base. Instead she was told to find a comfortable seat in court and stay there for the rest of the day.' (*The Times*, 8 August 2000).

'Mrs. Meredith was casually dressed yesterday in a purple tee-shirt bearing the legend 'nobody needs a nuclear weapon' and

Joan (left) at a blockade at Faslane, August 1999, with Josje Snoek and Billy Wolfe

matching purple socks poked from the end of her open-toed san-
dals. She clutched a small duffle bag containing the spare clothes
and provisions she had expected to need in a week-long stay at
Low Newton remand centre near Durham. The three middle-aged
men smiled warmly at her as she took her seat for the beginning
of the afternoon session and Mr. Burn (the court clerk) even
offered her a cup of coffee.' (*Scotsman*, 8 August 2000)

'She would go to more protests, she said yesterday, 'I can't see
this making any difference.' (*Guardian*, 8 August 2000)

Conclusion

I finished my first submission by saying,

From any objective global perspective, we three women were
acting morally and according to natural justice. From an international legal perspective, our arguments (that we had legal justification for trying to prevent the preparations for the use of
nuclear weapons that could not be used in accordance with the
intransgressible principles of international law and which would
lead to indiscriminate attack and mass destruction) were compelling. Our acquittal showed that at least one Judge ruled our
act as also being lawful.

However, we acted within the judicial boundaries of one of the five major nuclear powers – the UK – at a time when the Government's view was that their nuclear weapons of mass destruction (the Trident system) were necessary for deterrence and were lawful under international law. Such an acquittal could therefore not go unchallenged and the Lord Advocate of the time – Lord Hardie – bowed to political rather than legal pressure and sought a Lord Advocate's Reference. I say this advisedly in the light of the way the petition is framed and of the questions that have been brought to the High Court.

A LAR is meant to be a procedure whereby points of law that have arisen in a case in relation to an indictable charge can be examined and clarified by the High Court. Serious mistakes in law can thus be rectified and potential problems and conflicts solved.

Is Trident criminal, and if it is what can be done to remove it from Scotland and ensure changes are made to the government defence policy and its implementation to bring it within the law?

In my opinion, the major point of law – or legal question – that arose from the Greenock Trial can not be seen within the Lord Advocate's Petition. The missing question is quite simply 'Is Trident criminal, and if it is what can be done to remove it from Scotland and ensure changes are made to the government defence policy and its implementation to bring it within the law?'

In a letter from the present Lord Advocate – the Right Honourable Colin Boyd – in response to a Scottish MSP – Dennis Canavan – who wrote in support of including the question of whether Trident is unlawful in the present proceedings, Colin Boyd states that 'it is not appropriate for the Crown to invite the court to answer the question'. This is a classic example of government evasion and abuse of power. The Government is trying to have its cake and to eat it too. It seeks to obtain the Court's views on questions that do not fairly arise from the Greenock acquittal, while at the same time avoiding the issue that goes to the very heart of the matter. Of course it is appropriate to invite the Court to answer the underlying question. As a matter of grave, urgent, public concern, the Court should initiate an immediate full inquiry into the whole problem or indicate an effective remedy open to the respondents.

There is another legal issue that has arisen in this trial and which the High Court have not been invited to answer and that is to what extent domestic law can over-ride basic principles of customary humanitarian law. In other words if the domestic law of a country does not allow the prevention of an international crime by its citizens, for whatever narrow technical reasons, does this actually invalidate the crime prevention. I think not. At Nuremberg we saw that in fact narrow domestic German Law did not over-ride international law. Whatever the state of German law, if the actions within Germany broke international law then that is what they were tried for and died for, and German law could only act in mitigation, if at all.

A much more recent German High Court case reported in the leading German law journal *New Juristic Weekly* can shed some light on this issue. It concerned two soldiers of the former East German Volksarmee who did their service at the Berlin wall protecting the East German border against their own people. After the fall of the Iron Curtain, in 1993 they were charged with homicide for the shooting of a refugee in 1984 who had tried to climb over the wall in East Berlin. They were found guilty at the first instance and it was confirmed at the appeal even though East German law permitted the use of firearms to prevent such a crime and even though they had been ordered by superior officers to prevent such 'crimes'. The High Court referred to the International Covenant on Civil and Political Rights and 'found that the defendants must have seen and respected the command of humanity'. It is interesting to note that the High Court referred to the Nuremberg Trials and said 'The judge has to examine whether the state has crossed the limits set by the basic values and convictions of all civilised nations.'

The judge has to examine whether the state has crossed the limits set by the basic values and convictions of all civilised nations

In a letter from the present Lord Advocate, the Right Honourable Colin Boyd – in response to a Scottish MSP, Dennis Canavan – the present Lord Advocate stated that the issues which arise in these Reference Proceedings are 'primarily related to the relationship between international law and the criminal law of Scotland'. He also stated that 'a wide ranging enquiry into the legality of Trident is not one which can be accommodated in this procedure'. If this is so, which I dispute, then nevertheless I submit that enough evidence came to light in the original Greenock trial which has been reported and commented upon in these Reference Proceedings to indict the people responsible for running and maintaining the UK Trident system and this Court should order the immediate and complete disarmament of Trident in the interests of the whole of humanity and in accordance with international law. Otherwise there will continue to be conflict between the very large percentage of people in Scotland, and the vast majority of other countries, that consider the Trident system to be unethical and criminal, and the people running and supporting the Trident bases.

It is also inherently unfair that such a life and death issue be left unresolved – and especially unfair to the military and other civilian workers within and outside the nuclear weapons bases who are at present engaged in the deployment of Trident and also in protecting the bases – and I speak here of the submariners and Commanders of the Trident submarines (some of whom are known to be deeply uncomfortable and confused about their role) and of the MOD and Strathclyde police in particular – all of whom could face criminal proceedings in a future war crimes tribunal for their part in enabling the complex system of mass destruction to continue to operate through its outstretched tentacles that cover many of the lochs and hills of Scotland.

I hope that the High Court and Scots law rise to the challenge.

A legal system can be supported by people if, and only if, it remains firmly grounded on natural justice and morality.

Murder has always been recognised as a wrong and as being unlawful and criminal. Mass murder is probably one of the most heinous wrongs known to mankind.

Crime prevention is natural and as long as it is done nonviolently, safely and accountably forms a recognised right in the vast majority of cultures, societies and nations, many of which have incorporated it directly within their judicial systems.

Although the questions put to the High Court seem to be purely technical, nevertheless they challenge the right of ordinary citizens to try to put very great wrongs right. For this right to be undermined spells disaster for our society and will lead to a protracted conflict of interests between the state and ordinary people. People will no longer be able to remain responsible caring human beings as well as Scots law-abiding citizens. They will have to choose between the two.

It is clear that responsible, caring global citizens will choose life and people's disarmament over a legal system devoid of morality, humanity and natural justice. The **nuclear crime prevention will continue whatever the outcome of the Lord Advocate's Reference** but if the court is wise and courageous it will also grapple with the underlying problems arising out of the Greenock Trial – that of the vital question of the criminality of Trident and how to remove it from Scotland.

I would like to leave you with one last quote and urge the court to read the whole of the Opinion of Judge Weeramantry from whom it comes. He says,

'One wonders whether in the light of common sense, it can ever be doubted that to exterminate vast numbers of the enemy population, to poison their atmosphere, to induce in them cancers, keloids and leukemias, to cause congenital defects and mental retardation in large numbers of unborn children, to devastate their territory and render their food supply unfit for human consumption – whether such acts as these can conceivably be compatible with 'elementary considerations of humanity'. Unless one can in all conscience answer such questions in the affirmative, the argument is at an end as to whether nuclear weapons violate humanitarian law, and therefore violate international law'.

Resolving Culture Conflicts

by David Heller, *Faslane Full-timers Rapid Reaction Force Affinity Group*

At the time of the first Trident Ploughshares disarmament camp in August 1998, I was living at the permanent peace camp at Faslane. Life at the camp was turned upside down for a few weeks as 300 Trident Ploughshares activists, as well as the For Mother Earth peace walk from NATO HQ, arrived in the area. For those of us willing to get involved it was an amazing experience. Ploughshares brought a huge amount of energy, and inspiring actions, to the struggle against Trident. The Peace Camp has made some good friends, and many contacts around the world. Many of us living at Faslane also learnt new campaigning skills, from press and legal support to effective e-mail networking.

But, for those peace campers who had little or no experience of the wider peace movement, this influx was a threat to the virtual monopoly that the Peace Camp held over opposition to the base. There was a curious territoriality, a kind of 'we've been camping outside this base for 16 years, what gives these people the right to come and do actions here?' attitude. Equally, there was a great deal of mistrust from some of the Ploughshares people, who saw the camp's emphasis on living an alternative lifestyle (and putting energy into a campaign against an eviction) as a dangerous distraction from anti-nuclear work.

So, over the course of the camp, I found myself spending quite a lot of time in the unenviable position of trying to bridge the gap between the camp at Faslane, and the Ploughshares camp a few miles away at Coulport. It was a struggle to convince some people that being opposed to nuclear weapons might mean getting involved with Faslane Peace Camp, and with Trident Ploughshares. This job became so stressful that my first arrest, as part of a group of Ploughshares activists blocking the main gates of Coulport, came as a welcome relief from the heated arguments, the seemingly endless round of meetings, the long uncomfortable bus trips between the two camps, and the rain.

By the end of 1998, a lot of the conflicts had been sorted out, and the Faslania All-Stars affinity group had been formed, as an umbrella for Trident Ploughshares Pledgers who were living at, or regular visitors to, the Peace Camp. However, the lack of stability in the group (caused by a rapid turnover of people, as well as personal conflicts) meant that a serious disarmament action was never realistic. We also realised that if everyone in the group was put on remand it would leave virtually no one at the camp.

Faslane Peace Camp continues to offer a huge amount to Trident Ploughshares. In practical terms it is a convenient starting point for actions at Faslane, and it is always a relatively dry spot to get a cup of tea, or to spend a night when you're kicked out of the base at two o'clock in the morning. Faslane campers have also helped set up and take down the temporary camps at Coulport. Beyond this, those of us who have spent weeks, months or years living near the base have a huge amount of experience to share. Several Ploughshares affinity groups on their first trip to the base have benefited from guided tours of the area – to point out the Trident submarine berths, more secluded routes to the base, and good places to cut the fence. Peace Campers have also played an important role in blockades of the base, and we have introduced tactics such as the tripod, and lock-ons, to the campaign. The co-operation and practical support continues to develop, and the recent 'Big Blockade' in February 2001 was jointly organised by Trident Ploughshares, Scottish CND and people from Faslane Peace Camp.

Hoozie and Teapot on Tripod blocking the south gate to Faslane, 1 August 2000

I'm not living at the camp at the moment although I'm still part of the Faslane Full Timers Rapid Reaction Force Affinity Group (the successor to the Faslania All-Stars). The more anarchistic ideas of the Peace Camp also continue to be a major influence on my approach to 'people's disarmament'. In particular, spending time at the camp has shaped the way I look at the legal system.

There is still a general impression within the Trident Ploughshares campaign that British courts are a relatively neutral place to argue points of international law. But, the court in Helensburgh, where the majority of cases are heard, has consistently refused to take account of international law, and plays a vital role in protecting the interests of the nuclear state of which it is a part. Despite the great media coverage that the campaign generates, simply having peace activists in court is no longer a news story, in Helensburgh at least. And while the Dumbarton Procurator Fiscal's office is certainly finding it hard to cope with the number of arrests that the Ploughshares campaign is generating, they will undoubtedly be able to deal with any number of people who submit themselves willingly to the court.

David Heller (right) serving food at the summer disarmament camp with Jenny Gaiawyn

Over the past three years I've seen lots of people turn up to Helensburgh District Court expecting to be acquitted simply by offering an international law defence, or content to have their day in court, and pay a fine of a few hundred pounds. The result is often a guilty verdict based on really flimsy evidence, with activists doing the prosecution's job for them as they explain how and why they sat in the road and blocked the traffic. On the occasions that I have put my energy into arguing with the prosecution evidence this has more often than not led to a reduction in the charges and lower penalties, and in a couple of cases to the prosecution accepting a not guilty plea.

If we are serious about making sure that the courts cannot find us guilty, we have to start playing their game well. This probably means getting cases in higher courts, really doing our legal home-work, as well as challenging the prosecution evidence. Otherwise, as a few of us in the campaign have been suggesting for some time, we need to stop playing their game entirely and take direct action against the courts to stop them functioning.

Decommissioning in Baggy Pants – Can Pay, Won't Pay
by Roger Franklin, *Midlands Affinity Group*

Four of us from the Midlands Affinity Group came out of a three day trial in Newbury with demands for compensation to the MOD, and for the costs of the prosecution (the latter would not have been required in Scotland where the courts demand no costs but also pay no costs if you win). The trial had taken place seven months after we had started to decommission the Atomic Weapons Establishment (AWE) at Aldermaston one night in July 1999.

Two months later, 5 May 2000, I went, by appointment, to my local magistrates' court in Stroud, to which the enforcement of the penalty payments had been transferred. I was supported by the local peace group, friends, and local reporters. In court, I explained briefly why I was not willing to pay the £570 demanded. I had already sent three pages of explanation, plus related docu-ments, to the court some time in advance. The magistrates said they had read them.

After a short discussion, followed by whispered consulting between the magistrates and the Clerk of the Court, I was told that bailiffs would be sent to my house with a court order to take some of my property for sale at auction.

There followed the siege of Tickmorend (Nuclear Free Zone), which was not lifted for three months. First a very fierce notice, with red capital letters of warning from the London-based bailiffs, soon followed by a second fierce notice from the bailiff's removals dogsbody – also in London – each giving me a week to pay before they would arrive.

I made the house as impregnable as possible for a 330 year old building, and locked doors behind me when going out, even to the garden. A notice on the front door warned bailiffs to be careful with (non-lethal) booby traps around the back; and a copy of *The Guardian*'s report about uncomplimentary comments from Citizens Advice Bureaux about bailiffs.

Fortunately, no bailiffs arrived at the occasional times when I had to relax precautions because of visiting family. Then a friend in the village was asked by a bailiff he had met at a concert about what sort of profitable pickings might be had from Tickmorend House. The reply was that, with no car, and not many electronic treasures, the bailiffs might do better at some other place on his long list!

I returned from the camp at Coulport in August 2000, and I was told that no bailiffs had been seen during my two weeks absence. But next morning, 16 August, just after I'd had a comfortable and late breakfast, a local policeman arrived at my door with a warrant for my arrest. He drove me to Stroud police station, in the same building as the magistrates' court, and I was subjected to the usual arrestee processing: removal of possessions, carefully listed, including my belt – but no fingerprinting or photographing. After about half an hour in a cell, with a permitted book, I was tunnelled up to the secure dock in the court to face three magistrates and a Clerk – with no public audience, of course.

Holding my trousers as best I could, I was told that the bailiffs had not been able to collect, so the magistrates were deciding what else to do, short of prison. The decision was that they would give me another three months to pay. By this time, another compensation plus fine had been passed to Stroud court from Helensburgh court – what can one expect if one uses the walls of a pristine MOD holding cell for writing important messages on?

Anyway, the Stroud magistrates told me that, after the three months, the case would be transferred to the county court in Gloucester, which has the power to take 'Garnishee Proceedings' (removing money from bank accounts). It then dawned on me that this secret hearing, at which I had had to affirm that I would speak the truth – holding up one hand while the other clung on to my baggy jeans – was for the purpose of establishing that maybe I did have money in a bank. To lie in such circumstances might have been a bit unwise.

Fairly soon after, I was surprised to receive a notice to appear in the same Stroud magistrates' court again, three months and five days after the secret hearing – not so secret, actually, as the local press published reports based on what I told them.

Four weeks before the hearing, I received a helpful explanatory letter from the Principal Court Clerk in Stroud, saying that he would now be addressing the magistrates that 'Garnishee Proceedings' would be a rather costly way to take such a 'small' amount (now £721). Therefore, the magistrates may again have to consider imprisonment, and I may wish to have legal representation in court.

Incidentally, the first notice I received from the bailiffs added their fee of £90 to the payment demanded. But that fee was not carried over, presumably because of the lack of success by the bailiffs. I might say, also, that during the 'siege', in order to prevent the whole house being ransacked in pursuit of £660 worth of goods to sell at low auction prices, I had concealed cash in excess of that amount to hand over should the bailiffs succeed in gaining entry (and perhaps adding further charges for their efforts). The archaic rules for bailiffs allow them entry through any open window, on any floor, so it got a bit stuffy in my house over the summer months. Once inside, bailiffs can break into any locked room in the house.

I responded to the helpful letter from the Principal Clerk at my usual length, saying I would continue to represent myself, but I wanted to remind the court that imprisoning me would cost the state (i.e. taxpayers) quite a bit of money, and would do little to deter me from my duty of continuing to decommission illegal nuclear weapons. I asked if the court had considered community service as an alternative, pointing out that I have considerable skills at cutting down fencing; there might be some unwanted fencing in the local area upon which I could usefully exercise this talent.

So the third hearing in the Stroud court finally came in November 2000. I again welcomed a good number of supporters and some reporters. The less secure dock was on a comfortable level with the three magistrates and I was again allowed to comment on how I could pay but wouldn't. After the usual consultations, the chief magistrate said he would have to sentence me to 28 days in prison (if well behaved, I might get out after 14 days). But he would suspend the sentence until I had failed to pay instalments on the penalty of £15 per week, starting a couple of weeks after the trial. For the £721 then owing, this would take nearly a year to pay off.

I knew I could survive prison, after previous short residences resulting from ongoing tax resistance. However, the instalment arrangement rather intrigued me, and, after careful consideration and consulting with my Trident Ploughshares Affinity Group, I hit upon an experiment that didn't seem to compromise Trident Ploughshares principles too much.

I announced to the local press, who kindly publicised my plan, that I would accept £15 cheques from people who support the decommissioning of Trident by direct action but could not become Pledgers themselves. These cheques should be made out to 'The Clerk of the Justices'; I would then send them on each week, and would match them with my own £15 cheques paid to the Trident Ploughshares campaign – £15 buys a good pair of bolt-cutters... I called this the 'Franklin's Freedom to Decommission Fund', implying that I could continue decommissioning uninterrupted by prison.

Roger Franklin paying his fine in instalments

I am encouraged to have received 35 cheques already – none from Pledgers, of course. This indicates considerable support for nuclear decommissioning, and has raised £525 for Trident Ploughshares. I now have 8 months of freedom assured, and I hope for more contributions – smaller cheques of £5 or £3 would be good, as they would show even more people supporting.

However, in the 'pipeline', as it were, is another fine of £75 from Helensburgh, and £350 of penalties from Newbury for further decommissioning at AWE, Aldermaston (May 2000). And there is a trial coming up at Helensburgh for a charge of 'maliciously damaging' a fence at Coulport – 50 cuts made me runner-up in the sponsored fence-cutting competition of August 2000. C'est la vie! I'm collecting reading material for a time in the clink at some point.

Supplement

by Marlene Yeo, *Midlands Affinity Group*

The Loughborough Court issued a distress warrant in July 2000 – four months after my case for non-payment of damages had been transferred from Newbury. The bailiffs sent me a letter on 4 August, adding their fee of £53.65. The Citizens Advice Bureau provided me with up to date information of citizens' rights and bailiffs' powers. So I knew that bailiffs are not allowed to enter your house for the first visit without your invitation. We tried to keep the doors locked, including the porch door. We put more or less token padlocks on the garden gate and shed. I made an assortment of posters to alternate in the porch window – variations on the themes of Trident warheads are immoral, illegal and a waste of money. All ended with 'I won't pay for them. Bailiffs keep out.' This, I hoped, would be proof that I did not invite the bailiffs in, even if the door happened to be open. It incidentally spread the message among tradespeople and the burghers of Burton-on-the-Wolds. (I'm sorry to say that the cost of Trident made far more impact on them than its destructive potential!). We put a poster on the back gate, too.

To my knowledge, the bailiffs only came twice: once when we

Marlene Yeo (right) with Judith Pritchard (left) supporting Sylvia and River at their Manchester trial, January 2000

were out, neighbours saw them walking round the house. The second time I talked to him through the porch window. The porch door was locked, and Peter locked me out of the house for good measure. But the bailiff never tried the door to see if it was open. He did try to trick me into opening the door, though, by holding up a paper well out of reading distance, saying, 'I have some information that you require.' I asked him to put it through the letterbox. He didn't. He reminded me that I made myself 'liable for additional costs.' His eye swivelled from me to the car that stood on our drive, and to the half-open garage door. I'm told that bailiffs can't touch your car while it's on your property, though they can on a public road. All the same, when he eventually gave up and went back to his car, he wrote in ink on his pre-printed FINAL NOTICE: Removal Team in Area. Wheel clamping. He added another £75 for his fees. He put that through my letterbox and left, never to be seen again.

Seven months later, the court gave up and gave me a detention for three hours in court.

Dear Bailiffs

Angie Zelter does not live here at present – she is away. Virtually nothing in the house belongs to her. It belongs to various people including her children, brother, partner, friends and various NGOs. They will sue you if you steal their possessions.

She refused to pay the original fine because she was upholding international law and protesting about the UK's threat to use nuclear weapons. She was acting to prevent mass murder. She always acts peacefully, openly, nonviolently and accountably and told the magistrates she would not pay the fine and that she had no private possessions.

It cannot be nice being a bailiff, why don't you stop working for the forces of darkness, become a gardener and enjoy the natural world.

Harry Potter!

Notice put up on the front door of Angie's home while she was away on urgent disarmament work.

CHAPTER 6

Challenge to the Scottish Judiciary

THE HIGH COURT HAD cleared only five days for the reference proceedings but by Thursday 16 November, the 4th day, it was clear we would not even have completed the first round of submissions. We were therefore invited to speak to the judges in their chambers to discuss how many more days to allot to the process and when they should be held. It was strange to be shepherded into the plush room with leather chairs, to await the judges entrance and then to be able to see them for the first time at the same level as us, rather than on the raised bench. It did make a difference to be able to see the trousers and shoes peeping out from under the robes and to be able to look them directly in the eye.

It was difficult to find a time convenient to us all but eventually we found 4 days in November for the proceedings to continue. By the Friday we had, in fact, finished the submissions of Simon Di Rollo for the Lord Advocate, my submissions, and the submissions of Jerry Moynihan, the amicus curiae, but only just begun to hear John Mayer's submissions.

When we reconvened in November, John Mayer finished off his submissions, on behalf of Ulla, and then Aidan O'Neill made his, on behalf of Ellen. The Senior Counsel for the Crown, Duncan Menzies QC, then started the second and final round of submissions, which I then followed. After me came Jerry Moynihan QC, the amicus curiae once again, Ian Anderson for Ulla and then Aidan O'Neill QC doing the second round for Ellen.

I concentrated in this second round on answering the questions that had arisen from the judges in the course of their questioning and on rebutting some of the Lord Advocate's arguments.

16 November, 2000 – High Court of Justiciary, Edinburgh, 2nd submission of Angie Zelter, 1st Respondent in the Lord Advocate's Reference, No.1. 2000.

'The Crown submitted that 'the use of nuclear weapons are merely one example of the use of force'. In my view, nothing could be more misleading. This is because nuclear weapons have three main effects – blast effects, fire effects and poison/radioactivity

LAR proceedings in Court 3, Edinburgh , October 200.

Drawn by Peter Lanyon

effects and electro-magnetic effects which occur indiscriminately over great continent-wide distances.

The prevailing military mindset is that nuclear weapons are means of delivering forceful blast effects, encapsulated in notions of strategic or tactical 'strikes', which derive from bombing Germany to 'hit back' at the Kaiser or Hitler. They are rationalised by pro-nuclear politicians through the use of homely playground analogies such as 'hitting the bully back on the nose'. In all these cases the key here is to realise that we are dealing with different versions of a model involving only two actors. Let us call it the two actor model.

Come World War Two it was discovered that many conventional shells and bombs used together were capable of creating a synergy effect or fire-storm which, when used against cities, engulfed many hundreds or thousands of non-combatant residents in Rotterdam, London, Hamburg and Tokyo. Although such actions were always justified morally and legally as retaliation, or reprisal, or hitting 'back', their real consequences went beyond this model. Hence, the examples of Hamburg etc. were not acclaimed as good and lawful acts, which then might have established a new (low) standard of customary state practice. Both sides claimed that their bombing was discriminating and focussed, and both continued to reinforce the norms of discrimination and non-combatant immunity through their denunciations of the 'deliberate atrocities' of the other side's area bombing of cities.

Looking back at these events, it is quite clear that both sides' area bombing, far from striking-back at the aggressor, actually struck at the heart of civil society, at the innocent bystanders, the non-combatants of London and Dresden. Yet, even so, with conventional explosives conventional bombing could be used in ways which could be focussed in time and place in a defensive war; for example, the use of air power in north west France in preparation for the Normandy invasion of 1944. With conventional explosives the two party model could still pertain.

However, with the use of nuclear weapons against Hiroshima and Nagasaki in 1945 we are immediately in the presence of a new paradigm.

Nuclear devices no longer fit the classical paradigm of a weapon: a means of extending force *vis a vis* an enemy

Nuclear devices no longer fit the classical paradigm of a weapon: a means of extending force *vis a vis* an enemy. This old model of force projection had already been stretched beyond breaking point in the course of area bombing of military-industrial complexes in city centres, as J.M. Spaight, the Air Ministry's top legal adviser during the war, admitted in *Air Power and War Rights* (London 1946). However by 1946 Spaight (now retired) had concluded that the inherently poisonous nature of nuclear weapons put them in a new category which could never be used in conformity with international law.

No rational person can imagine that they can 'defend themselves' or 'retaliate' against the unborn children of the next 1,000 generations

Nuclear weapons break out of the classical two actor model of weapons, retaliation, strike, etc. They necessarily involve civilians, emergency service workers, neutral nations, the environment, future generations. No rational person can imagine that they can 'defend themselves' or 'retaliate' against the unborn children of the next 1,000 generations –

to refer only to the 24,000 year half life of plutonium and its irreversible and cumulative vandalism of the gene pool of 'succeeding generations'.

So may I beseech the bench not to over identify with conventional, outdated and blinkered two actor views of the social relations involved between the statesmen and generals of 'our side' and the statesmen and generals of 'the enemy side'. May I beg you to identify with another 'our side' – that of the majority of those affected by nuclear weapons. This non-combatant community of peaceful life on earth is put in fear by inherently indiscriminate threats.

In the light of all this, let us revisit the analogy of using reasonable force to stop a neighbourhood thug. The appropriate analogy is not hitting the bully back on the nose. Rather the UK's posture can more accurately be likened to standing prepared at any minute to burn down the bully's home, thus murdering the bully's wife, child, aged parents, as well as endangering neighbouring houses and spreading poison throughout the entire neighbourhood.

These Reference Proceedings are addressing 'the most serious crimes of concern to the international community as a whole', the unlawful threat of destruction of all life on our planet.

Now, let me very briefly deal with the 'spanner in the works' as Mr. Moynihan put it, in his first submission, or what we have been referring to as:

The hypothetical extreme case

I think we have to ask just one question – is it believable or likely? The whole discussion depends on the concurrence of two incompatible events i.e. a state's survival being at stake and its response of exploding a low-yield nuclear weapon on a group of soldiers in the middle of a desert, and then if this doesn't work not using any other nuclear weapons. This is legalistic nonsense. It is quite obvious to any honest person that Trident is deployed to threaten mass destruction not to blow up a ship in the middle of the ocean or a tank unit in the middle of a desert – conventional weapons can do that perfectly adequately. This lie was at the heart of the problems within the ICJ Advisory Opinion. One does not need a 100 kiloton nuclear weapon to blow up a tank unit or a ship. Please don't allow such a ridiculous and misleading proposition to put a 'spanner in the works' of this court's rulings. We are here dealing with the realities of the UK Trident system as presently deployed and so are in a much better position than the ICJ which was asked to rule on a general question which had to take account of possible future inventions. This court therefore can be more specific and leave no loopholes for the unscrupulous to wriggle through.

It is quite obvious to any honest person that Trident is deployed to threaten mass destruction not to blow up a ship in the middle of the ocean or a tank unit in the middle of a desert – conventional weapons can do that perfectly adequately

Imminent, ongoing, ever-present, danger

There has been some discussion in this court of whether there is any imminent danger at all in the deployment of Trident and I would like to address this issue directly. In the process I invite you to note that more light is shed on the unlawfulness of deterrence itself by virtue of the plans, operations and deadly risks it entails.

I would like to bring to your attention a document which I gave in as evidence from the witness box at Greenock. It is a speech given by General Lee Butler. It is important because it helps provide an objective, rational explanation of why the deployment of Trident along with the expressed conditional intent to use it is an ever present, imminent source of danger that we should all be aware of and continually strive to eliminate.

Although it is about the nuclear weapons of the United States it applies to the UK too. In this regard please remember that the unrebutted facts at Greenock showed that:

• US nuclear weapons are still stationed at Lakenheath airbase (very close to where I live in Norfolk);

• UK nuclear forces are closely allied to those of the United States with whom we work closely in NATO and with whom we practise joint nuclear weapons exercises which involve scenarios of exploding thousands of NATO nuclear weapons;

• the targets for the UK Trident system are integrated into the overall targeting plan of the US;

• Prime Minister Blair has said he would be willing to press the nuclear button;

• Britain's refusal to take its nuclear weapons off alert is to continue to enable Trident to be used at any time – that is what the term 'credible deterrence' means;

• deployment of Trident is a way of keeping nuclear weapons in a state of readiness for use in a war – as Commander Tall said 'There was no doubt that when we went to sea we went to war'. A military unit on a short period of notice to fire is a status which would normally only be assumed in wartime. This term is not used with regard to any of the other British military forces listed in the Strategic Defence Review. This fact alone is enough to rebut Mr. Menzies' suggestion that Trident deployment is like an RAF practice flight over Scotland.

I would like you to read the whole of General Lee Butler's speech but will just highlight the most significant passages for you. General Lee Butler made this speech in Ottawa in 1999. He retired from the United States Air Force in 1994 after 33 years of military service where he had served at the very highest level. He was the Commander in Chief of the United States Strategic Command and had the responsibility for all US Air Force and US Navy strategic nuclear forces.

He states 'nuclear weapons are the enemy of humanity. Indeed, they're not weapons at all. They're some species of biological time bombs whose effects transcend time and space, poisoning the earth and its inhabitants for generations to come'. I shall return to this point later as it is crucial. He goes on to say, 'It required 30 years simply to reach the point in my career where I had the responsibilities and most importantly, the access to information and the exposure to activities and operations that profoundly deepened my grasp of what this business of nuclear capability is all about ... Let me .... give you some sense of what it means to be the Commander of Strategic Nuclear Forces, the land and sea-based missiles and aircraft that would deliver nuclear warheads over great distances. First, I had the responsibility for the day-to-day operation, discipline, training, of tens of thousands of crew members, the systems that they operated and the warheads those systems were designed to deliver. Some ten thousand strategic nuclear warheads. I came to appreciate in a way that I had never thought, even when I commanded individual units like B52 bombers, the enormity of the day-to-day risks that comes from multiple manipulations, maintenance and operational movement of those weapons. I read deeply into the history of the incidents and the accidents of the nuclear age as they had been recorded in the United States.

Missiles that blew up in their silos and ejected their nuclear warheads outside of the confines of the silo. B52 aircraft that collided with tankers and scattered nuclear weapons across the coast and into the offshore seas of Spain. A B52 bomber with nuclear weapons aboard that crashed in North Carolina – on one of these weapons, six of the seven safety devices that prevent a nuclear explosion had failed as a result of the crash. There are dozens of such incidents. Nuclear missile-laden submarines that experienced catastrophic accidents now lie at the bottom of the ocean.'

He goes on to explain how imminent the threat was when he says that as the 'principal nuclear advisor to the President of the United States' he had to be prepared 'on a moment's notice, day or night, seven days a week, 365 days a year to be within three rings' of his telephone, ready to recommend to the President what to do in the event of a nuclear attack. In explaining how the President 'had 12 minutes' to make his mind up he also shows how the military accept the reality of escalation from the use of one to many nuclear weapons. He says 'In the 36 months that I was a principal nuclear advisor to the President, I participated every month in an exercise known as a missile threat conference ... a scenario which encompassed one, then several, dozens, then hundreds and finally thousands of inbound thermonuclear warheads to the United States.'

It is interesting to note that he is as appalled as any of us that the 'fate of mankind in its entirety' hangs on a decision that has to be made in 12 minutes. This is not a peace protester saying this but a top military general.

He continues, 'sad to say, the poised practitioners of the nuclear art never understood the holistic consequences of such an attack, nor do they today. I never appreciated that until I came to grips with my third responsibility, which was for the nuclear war plan of the United States'. In January 1991 he 'finally for the first time in 30 years was allowed full access to the war plan' and says, 'I was shocked to see that in fact it was defined by 12,500 targets in the former Warsaw Pact to be attacked by some 10,000 nuclear weapons, virtually simultaneously in the worst of circumstances, which is what we always assumed. I made it my business to examine in some detail every single one of those targets. I doubt that that had ever been done by anyone, because the war plan was divided up into sections and each section was the responsibility of some different group of people. My staff was aghast when I told them I intended to look at every single target individually. My rationale was very simple. If there had been only one target, surely I would have to know every conceivable detail about it, why it was selected, what kind of weapon would strike it, what the consequences would be. My point was simply this. Why should I feel in any way less responsible simply because there was a large number of targets. I wanted to look at every one. At the end of that exercise I finally came to understand the true meaning of MAD, Mutually Assured Destruction. With the possible exception of the Soviet nuclear war plan, this was the single most absurd and irresponsible document I had ever reviewed in my life.'

He says, 'we escaped the Cold War without a nuclear holocaust by some combination of skill, luck, and divine intervention, and I suspect the latter in greatest proportion' and then continues to explain how he recognised that he 'had the responsibility to be at the forefront of the effort to begin to close the nuclear age' and how he persuaded the President to cancel millions of dollars worth of nuclear weapons programmes, accelerated the START I Accords, recommended that the bombers be taken off alert, put 24 bases on the closure list and 'cut the number of targets in the nuclear war plan by 75%'. He then went into retirement with 'a sense of profound relief and gratitude'.

That should have been the end of the story, but unfortunately he goes on to tell of his 'growing dismay, alarm and finally horror that in a relatively brief period of time, this extraordinary momentum and unprecedented opportunity had begun to slow down. So that today unbelievably United States policy is the same as what Ronald Reagan introduced in 1984. That our forces with their hair-trigger postures are effectively the same as they have been since the height of the Cold War ... NATO has expanded up to ... [Russia's] ... borders, and Moscow has been put on notice that the United States is presumably prepared to abrogate the ABM Treaty in the interest of deploying limited national ballistic missile defence'.

Now the UK is conspiring with the US in the support and development of the National Ballistic Missile Defense System and allowing military facilities in the UK to be developed for this purpose. Not only is this leading to the weaponisation of space and a new nuclear arms race (this time probably mainly with China) but once again the UK is backing the rule of power rather than the rule of law – undermining the international legal system through supporting the US in its planned breaches to the Anti-Ballistic Missile Treaty and the Outer Space Treaty.

To sum up – I have tried to give you a flavour of the evidence we gave at Greenock – to show the immediacy of the danger we are all in by design or accident.

No *true choice and the necessity defence*

With this information the court can appreciate more fully why Sheriff Gimblett was able to rule, without fear or favour as she put it, that we were justified in our attempts to disarm the Trident system. You may also be more able to understand why I feel that I am impelled to do all I can to prevent a nuclear holocaust, that I feel the necessity to act with others to try to disarm the Trident nuclear weapon system based here in Scotland, and why Trident Ploughshares will continue to encourage people's disarmament, or citizen intervention, until an official body takes over this urgent and necessary task. I consider my work here in this court as part of the people's disarmament attempts, as part of our work to reclaim the law for the protection of the innocent and helpless, for justice, fairness, equality, and the right to life. If this court does its duty in the light of the underlying principles of law

it would be against all logic and rationality for the court to be persuaded that citizens have a right to destroy property in ordinary cases of necessity but have no right to protect themselves in this way against the greatest evil of all

and justice and it rules appropriately then the executive will have no choice but to bow under the pressure of the law and disarm Trident of its nuclear weapons.

The court should be aware of the trap of too narrowly defining 'immediacy' – the timeframe for realising and acting on a threat and for those actions to yield efficacious results. The nature of the evil that my colleagues and I seek to prevent is on a unique scale totally different from say, creating a firebreak on someone's property to prevent a greater conflagration or breaking and entering to prevent a murder. The temporal element is quite different too. In ordinary necessity cases the immediacy of the greater evil is easy to discern and is a decisive element of justification. But, in the complex systems of mass destruction that have been set up for nuclear deterrence, the point at which the emergency is obviously apparent depends on the amount of information one has about the system, and the amount of information that a particular character may need to have, before they are convinced of the imminent danger. It takes some people much longer to realise the danger. It took General Lee Butler 33 years to realise how perilous and tenuous our survival is. How long will it take all those present in this court today?

I submit that it would be against all logic and rationality for the court to be persuaded that citizens have a right to destroy property in ordinary cases of necessity but have no right to protect themselves in this way against the greatest evil of all, the 'ultimate evil' as Judge Bedjaoui called it.

The right to intervene and the Nuremberg extension

One example of the 'extension' of the Nuremberg Principles to allow intervention to prevent international crime is the story of Paul Grueninger. He was the Chief of Police of St. Gallen, Switzerland, who allowed refugees from Nazi persecution to enter the canton of St. Gallen in the years 1938 and 1939 by disregarding federal directives and violating laws in order to protect them. He intervened to uphold human rights and dignity and to prevent crimes against humanity. He was dismissed from office and convicted by the district court of St. Gallen of violating the duties of his office and of falsifying legal documents. He was ostracised and lived in poverty the rest of his life. However, in 1995 Paul Grueninger was rehabilitated judicially when his trial was re-opened at the district court and he was acquitted and his descendants were given compensation for the losses in salaries and pension claims caused by his dismissal without notice.

Paul Greuninger's exemplary acts of humanity and international crime prevention are in marked contrast to the lawyers and judges who were tried at Nuremberg in the case of US v. Josef Altstoetter *et al* also known as The Justice Case. They were found to be complicit in war crimes and crimes against humanity. 'Some of the defendants took part in the enactment of laws and decrees the purpose of which was the extermination of Jews and Poles in Germany and throughout Europe. Others, in executive positions, actively participated in the enforcement of those laws'.

German law was no justification, no defence. 'This tribunal is not concerned with the legal incontestability under German law' of the cases against the Jews, Poles or other persecuted minorities, 'the defendants are not charged with specific overt acts against named victims. They are charged with criminal participation in government organised atrocities and persecutions unmatched in the annals of history'. The Tribunal was acutely aware that the accused jurists were enforcing domestic law that under German legal doctrine took precedence within Germany over international law. The Tribunal thus took special care to emphasise that the jurists nonetheless could be held responsible – the implication being that German legal theory was mistaken in endorsing the violation of international law if required by domestic law. The Tribunal states, 'The conclusion to be drawn from the evidence presented by the defendants themselves is clear. In German legal theory Hitler's law was a shield to those who acted under it, but before a tribunal authorised to enforce international law, Hitler's decrees were a protection neither to the Fuehrer himself nor to his subordinates, if in violation of the community of nations.'

These quotes show the 'universality and superiority of international law' over local State law. The Tribunal explained, 'It is therefore clear that the intent of the statute on crimes against humanity is to punish for persecutions and the like, whether in accord with or in violation of the domestic laws of the country where perpetrated, to wit: Germany. The intent was to provide that compliance with German law should be no defence.'

Just as international law provides for the prosecution of international criminals it also logically has to provide for the intervention by individuals to prevent those crimes from taking place. The rights of a state to intervene are explicitly recognised by – 'Sir Hartley Shawcross, the British Chief Prosecutor at the trial of Goering *et al*: The rights of humanitarian intervention on behalf of the rights of man trampled upon by a state in a manner shocking the sense of mankind has long been considered to form part of the [recognised] law of nations. Here, too, the Charter merely develops a pre-existing principle.' If no state intervenes then I submit there is a right of individual nonviolent intervention to prevent war crimes and crimes against humanity from taking place.

I submit that whatever the state of UK law on the deployment of Trident, the risks of a nuclear holocaust by design or by accident, and the practice of nuclear deterrence with 100 kiloton nuclear warheads is a war crime and a crime against humanity and should be stopped by this court. This court has a responsibility under the superiority of international law to back up global citizens like myself to reinforce the decision of Sheriff Gimblett and to use whatever powers it may have to enforce international law by ordering the UK to cancel their unlawful nuclear plans and operations and to immediately disarm Trident. Anything else would in fact be giving support to the illegal policies of the UK state and would be undermining international law.

Judge Panzer, who gave evidence at Greenock, explained how hundreds of lawyers and judges in Germany have learnt, from the terrible experiences under the Nazis, not to be complacent or to remain silent when their government acted unlawfully but to take their responsibilities for upholding international law seriously – to peacefully intervene to try to prevent war crimes and crimes against humanity before they could take place. They joined the Judges for Peace organisation – 20 judges were arrested for blockading the US nuclear base at Mutlangen in the 1980s. Before they could appeal against their convictions the Pershing missiles at Mutlangen against which they were protesting were removed from Germany.

it is the mark of a civilised country that its members are prepared to assist in the maintenance of good order

If the Crown is right, and private individuals have no right or role in preventing crimes organised and supported by the state, then this leaves only the servants of the same criminal state to address the problem. Leaving it to the criminals to stop the crime may not be a totally effective strategy.

I would also like here to address directly the concern that anarchy will arise if anyone arrogated to themselves the role of prosecutor, judge and jury and takes the law into their own hands. The right of nonviolent, open and accountable citizen intervention to prevent the most serious crimes known to humanity, when the state actors themselves will not enforce international law, is itself a safeguard against lawlessness. It is the mark of a civilised country that its members are prepared to assist in the maintenance of good order and it would be a mark of a wise judiciary to endorse such action as a necessary antidote to abuses of state power. At the moment it is the State that is encouraging international anarchy by undermining international law.

This is why it is essential, in considering the issues before this court, to start from an evaluation of whether Trident is unlawful. If in fact Trident is unlawful then our actions are defending rather than undermining the rule of law.

The uniqueness of nuclear weapons

President Bedjaoui said that the existence of nuclear weapons 'is a major challenge to the very existence of humanitarian law'. Judge Weeramantry argued that no credible legal system could contain a rule within itself which rendered legitimate an act which could destroy the entire civilisation of which that legal system formed a part. Such a rule could only find a place in the rules of a suicide club, and could not be part of any reasonable legal system. In a world where a number of states possess and deploy nuclear weapons, a very small part of which, if used, could destroy civilisation, it is clear that these weapons and weapon systems really are unique in an unparalleled sense. For any use of them necessarily exposes the world to the possibility of escalation to a truly apocalyptic nuclear exchange. The threat of use of a nuclear weapon is a threat to the world.

A legal system is usually distanced from the objective events on which it is required to make an impartial judgement. It limits its involvement to preserving its own integrity and reasonableness. However, in the case of the threat posed by nuclear weapon systems, any judgement that the law provides, because of its possible reflexive effect in terms of destruction, has consequences for itself. The law cannot condone as lawful actions which potentially are destructive of itself, for if the full consequences of a nuclear war should follow, the law itself would disappear, along with its courts, judges, jurists, precedents, records, indeed its very memory. (Perhaps the ultimate contempt of court?).

A legal system that allows the legality of indiscriminate nuclear threats would be the rule of a suicide club indeed. For this court to fail to condemn the continuing threat from the deployment of the Trident nuclear weapon system would be to assent to its own demise.

Do the NPT and other treaties legitimise possession, threat to use or use of nuclear weapons?

There has been some argument that the Non-Proliferation Treaty (NPT) and other treaties legitimise the possession of nuclear weapons in that they recognise and even presuppose the existence of nuclear weapons. I would like to rebut this. The ICJ nowhere states that the NPT or other treaties legitimate possession. It merely accepts the reality of possession. In other words the NPT recognises the *de facto* possession by the five nuclear weapon states but nowhere confers *de jure* possession. Moreover, these treaties certainly do not recognise or imply the legality of the threat or use of nuclear weapons. The position of the non nuclear weapon states is that they make the best of a bad job. They have accepted a temporary right to possess whilst simultaneously the possessors negotiate disarmament. Any scintilla of legitimacy for their possession (should that be conceded) has worn away with the passage of 32 years and the failure of the nuclear weapon states to nail down the Article VI negotiations. To suggest that possession in accordance with the 1968 NPT implies legality of use, as the UK and US contended in the ICJ hearings, amounts to saying that the NPT is a licence to use or threaten to use nuclear weapons which it is obviously not.

On the first day of the oral hearings at the ICJ on October 30 1995, Gareth Evans QC, Foreign Minister of Australia, argued that the norm of non possession of nuclear weapons under Articles I and II of the NPT 'must now be regarded as reflective of customary international law'. He stated that 'if humanity and the dictates of the public conscience demand the prohibition of such weapons for some states, it must demand the same prohibition for all states. And following the end of the Cold War, there can no longer be, if there ever was, any practical imperative for treating nuclear weapon states and non nuclear weapon states differently.'

The court essentially accepted that argument, unanimously concluding that: 'There exists an obligation to pursue in good faith and bring to a conclusion negotiations leading to nuclear disarmament in all its aspects under strict and effective international control'. Although not stated explicitly, the court's reasoning made it quite clear that this obligation applies to all states, including those outside the NPT.

As Judge Weeramantry summed up:

'These are clear indications that, far from acknowledging the legitimacy of nuclear weapons, the Treaty was in fact a concentrated attempt by the world community to whittle down such possessions as there already were, with a view to their complete elimination. Such a unanimous recognition of and concerted action towards the elimination of a weapon is quite inconsistent with a belief on the part of the world community of the legitimacy of the continued presence of the weapon in the arsenals of the nuclear powers.

Even if possession is legitimised by the treaty, that legitimation is temporary and goes no further than possession. The scope and the language of the treaty make it plain that it was a temporary state of possession simpliciter and nothing more to which they, the signatories, gave their assent – an assent given in exchange for the promise that the nuclear powers would make their utmost efforts to eliminate those weapons which all signatories considered so objectionable that they must be eliminated. There was here no recognition of a right, but only of a fact. The legality of that fact was not conceded, for else there was no need to demand a *quid pro quo* for it – the *bona fide* attempt by all nuclear powers to make every effort to eliminate these weapons, whose objectionability was the basic premise on which the entire treaty proceeded.'

Equally, such temporary possession cannot cure an illegality of use and threat to use. All these treaties see nuclear weapons as a 'bad thing' – why else would states undertake to keep certain areas nuclear weapon free, or prevent proliferation and negotiate nuclear disarmament? In fact the legality or illegality of the threat or use of nuclear weapons can only be determined with reference to the law of the UN Charter and the requirements of the law applicable in armed conflict, in particular the principles and rules of humanitarian law.

There is nothing inconsistent with recognising that states possess certain weapons whilst denying their right to use them or to threaten their use. That was exactly the position for many states with asphyxiating gases under the 1925 Geneva Protocol, before the more recent Chemical Weapons Convention made even pos-session unlawful. The court should also note the ICJ Advisory Opinion that it is the 'strong adherence to the practice of deter-rence' by states like the UK that hampers the emergence of a spe-cific rule prohibiting the use of nuclear weapons.

The fact that there are treaties, which admit the existence of nuclear weapons, does not legitimise their use. In any event these Lord Advocate's Reference proceedings are about the specific illegality and criminality of Trident in the context of government policy, not of nuclear weapons in the abstract or in general. And the threat or use of 100 kiloton nuclear warheads is indisputably unlawful.

State practice and opinio juris

The core of this question concerns not mere state practice but the practice of states coupled with acts to reflect and constitute *opinio juris*. In this connection it is not a matter of whether a handful of powerful and populous states would rather that inter-national humanitarian norms of great antiquity and widespread support were held not to apply – rather inconveniently – to cer-tain kinds of weapons (or rather, poison-scattering devices) to which they are attached. The question is, have they come out publicly and shamelessly to say, 'We believe that incinerating civilians and poisoning neutrals are lawful things to do'? No, of course they have not. In fact, they repeatedly denounce such actions when other states engage in them, thus re-inforcing their shared adherence to the global consensus as to *opinio juris* and also on intransgressible norms or *jus cogens*.

Moreover, as yesterday Lord Prosser canvassed several contrac-tual analogies from civil law, it may be helpful to remind the court that states parties to international conventions are no more capable of concluding valid agreements if their object is to vio-late more general legal norms (for example, the Nazi-Soviet pact to dismember Poland) than any two commercial companies would be free to conclude a pseudo-legal agreement to smuggle cigarettes or guns etc. Thus the Vienna Convention on the Interpretation of Treaties confirms that international agreements cannot be validly concluded violative of prior norms of interna-tional law *jus cogens* or 'intransgressible' norms to use the lan-guage of the ICJ. If this is true of whole treaties, how much less scope is there for one or two of a handful of states parties to a treaty to seek to establish formally entered reservations which run counter to norms of *jus cogens*.

Had the UK entered its 'understanding' as a formal reservation all anti nuclear states parties to the Geneva Protocol negotiations would have challenged that alleged reservation with their own counter reservations deposited on signing or ratification which would have stated that they did not consider that the reservation of the UK rendered them *bone fide* participants in the Additional Protocols. It was precisely for this reason that as a matter of political expediency the UK sought to have it both ways in 1977 by entering merely an 'understanding' which they knew was unlikely to risk any counter reservations. If the anti nuclear states had entered such counter-reservations it would have conferred legal significance on what was and remained a mere political declaration devoid of legal import. The arguments of the UK and US concerning their pseudo reservations were canvassed before the ICJ at some length. It is in that context that the 'understandings' in the 1998 ratifications have failed to lift the class of nuclear weapons clear of the scope of the 'grave breaches' provisions of the Protocols and Act of 1995. I refer you once again to paragraph 84 of the ICJ Advisory Opinion, which makes it quite clear that the Protocols do apply to nuclear weapons.

Crime in war/legal in peacetime?

It has been suggested that international humanitarian law, because it deals with armed conflict, is not applicable in times of peace. (Can the UK be said to be at peace, or not in a state of armed conflict, if is engaged in dropping bombs in Iraq at the present time?) This suggestion if it were true would lead to a very surprising conclusion – namely that if a certain mode of deployment of Trident was unlawful only in wartime, the UK would be in the position of having a weapon that can only be so deployed in peacetime and which would have to be withdrawn in times of war – hardly what the war-planners have in mind.

What is an illegal threat?

In its Advisory Opinion, the ICJ does not offer a comprehensive definition of 'threat'. Its approach to the concept is, however, apparent from a sentence in which it discusses threats. It says,

'Whether a signalled intention to use force if certain events occur is or is not a 'threat' within Article 2, paragraph 4 of the Charter depends upon various factors.' Several points are implicit here. First, the existence of a threat is not predicated on the actor saying, overtly, 'we threaten you'. A threat may be inferred from actions taken. Second, there is a certain contingency about a threat; there is an 'or else' associated with it directed at the target state. Thirdly, the court was not ready to pin itself down to particular 'factors'. Evidently the test is a flexible one depending on the circumstances.

Thus to answer the question 'what is an illegal threat?' will depend on the circumstances surrounding Trident's deployment and on adducing the necessary evidence. We gave this evidence at Greenock and it was unrebutted. The ICJ acknowledges the importance of circumstances and necessary evidence in some of its cases.

For instance in the Nicaragua Case the ICJ held that US military manoeuvres near the Nicaraguan border were not an illegal threat of force. It said: 'The Court is however not satisfied that the manoeuvres complained of, in the circumstances in which they were held, constituted on the part of the United States a breach, as against Nicaragua, of the principle forbidding recourse to the threat or use of force'. The court thus implied that the manoeuvres could or would have constituted an illegal threat if the circumstances had been different.

The term 'illegal threat' is sensitive to context. Within the context of the evidence given at Greenock it is quite clear that the ongoing deployment of 100 kiloton nuclear warheads on Trident is seen as an illegal threat by many non-nuclear states.

To define any word in the English language, the *Oxford English Dictionary* (OED) is a good start. It is necessary to find a comprehensive meaning for the word 'threat' because there is no clear, unambiguous definition, by Treaty, by the General Assembly of the UN, or by the ICJ. The OED defines 'threat' as a 'declaration of intention to punish or hurt', 'menace of bodily hurt or injury', 'indication of something undesirable coming'. A threat, in other words, may be something short of a warning shot. I submit that the deployment of Trident must be within the core meaning of 'threat' as the ICJ seems to be using it.

As to the 'illegality' of such a threat, a threat to use Trident's nuclear weapons is illegal because such use would be contrary to international humanitarian law.

I think it is important to once more draw to your attention the discussion of the illegality of nuclear threat or deterrence put so very clearly by Judge Weeramantry where he discusses the illegality of nuclear deterrence.

'Deterrence as used in the context of nuclear weapons is deterrence from an act of war – not deterrence from actions which one opposes.

One of the dangers of the possession of nuclear weapons for purposes of deterrence is the blurring of this distinction and the use of the power the nuclear weapon gives for purposes of deterring unwelcome actions on the part of another state. The argument of course applies to all kinds of armaments, but *a fortiori* to nuclear weapons. As Polanyi observes, the aspect of deterrence that is most feared is the temptation to extend it beyond the restricted aim of deterring war to deterring unwelcome actions...

It has been suggested, for example, that deterrence can be used for the protection of a nation's 'vital interests'. What are vital interests, and who defines them? Could they be merely commercial interests? Could they be commercial interests situated in another country, or a different area of the globe?

Another phrase used in this context is the defence of 'strategic interests'. Some submissions adverted to the so-called 'sub-strategic deterrence', effected through the use of a low-yield 'warning shot' when a nation's vital interests are threatened... This Opinion will not deal with such types of deterrence, but rather with deterrence in the sense of self-defence against an act of war...

Deterrence can be of various degrees, ranging from the concept of maximum deterrence, to what is described as a minimum or near-minimum deterrent strategy. Minimum nuclear deterrence has been described as:

'nuclear strategy in which a nation (or nations) maintains the minimum number of nuclear weapons necessary to inflict unacceptable damage on its adversary even after it has suffered a nuclear attack'.

The deterrence principle rests on the threat of massive retaliation, and as Professor Brownlie has observed:

'If put into practice this principle would lead to a lack of proportion between the actual threat and the reaction to it. Such disproportionate reaction does not constitute self-defence as permitted by Article 51 of the United Nations Charter.'

In the words of the same author, 'the prime object of deterrent nuclear weapons is ruthless and unpleasant retaliation – they are instruments of terror rather than weapons of war'.

Since the question posed is whether the use of nuclear weapons is legitimate in any circumstances, minimum deterrence must be considered...

One of the problems with deterrence, even of a minimal character, is that actions perceived by one side as defensive can all too easily be perceived by the other side as threatening. Such a situation is the classic backdrop to the traditional arms race... With nuclear arms it triggers off a nuclear arms race, thus raising a variety of legal concerns. Even minimum deterrence leads to counter-deterrence, and to an ever ascending spiral of nuclear armament testing and tension. If, therefore, there are legal objections to deterrence, those objections are not removed by that deterrence being minimal.

Deterrence needs to carry the conviction to other parties that there is a real intention to use those weapons in the event of an attack by that other party. If deterrence is to operate, it leaves the world of make-believe and enters the field of seriously intended military threats.

Deterrence therefore raises the question not merely whether the threat of use of such weapons is legal, but also whether use is legal. Since what is necessary for deterrence is assured destruction of the enemy, deterrence thus comes within the ambit of that which goes beyond the purposes of war. Moreover, in the split second response to an armed attack, the finely graded use of appropriate strategic nuclear missiles or 'clean' weapons which cause minimal damage does not seem a credible possibility.

The concept of deterrence goes a step further than mere possession. Deterrence is more than the mere accumulation of weapons in a storehouse. It means the possession of weapons in a state of readiness for actual use. This means the linkage of weapons ready for immediate take off, with a command and control system geared for immediate action... There is clearly a vast difference between weapons stocked in a warehouse and weapons for immediate action. Mere possession and deterrence are concepts which are clearly distinguishable from each other...

If one intends to use them, all the consequences arise which attach to intention in law, whether domestic, or international. One intends to cause the damage or devastation that will result. The intention to cause damage or devastation which results in total destruction of one's enemy or which might indeed wipe it out completely clearly goes beyond the purposes of war. Such intention provides the mental element implicit in the concept of a threat.

However, a secretly harboured intention to commit a wrongful or criminal act does not attract legal consequences, unless and until that intention is followed through by corresponding conduct... If, however, the intention is announced, whether directly or by implication, it becomes the criminal act of threatening to commit the illegal act in question.

Deterrence is by definition the very opposite of a secretly harboured intention to use nuclear weapons. Deterrence is not deterrence if there is no communication, whether by words or implication, of the serious intention to use nuclear weapons. It is therefore nothing short of a threat to use. If an act is wrongful, the threat to commit it, and more particularly, a publicly announced threat, must also be wrongful.

Another aspect of deterrence is the temptation to use the weapons maintained for this purpose. The Court has been referred to numerous instances of the possible use of nuclear weapons of which the Cuban Missile Crisis is probably the best known. A study based on Pentagon documents, to which we were referred, lists numerous such instances involving the possibility of nuclear use from 1946 to 1980...

Either all nations have the right to self defence with any particular weapon or none of them can have it – if the principle of equality in the right of self-defence is to be recognised. The first alternative is clearly impossible and the second alternative must then become necessarily the only option available...

As already observed, the Declaration of St. Petersburg, followed and endorsed by numerous other documents declared that weakening the military forces of the enemy is the only legitimate object which States should endeavour to accomplish during war. Deterrence doctrine aims at far more – it aims at the destruction of major urban areas and centres of population and even goes so far as 'mutually assured destruction'... Such policies are a far cry from the principles solemnly accepted at St. Petersburg and repeatedly endorsed by the world community.'

Can state practice legitimise the threat to use nuclear weapons?

Is the standing of a rule of humanitarian law vitiated by acts which are in breach of it? For example, does the practice of gassing whole groups of citizens by a state count as evidence for deciding what is law or not? Can the awful practice of 'ethnic cleansing' by various states over the last decade make it lawful? Can the practice of the most powerful nuclear weapon states undermine and displace intransgressible principles that they themselves once adhered to? If it can then we are at the mercy of the powerful and the law will no longer be able to protect us from violence. It is up to all of us to make sure that this does not happen.

I submit that the practice of the powerful nuclear weapon states who threaten to use their nuclear weapons is contrary to the very essence and spirit of international humanitarian law and can never be legitimate however long they continue to practise nuclear deterrence.

Judge Shi's Declaration says that the policy of nuclear deterrence 'has no legal significance from the standpoint of the formation of a customary rule prohibiting the use of nuclear weapons as such. Rather, the policy of nuclear deterrence should be an object of regulation by law, not *vice versa*. The Court, when exercising its judicial function of determining a rule of existing law governing the use of nuclear weapons, simply cannot have regard to this policy practice of certain States as, if it were to do so, it would be making the law accord with the needs of the policy of deterrence. The Court would not only be confusing policy with law, but also take a legal position with respect to the policy of nuclear deterrence, thus involving itself in international politics – which would be hardly compatible with its judicial function.

Also, leaving aside the nature of the policy of deterrence, this 'appreciable section of the international community' adhering to the policy of deterrence is composed of certain nuclear weapon States and those States that accept the protection of the 'nuclear umbrella'. No doubt, these States are important and powerful members of the international community and play an important role on the stage of international politics. However, the Court, as the principal judicial organ of the United Nations, cannot view this 'appreciable section of the international community' in terms of material power. The Court can only have regard to it from the standpoint of international law. Today the international community of States has a membership of over 185 States. The appreciable section of this community to which the Opinion refers by no means constitutes a large proportion of that membership, and the structure of the international community is built on the principle of sovereign equality. Therefore, any undue emphasis on the practice of this 'appreciable section' would not only be contrary to the very principle of sovereign equality of States, but would also make it more difficult to give an accurate and proper view of the existence of a customary rule on the use of the weapon.'

In other words international law cannot just be what the powerful nations say it is – because as the Malaysian Ambassador put it 'Otherwise we would be legitimising the principle that might is right and we would have to come to the frightening conclusion that international law is on the side of the powerful, as interpreted by the powerful.'

Perhaps it is enough to note the fact that many non-nuclear weapon states see us as the pariah or rogue states.

The evidential basis of the Lord Advocate's Reference

Lastly, I must come back once again to a major problem with this LAR. I have argued from the start that the most serious legal question that arose from our trial at Greenock was the issue of the legality of the UK Trident nuclear weapon system. This is the question above all others that should be discussed at this Hearing. However, we have never clarified and agreed on what evidential basis these proceedings are working. We have been denied the complete evidence from Greenock. For instance the testimony of the three respondents and two of our witnesses has been denied to this court. Although we have been allowed to raise some of the issues and arguments about the legal position of Trident it has been with many constraints, not least of which has been the inability of the respondents to call expert evidence and the constraints of having to work within the framework of the four questions however widely interpreted.

In other words we are in fact having a legal discussion on a major issue of public importance without either the full testimony from Greenock and also without being allowed to call expert witnesses to give their testimony directly to this court. It would be unfair and misleading if the judges were to infer from this that there is no factual base to the illegality and criminality of Trident's possession, deployment, threat to use and use.

Although the court has allowed a wide interpretation of the Lord Advocate's questions it has become clear that the court has not been given the factual nor the legal information that they require to come to a wise, just and fully informed decision as to the legality of Trident. I may be mistaken in this and if I am and this court rules that it is evident – even on the incomplete evidential basis and the incomplete international law submissions put by advocates before this court – that Trident is unlawful under International law and that international humanitarian crimes are being committed, then I will, of course, be content. However, it is fair to notify the court that if it rules that Trident is lawful on the basis of these proceedings that I will not consider justice to have been done.

> **if the court rules that Trident is lawful on the basis of these proceedings then I will not consider justice to have been done**

This is because the legality of Trident is being looked at through the back-door.

In response to Mr. Menzies' point that there are no facts that arise from Greenock I would like to ask, if there were no facts at Greenock are there also no facts here in this court? And if so how can this court rule whether there is a crime or not? Therefore this court may not be able to make headway in deciding whether Trident is lawful or not because it needs facts about proportionality and discrimination. As the ICJ said, it couldn't make a more precise ruling because it didn't have the facts or specific systems in front of it. I had been assuming that this court did have some cognisance of facts about Trident.

Until a court has called to the witness box the commanders of Trident and the nuclear policy makers and have before them the true and complete picture of the facts of Trident and have before them international lawyers who can adequately answer the questions as to the intricacies of what precisely international law does and does not permit in relation to the specifics of Trident then I will not have confidence in any ruling that suggests that international law can not protect us from Trident. If after a full and independent and publicly accountable judicial inquiry into Trident a court then decides that Trident is lawful, then and only then would I believe that international law is weak and not developed enough to protect us and to live up to the fine principles of the de Martens Clause.

Our capacity to prevent harm

I wish to address this court on the capacity to prevent crime as several times the court has pointed out that in the necessity/crime prevention defences one has to be able to prove that the act is actually capable of preventing the harm or preventing the crime. It has been insinuated that acts by Trident Ploughshares Pledgers, and specifically our act of destroying all the equipment on the barge *Maytime*, was not a direct enough causal link to provide the element necessary to found a valid legal defence. I refute this – our act on *Maytime* was capable of preventing crime.

Firstly, *Maytime* was an essential link in the Trident programme. Secondly, our action effectively broke that essential link. Thirdly, although the essential link, without which the whole Trident deployment system would soon have come to a grinding halt, was soon repaired and the equipment replaced, this does not invalidate the crime prevention or the necessity to act. In the same way as a policeman taking a gun away from a criminal is not said to have failed in his crime prevention just because the gunman procures another gun. Fourthly, our act cannot be seen as a single act – in the same way as a single policeman's act needs to be put into the context of the crime prevention acts of the whole police force. Trident Ploughshares nuclear crime prevention acts are not isolated one-off acts. Trident Ploughshares has a consistent policy, training and plans to prevent the threat and use of nuclear weapons. We are in a continuing process and getting better at it. Only a couple of weeks ago yet another team disabled a vehicle used to transport dangerous nuclear warheads for Trident from Burghfield to Coulport. And don't forget the two women who disabled the equipment on *Vengeance* delaying it for some months.

But we are working within a basic moral and legal framework that insists upon total nonviolence. Our *Handbook* states our total commitment to accountable, nonviolent, open and safe disarmament of mass destruction weapons. We emphasise that to be completely effective may take many different disarmament actions over an extended period of time because the Trident system is so large, complex and entrenched within the thinking and structure of the institutions of our nuclear weapon state. However, each act of disarmament is also a separate crime prevention act if you see the equipment and the specific job as part of a complex conspiracy. We also emphasise that just getting rid of the nuclear weapons at one particular time or in one country is not enough – that we will have to work over time and in all the nuclear weapon countries. And we acknowledge that continuing nuclear disarmament eventually requires the state to do its part. Citizens cannot complete the nuclear disarmament as it requires amongst other things the guarding of long-term storage of nuclear wastes that are actively dangerous for hundreds of thousands of years.

I know that we would ostensibly have had a better defence in law if we had blown up all four Trident nuclear submarines at once. On a superficial level such an act could be seen as proportionate to the crime that we say is being committed – namely the threat to all life on earth. I am sure that a small group of determined citizens could do this but I would never suggest or back any such plan because it is not nonviolent or safe, and could trigger off the very thing we are trying to prevent, i.e. the destruction of all life on earth.

When I was told many years ago by a judge at Kings Lynn Crown Court after I had taken part in a demonstration that I would have had a better defence in law if I had blown up a plane, I thought very carefully about the implications of this. It eventually led me to take part in the successful nonviolent and safe disarmament of a jet plane being exported to Indonesia that would have been used in the continuing genocide of various tribes in East Timor. That particular plane was still out of action six months later when we came to trial and the Indonesians in the end refused to have it even when it was eventually rebuilt. The destruction of that plane was safe. It was easy to do safely. And the jury eventually found us not guilty.

But a complex nuclear weapon system like Trident cannot be safely, nonviolently, directly and totally disarmed by untrained citizens in one action at one moment in time. They cannot even be deployed safely (look at the problems the UK is having with the nuclear powered hunter-killer submarines which have been recalled and look at General Lee Butler's and Professor Paul Roger's testimony on the danger from nuclear accidents). Such safe and nonviolent citizen disarmament will take time and care to be effective and on the way will bring in various state actors who will finish the whole process off. Nevertheless just because preventing some of the international criminal actions taking place cannot be equated with preventing the whole massive nuclear weapons crime doesn't mean to say that we are not preventing crime or acting out of necessity. We did disarm *Maytime* – one link was taken out.

Morality and law

There have been some comments during this trial to the effect that morality has no part to play in the law. I submit that this can never be so and particularly in a case like this. Morality underpins the law and without it the law has no legitimacy and our society would descend into selfish brutality. If the technicalities of the legal process and legal reasoning itself become so convoluted as to make no sense to the ordinary person in the street; if their own natural sense of what is right and wrong, just and unjust is completely at odds with the law; or if a ruling leaves everyone confused about what is lawful and what is not; then in all these cases the law has failed us. We must not be scared to look directly at Trident and to make an honest appraisal on moral and legal grounds.

Morality and legality are intertwined perhaps more so in humanitarian law than in other branches of the law. We have frequently had our attention drawn to phrases like 'the dictates of public conscience' because it is a common human morality that underpins all international humanitarian law. It is indubitable that the firing of a 100 kiloton nuclear warhead from the British Trident system would shock all of mankind and would be a crime in most people's eyes. The submariners carrying out orders to fire these warheads would be committing war crimes. The court has a duty to us all to say this fairly and squarely before the war crime is committed. Such a pronouncement from this court would help prevent the launch of these mass-destruction nuclear warheads from ever taking place and do a great deal to encourage our government to disarm all its weapons of mass destruction and put its efforts into addressing the underlying causes of conflict.

When all is said and done, and the very necessary legal technicalities completed, and we are left with the rulings from this court – will justice have been done? Will the law have proved capable of protecting us? Will the scales of justice come down on the side of annihilation or peace? It is in your hands.

Conclusion and motions to this court

The ICJ states that 'In the long run, international law, and with it the stability of the international order which it is intended to govern, are bound to suffer from the continuing difference of views with regard to the legal status of weapons as deadly as nuclear weapons. It is consequently important to put an end to this state of affairs: the long promised complete nuclear disarmament appears to be the most appropriate means of achieving that result.'

This court should consider a similar ruling in its conclusions and challenge the UK government to disarm its own nuclear weapons system and by this action lead other nuclear weapon states to the long promised nuclear disarmament we all desire.

Many countries go the ICJ to have an impartial examination of territorial disputes, so that they can resolve problems without recourse to war. Governments can use the ICJ as a face-saving device to enable the giving up of territory without being forced to extreme nationalistic posturing. It is difficult for a government to give up power voluntarily but if a government can point to a judicial decision this can let them off the hook politically. Giving up its nuclear weapons would be difficult politically for any UK government because of their powerful status symbol and use as a Security Council ticket, and because it would put severe strains on the UK's position as the chief ally and supporter of the USA.

However, a ruling from the highest court in Scotland indicating that Trident is illegal could not be ignored. A clear message that the Trident system undermines international law would be a powerful step on the way to nuclear disarmament. At last the uncomfortable fudging would be over – the fudging that cannot be entertained in a situation of life and death.

Apart from the specific answers to the four questions from the Lord Advocate, which I specified in my skeleton argument and first submission and do not need to repeat, I would like to put the following motions to this court and I therefore ask for the following:

• A clear statement that international humanitarian law applies in Scotland, and in England, Wales and Northern Ireland, that is to say, throughout the UK;

• A clear statement that international humanitarian law applies to the UK Trident system;

• A clear statement that any use of the 100 kiloton nuclear warheads on Trident would necessarily breach the intransgressible principles of humanitarian law as specified in the ICJ Advisory Opinion of 1996 at para. 78;

• A clear statement that any order to launch a Trident missile armed with 100 kiloton nuclear warheads would be unlawful, as would any compliance with such an illegal incitement, such as to transmit or facilitate or execute such an order;

• A clear statement that 'there exists an obligation to pursue in good faith and bring to a conclusion negotiations leading to nuclear disarmament in all its aspects under strict and effective international control', that such good faith is not exhibited by the UK's continuing deployment of nuclear weapons of such a size that they could never be lawfully used, and that therefore the active deployment of Trident should cease herewith and all warheads should be taken off the Trident missiles and stored separately from their delivery systems whilst further disarmament measures are undertaken;

• A clear statement that the Nuremberg Obligation of Individual Responsibility applies to individual citizens acting nonviolently and safely and gives them authority to try to prevent any individual or state actor from preparing or carrying out 'the most serious crimes of concern to the international community as a whole' even when this may contravene other legal norms of the law of the country in which they are acting.

• Clear advice to members of the armed forces and civil servants who because of their involvement with the nuclear chain of command may find themselves placed in an excruciating dilemma by current government policy.

And if the court cannot or will not make the motions above then to grant the following:

• The court should place on record its understanding of the urgent necessity and desirability of a full, independent and publicly accountable judicial inquiry into the implications for the integrity of the Scottish legal system of the continuous hosting by Scotland of the UK Trident nuclear weapon system in the light of international humanitarian law.

• Advice on what a court such as this can be asked to do that would provide an effective remedy to our distress at living with the threat of mass murder hanging over our world community.

• Bearing in mind that the ICJ, in its attempt to help the world community, made a concluding and unanimous decision on a matter not put before it in the original question, i.e. the international obligation to perform nuclear disarmament in all its aspects, under strict and effective international control, this court might similarly wish to consider any rulings that might help the Scottish community.'

The Japanese Connection
by Astrid Ubas, *Peace Pagoda Affinity Group*

Our Group is made up of the Buddhist monks and nuns of the Nipponzan Myohoji temples in London and Milton Keynes. For us, nonviolent action is very much part of our religion.

Life is an equal treasure to all living beings, big or small – good or bad, and the Buddha has compassion for all, without discrimination. Therefore, the first among all the various precepts and practices he laid down is the precept of non killing, non violence.

Our order is particularly following a teaching of the Buddha called the Lotus Sutra. The founder of Nipponzan Myohoji, the Most Venerable N. Fuji, said, 'The Lotus Sutra contains a prophecy. It says that there will come a time when all living beings will be about to be burned in a total conflagration. The survival, not only of human beings, but of all life, is endangered ... But it also says that deliverance will be brought about when the threat is greatest; it will appear in the hearts and minds of human beings ... The earth will open and produce innumerable people who will relieve the sufferings of the world ... the skies will open and the rain of correct faith will fall, nourishing and cultivating all life on earth. This prophecy must be made to come true now.'

By joining Trident Ploughshares actions, we follow in the footsteps of those who have worked on materialising this prophecy in

Gyosei Handa arrested whilst in prayer

Yuko Ohara praying for peace during the Trident Three trial

Nagase Fyoro praying for us all

Yoshie Marute being arrested, Faslane, 1 August 2000

Credit: Andrew McColl

Peace Pagoda Affinity Group at their temple in Milton Keynes

Credit: Doug Blane

Astrid Ubas drumming at blockade at Faslane, 1 August 2000

Credit: Roger Franklin

the past. For instance, St. Nichiren, a 13th century Japanese monk, searched the scriptures for years to find a way to bring relief to the disasters in his society, he finally found a way to practice the essence of the Lotus Sutra, and bring the Buddha's medicine to the people, by chanting the prayer 'NA-MU-MYO-HO-REN-GE-KYO'. He admonished his government in a major treatise 'rissho ankoku-ron' (establish the righteous law to secure peace among nations) and was imprisoned, exiled and almost executed for it.

Most Venerable N. Fuji, our direct teacher, who died aged 100 in 1985, dedicated his life to chanting this sacred prayer for peace. He beat a hand-drum, walking and bowing to everyone – to awaken the Buddha-nature we believe is present in all living beings. To fulfil part of the prophecy, he set out to India in the 1930s, where he met and walked with Mahatma Gandhi. After World War Two, after the nuclear bombing of Hiroshima and Nagasaki, he sent his followers out over the world, to construct peace pagodas and work with local people everywhere for general and nuclear disarmament.

Our teacher knew the Ploughshares movement well, and held them up as examples to his followers, saying we should be 'not just taking the superficiality of the words we recite from the Sutra by the mouth, but by the mind (and body)', and 'only they who have created the righteous movement with the experience of imprisonment can declare themselves true pacifists'.

This is where we come from: honoured to be part of Trident Ploughshares, beating the drum, chanting and bowing to awaken the best part of everyone. We support blockades, sometimes encouraging others from the side, sometimes as part of the blockade. We walk, raising awareness of Trident and direct action, and do a little prison support. There is no more important place to be with the drum than 'where a nonviolent revolution takes place'.

International Mosquitoes Buzzing Around Trident

by Katri Silvonen, *Titanic Trident! Affinity Group*

Four of us had come to Scotland from For Mother Earth in Gent, Belgium in October 1998 to defend our attempts to disarm Trident nonviolently and openly in court. On the same day we were standing at the bank of the Gareloch, and watched one of the Trident subs quietly leaving the base. People said it was heading towards Iraq, where bombings by Britain and US were taking place because of Hussein's refusal to allow UN weapons inspection teams to enter suspected sites of illegal weapons of mass destruction. These bombings were backed up by the UN Security Council whose five permanent members Britain, China, France, Russia and the US deploy enough illegal weapons of mass destruction to destroy our entire planet multiple times.

Abolition Days

We started a new campaign on nuclear weapons with For Mother Earth in 1997, following the ICJ decision of the previous summer. The idea was to create a network of direct action activists, lobbyists, and legal campaigners and to combine the experiences and expertise of these different people into a common strategy, which would be efficient, both legal-defence and direct-action wise. The idea was also to organise direct action at nuclear weapons bases around the world at the same time in solidarity with each other. We named the network 'Nuclear Weapons Abolition Days', and kicked off in Madrid, Spain during a NATO summit by delivering the representatives of each member state a notarised citizens' summons. In the summons we announced a campaign of nonviolent direct action at NATO nuclear weapons sites unless the Alliance took an immediate initiative to disarm their nuclear weapons.

Inspection Teams Enter Nuclear Bases

As NATO failed to respond to our demands during the summit in Madrid, or afterwards, the announced actions started three weeks later with an international action camp at NATO HQ in Brussels, Belgium. On the anniversary of Hiroshima we followed the action model of UN weapons inspection teams, and entered the NATO territory to look for information on the nuclear deterrence of NATO.

Three days later, on Nagasaki day, 'inspectors' entered nuclear weapon-related sites in Belgium, England, France, Germany, the Netherlands, Scotland and the USA.

The action model of inspections has been part of our campaigning ever since in Belgium, both at NATO HQ and in the NATO nuclear weapons base of Kleine Brogel. With the inspections we have been hoping not only to find out information about the 'secret' deployment of 10 US B61 nuclear bombs in Kleine Brogel, but also to bring nuclear weapons to court. So far there has been one court case, in which the court declared itself incompetent.

Joining Trident Ploughshares

When we heard the call to form affinity groups for Trident Ploughshares at the end of 1997, it seemed like a natural follow-up to the inspections to join the campaign. The illegal weapons of mass destruction of Britain had been located, it was the time to send in disarmament teams.

We felt connected to Trident Ploughshares also because of its non hierarchical structure of autonomous affinity groups and direct democracy. For Mother Earth has always worked with consensus, as we want our means of working to match with our goals of a nonviolent society.

While organising another international action camp at the NATO HQ for July 1998, we started an affinity group for Trident Ploughshares. We decided that two members of our seven headed affinity group 'Titanic Trident!' would attempt major disarmament actions during the first Trident Ploughshares camp. For Mother Earth has a history of organising long peace walks, and we decided to gain strength and support for the upcoming

Ploughshares camp by organising a walk from our action camp at NATO HQ to the Trident Ploughshares camp in Scotland. The aims of the 'Walk for Nuclear Disarmament' which we realised in co-operation with local people, CND groups and Quakers, were to inform people along the route about NATO's nuclear policy, Trident and the Trident Ploughshares Campaign by spreading leaflets, petitioning, organising information events and vigils, having meetings at city halls, doing local media work, and simply by talking to people in the villages and cities we walked through. The walkers came from ten different countries to give a clear signal that Trident is not just a national issue, it threatens the whole world with nuclear genocide. The Walk for Nuclear Disarmament linked NATO HQ, where decisions about nuclear weapons policies are taken, to Faslane, where these decisions are carried out.

Walking on the Path of Nuclear Destruction

The Walk for Nuclear Disarmament partly followed the convoy route of British nuclear warheads. We walked by the Atomic Weapons Establishment in Aldermaston, Rolls Royce Nuclear in Derby where the Trident submarines' nuclear reactors have been built, Springfields nuclear fuel factory, Inskip communications site, Sellafield where used nuclear fuel is reprocessed into weapons grade plutonium and where nuclear waste is stored and dumped into the Irish sea, and Chapelcross nuclear power station where Tritium is produced. Thus we got to see many of the links in the Trident nuclear chain. It was shocking and made the walkers feel very strong about stopping the nuclear age. Many people who had planned to join the walk just for a while decided to stay on the Trident Ploughshares camp for support. Some became Pledgers and decided to join in the attempts to disarm Trident during the camp.

In addition to all the sites of nuclear crime we passed on our way to Faslane, we should not forget the other parts of Trident's nuclear chain which are located outside of Britain. These are the uranium mines and nuclear test sites, mostly on indigenous peoples' lands, contaminating their traditional living areas with deadly radioactivity.

The first Trident Ploughshares camp was very intense for many of us because of the experiences of the walk. Three members of 'Titanic Trident!' were remanded for five weeks after their fifth arrest. There have been volunteers of For Mother Earth and members of Titanic Trident! on all the long Trident Ploughshares camps ever since.

International Anti-Nuclear Conspiracy is Blossoming

Being part of Trident Ploughshares has inspired us a lot, and has given us good experiences both for our campaigns and personally. One of the positive things we have been able to bring in to the campaign is international participation. The participation, arrests, court cases and imprisonment of For Mother Earth volunteers have inspired groups and individuals in our countries of origin to support the campaign, keep on working locally to reach a nuclear weapons-free world, and to join the Trident Ploughshares action

Katri Silvonen (on right) balancing on the main gate entrance to Coulport (summer 2000) with Hanna Jarvinen.

camps. Trident Ploughshares has received much media attention in some of these countries, like Belgium, Finland and the Netherlands. The publicity about For Mother Earth volunteers being in prison in Scotland inspired many new people to join our actions in Kleine Brogel in Belgium. As said earlier, Trident is an international issue, and therefore it is important to have international resistance to it.

In spring 1999 For Mother Earth organised yet another peace walk, this time from the ICJ in the Hague, the Netherlands, to NATO HQ in Brussels. The walk lasted for ten days, and several Trident Ploughshares Pledgers joined in to tell NATO that nuclear weapons have got to go. There were 272 arrests at the NATO HQ at the end of the walk, some of which were after trying to gain access to the headquarters nonviolently to look for information of NATO's genocidal nuclear weapons, and some of which took place because NATO was busy bombing people of the former Yugoslavia, and the Freedom of Assembly had been called off by the Mayor of Brussels.

The story of our international resistance to Trident, NATO and all nuclear weapons continues.

For Mother Earth in Action

by Bernard De Witte, *Titanic Trident! Affinity Group*

With ten people from For Mother Earth we left for Scotland to participate in the big blockade of the Faslane Trident base on 12 February 2001. David Heller took off on his own on Friday evening, the others went together in a nine-seater minibus from Gent in Belgium (Julien Vacher and Regis Lequin from France, Katri Silvonen, Eveliina Lundqvist and Hanna Järvinen from Finland, Krista Van Velzen from the Netherlands, Pol D'Huyvetter, Iwan Meerhaeghe and Bernard De Witte from Belgium).

After a long ride we arrived at the meeting place in Glasgow and took part in the last briefings and an action training. Next morning we drove to the base, to find the entrance already blocked on our arrival, with hundreds of participants and also hundreds of policemen.

Early during the blockade Julien Vacher and Regis Lequin were arrested and brought to a Glasgow police station.

With the others of our group we had decided not to be arrested during the blockade itself, but to try to get inside the base, in order to trigger the 'bandit alert' which means that, as soon as someone gets arrested inside the base, the work on the base has to be stopped and everyone on the base is supposed to go and look for the 'invaders'. Since at the peace camp they managed to get hold of documents which describe this emergency scenario, we know exactly how this alert works. The alert lasts for at least half an hour, during which the whole base is inoperative.

At about 12.30 Krista Van Velzen, Iwan Meerhaeghe, David Heller and Eveliina Lundqvist managed to cut through the fence, but were discovered getting inside the base and arrested, which of course triggered the 'bandit alert'. Meanwhile Katri Silvonen and Bernard De Witte tried to get into the base north from the main entrance, but since they were just alongside the main road, they were discovered before they could cut enough. They also got arrested, and both groups were held for about three hours at the police station inside the Faslane base. About four in the afternoon we were all released and brought to Faslane peace camp.

After some rest at the peace camp we decided to try once again to get inside the base, so we could stop them for some more time. But from a first reconnaissance it appeared that there were too many police cars patrolling still, and we postponed our plan for an hour. But at nightfall we got into our minibus, and somewhere at the beginning of the fence, Krista, Katri and Bernard got out and climbed the slope up to the fence, where we started cutting. It took a long time, because every time a car passed we ducked down so we could not be seen by the police patrols.

Once inside things got smoother, we cut a passage through the rolls of razor wire and took off behind some administrative buildings. After a while we got on the main road which connects the south gate with the north gate. There were still workers passing on this road, and several cars drove by, but no one took attention of our presence. So we sauntered further on that road, it was a queer feeling, walking in the middle of that military base, being seen by passers-by and still not being embarrassed.

Bernard de Witte (right) relaxing at the disarmament camp between actions, with Grace Nichol

After a walk of some twenty minutes we got to the rear of the first berth (where Trident and other submarines are inspected), but there we were seen by two policemen, Katri being recognised by one of them.

'Can we see your passes?' – well of course, we could not show anything of that kind, and were arrested immediately, while the 'bandit alert' sounded from loudspeakers all around, so once again we blocked the whole system for some time.

We got taken to the police station inside the base, but only a few minutes after we arrived there, Pol D'Huyvetter, Hanna Järvinen and Martin Kelly (from Ireland, who joined us for this action) appeared. They had managed to cut through a first fence but were arrested while trying to cut through a second fence.

This time we were held about six hours, until four in the morning, and then we got brought back to Faslane Peace Camp.

CHAPTER SEVEN

The Scottish High Court Gives Its Opinion

OFFICIAL SPEAK CAN BE quite amusing. I received a letter on Friday March 23 2001, headed 'Lord Advocates Reference – Trident Appeal.' Was that Trident appealing? If so we had succeeded in something. The letter, we had all been waiting four months for, was quite short: 'I am instructed by the Right Honourable Lord Prosser to intimate to you that the above will be Advised on Friday 31 March at 10am in Court 3, Parliament House, Edinburgh.'

At last the day had been announced. The day we would hear what the Scottish legal system had to say about weapons of mass destruction and the right of individuals to try and prevent their government from threatening to use them. Would Lord Prosser, who had promised in court that he would not duck the issue, tackle it head on or would there be a fudge? Would the Court come out in favour of human rights or in favour of militaristic might? Would the Scottish judiciary prove its independence from the nuclear establishment or would it follow the official line? What would this Opinion say?

I rang Jane and David to let them know it was on, and we all started putting out email messages to inform our supporters. We had made some preliminary plans – the main issue had been resolved a long time previously. Whatever the decision of the court we would not stop our direct disarmament work while Tridents were still fully armed in the dock at Faslane. We are a practical grass-roots campaign based on what is happening in the real world – not merely on what is talked about on the internet, or on a piece of paper, or in a Court Opinion. While Trident is threatening mass destruction and is still operational then we had to continue our disarmament work. We will only stop when we are assured that the military and government will take over and complete our work, and when we can verify, to our own satisfaction, that this is happening.

Notwithstanding that decision we were eager, excited and nervous to hear what the Court would say. If Lord Prosser and the High Court answered in our favour a tremendous victory would have been won, and the legal and political pressure for immediate nuclear disarmament by the UK government would be immense. It would save us a lot of time and effort.

We would be looking at the Opinion from two perspectives – our right as global citizens to intervene to uphold the law and the position of the Trident nuclear weapons system in the light of international humanitarian law.

On the first issue we would be noting what the judges said about the Defence of Necessity in Scots law and what its limits are. We would also look at anything they might say about the state of mind of defendants and the objective analysis they have made of the situation. We would see if they expressed any worries about anarchy and vigilantism if the right to intervene was too loosely defined. We wanted to know what they made of the proposed extension of the Nuremberg Principles, which claims the right of citizens to take action to prevent unlawful 'official' actions?

On the second issue, we would be looking at any statements made about the relationship between international humanitarian law and Scots law and the extent to which it is within the competence of the courts to examine state policy on nuclear weapons.

What would be said about Trident? Would the court accept that the principles of international humanitarian law apply to it and that there is at least a *prima facie* case against Trident? These were some of the questions that were pounding around in our heads with only a week to go.

Jane asked who I was going to have as a Mackenzie Friend and I replied that I would be happy if she would join me with all the men in their black garb. We began to laugh as we realised that we could celebrate the end of this legal process by wearing our more brightly coloured clothes rather than dressing conservatively for the court. Whatever the outcome, there was no going back.

I packed my sleeping bag and laptop and left my home in rural Norfolk at 6am for yet another long trip up North. Arriving off the train at 4pm I was met by friends and TV cameras who wanted to know what I thought the High Court might say. There was to be an over-night vigil outside the Court which is housed in the ancient Scottish Parliament, so we all made our way to the statue of Walter Scott in Parliament Square. It was a great occasion – full of hope and anticipation. Some of the members of the drumming band – Commotion – played. There was singing; shared food; the handing out of leaflets encouraging people to come to Faslane on Saturday; intense debates on democracy, the powers of the judiciary and the rights of people who feel under immense danger because of their government's policies. The lit candles glowed as the darkness closed in. Around twenty people stayed up all night but I went off to have a good night's sleep so I wouldn't be too tired to think the next day.

By 9.45am, on 30 March 2001, Court 3 of the Edinburgh High Court was full with over a hundred concerned people. They had come to hear what the highest court in Scotland was going to say about their right to prevent their government from threatening mass murder. There were police in the well of the court looking rather officious – perhaps the court was preparing to deal with an immediate uproar of protest. But from the public gallery there was a friendly and expectant air of intense curiosity. Most people expected a complex ruling that would probably give each side something. But there was the exciting possibility and hope that the Scottish judiciary would take their responsibilities for the rule of law seriously and provide a very necessary rebuke to the British state for threatening the peace of the world by continuing to deploy Trident.

10am prompt – Lord Prosser appeared without his wig and without looking anyone in the eye, in a weak and unconvincing manner, he stated shortly that the answers to all four questions put by the Lord Advocate were negative. He was not accompanied by Lords Kirkwood and Penrose – but by two others.

30th March 2001 – Lord Prosser, High Court of Justiciary, Edinburgh, Advice of the High Court.

The Reference contains four questions for the Court. The first raises a question of competency in law and we find in the negative. Each of the other three questions raises an issue of substantive law. All of these issues concern different aspects of possible defences to criminal charges on the basis that the act charged might be justified either as a matter of customary international law or as a matter of Scots law necessity. We answered each of these three questions in the negative.

He then scurried out and there was a stunned silence as we all took it in. The Clerk began handing out sealed brown envelopes with a 70 page Opinion in it. I felt numb, shocked, and then angry and hurt. The establishment, the system, had won again. The humanity within us all was diminished.

Lord Prosser especially, had not only let us down but himself as well. The Scottish judges had acted in the interests of the status quo – but they did not have the excuse of being under an authoritarian and repressive regime. This was a supposed democracy. They had not taken to heart the examples of the German judges and lawyers condemned at Nuremberg in the Justices Case. Did they somehow think that deliberately killing millions in gas chambers was somehow worse than killing millions by using nuclear bombs?

The Scottish judiciary prides itself on having a legal system that works from principles rather than precedent. And yet it could not do what the vast majority of the Scottish population can do – make a judgement that Trident is criminal and immoral.

The press, of course, wanted to know what we thought immediately. I only wanted to have time to study the Opinion and see how bad it was. But I made some comments to the press, as did others from the campaign. I then sat down on a bench in the sun and as I finished reading one page handed it to the person next to me, who read it and passed it on to the next person.

An enthusiastic young man from the Scottish National Party came up and offered to get photocopies done for us free. Within half an hour thirty copies appeared and everyone interested was able to see it directly. I wonder if there has ever been a ruling of the High Court read so immediately and assiduously by non-lawyers.

We were certainly taking the law into our own hands. We wanted to reclaim it for humanity's sake.

Ellen, Ulla and I had a quick meeting with their lawyers to ask them to write an opinion for us on whether there were any other legal remedies open to us to challenge the Opinion. They felt that although there might be possibilities at the European level on various

Reading the Opinion outside the High Court, Edinburgh, 30 March 2001.
From left to right – Angie Zelter, Keith Mothersson, Ulla Roder,
John Ainslie, John Mayer

minor points, it would probably be impossible to get the real issue of Trident's threat of mass murder examined judicially. However, some of them were still convinced that Trident was criminal in international law and were willing to study the Opinion and give us their analyses in the coming weeks.

In the days following we sent the Opinion to international lawyers around the world to see what they would make of this first detailed response to the ICJ's Advisory Opinion by a national High Court. The responses we received indicated that many of them found the Opinion to be biased, muddled and contradictory. It was certainly going to cause a furious debate in legal circles.

We set up a page on our Trident Ploughshares website (www.tridentploughshares.org) dedicated to the Opinion and to these responses so that the public could follow the debate. The law was too important to be left to lawyers and public interest was such that many people were very well informed and wanted to join in the debate at a deeper level than the mass media could or would provide.

A group of us discussed the Opinion, and then Keith Mothersson produced a quick written analysis of the Opinion to which I added other useful comments that were coming in. I then produced the Trident Ploughshares Initial Response which we sent to our supporters. It is a continuation of the very necessary public legal debate which will no doubt be developed over the coming months and years.

5 April 2001, Trident Ploughshares initial response to the Appeal Court Opinion on the Lord Advocate's questions.

We are disappointed that the Scottish Court system has let itself and us down and did not rise to the challenge we presented it with. It had an historic opportunity to back the rule of law and instead it chose to back state terrorism posing as self-defence.

Fortunately, our legal system is not just dependent on a few Judges but still retains a recognition that the law must be based upon the common person's reasonable appreciation of the facts and morality – this is what a jury is all about. The jury system is one of the safeguards of our democratic system and ensures that the legal system does not get too out of contact with real life and common sense.

It is significant that in nearly every one of the major Trident Ploughshares cases, that end up in front of a jury, we have been acquitted. At Greenock, if the Sheriff had not decided in her own right on matters of law that we were not guilty, then we would most likely have had a jury acquittal. Instead we were fortunate to have a brave woman, Sheriff Gimblett, who, without fear or favour, acquitted us on international law grounds. This was such a challenge to the 'legitimacy' of the Trident nuclear weapons system and had such wide ramifications – for instance if the use of Trident is criminal then the current Trident Commanders are actually conspiring to commit war crimes at the present time – that the State had to step in. We were then forced into an 'appeal by the backdoor' through the mechanism of the Lord Advocate's Reference.

Advice from lawyers around the world was that there was little chance that any High Court within a nuclear weapon state would be allowed to outlaw nuclear weapons however strong the arguments. But this did not put us off. We felt that however distorted the legal system was, the law is not just for the powerful

if the use of Trident is criminal then the current Trident Commanders are actually conspiring to commit war crimes at the present time

but is for us all. We were not prepared to be so cynical that we would not even attempt the struggle. We are not naïve, we knew there would be tremendous pressures on the Judges and the system behind the scenes but we would do our best and we would appeal to all that was best in the law. Our

basic premise was that the law must be based upon common human morality or else lose its legitimacy in the eyes of the people. We also assumed that it applied to everyone, poor or rich, weak or powerful. Surely this is what is meant by the rule of law? We wished to reclaim the law from the abuse of the powerful and put it to its proper use – the protection and defence of the weak and powerless. Say not the struggle naught availeth!

On March 30 at 10am our hopes in the Scottish Courts were dashed. The Opinion could have been written by the Ministry of Defence itself – so much for the separation of executive and judiciary. Our only consolation after a close reading is that the Opinion is muddled, inaccurate and does not deal with (and therefore does not undermine) any of our strong arguments.

The Judges' Opinion is based upon the same underlying lie as the UK Government's position at the World Court, the same lie as deterrence is based upon – that deterrence is just a bluff and that we would never actually use our nuclear weapons, and that they are therefore lawful. The Government does this at the very same time, mind you, as they tell Iraq and other 'enemy' states that nuclear weapons would be used – and the Government does not mean, as the Crown pretended in the LAR, just to use them against an isolated group of ships in the middle of the ocean in a crisis situation of last resort to ensure the survival of the UK. The UK does not deploy four submarines with 192 nuclear warheads to use against isolated targets – they are there to threaten mass destruction.

The Opinion is based upon the outrageous justification that threatening mass destruction is lawful in times of peace and only becomes unlawful in times of war when one knows the exact target. This leaves them able to hang on to their nuclear deterrence and their hope that we will all leave it at that and stop asking awkward questions. However, reading between the lines we can detect that Britain feels justified in preparing to break international humanitarian law and is in fact practising daily to break almost every single international convention and law on armed conflict. The UK Government said as much at the ICJ Hearings when Sir Nicholas Lyell asked, 'If all other means at their disposal are insufficient, then how can it be said that the use of a nuclear weapon must be disproportionate?'

The Opinion is a perverse opinion and against the people's interest. Protecting a State's interests is not the same as protecting people's interests. The justified anger at the Court backing threats to commit mass murder has turned into a fierce determination that the struggle will continue, that People's Disarmament will continue. We will go to Faslane on Saturday 7 April to continue to take the law into our own hands, to uphold international humanitarian law, to insist that the law is in step with common human ethics. We are not going to give up on the law or our own humanity.

The Opinion is a perverse opinion and against the people's interest

To sum up the main points raised in the Opinion:

Positives

P1. Customary International Law is part of Scots law.

'A rule of customary international law is a rule of Scots law' [para 23]. It is directly a matter for the judge. It isn't 'foreign law' [para 24]. But it may be complicated so they don't rule out the possibility that experts may be heard to determine whether a particular rule has won the general acceptance necessary to constitute a rule of customary international law (ie whether an *opinio juris* has emerged) [para 27]. But such expert opinion would be presented without the presence of a jury, in order to clarify matters for the Judge who would then instruct the jury.

This means that the Procurator Fiscal Mr. Donnelly will have to eat his words – he has said on numerous occasions at the District

Court in Helensburgh that international law... does not apply in Scotland. One of the major successes of our campaign has been the education of ourselves and others, including the legal profession, about international humanitarian law.

P2. The Necessity Defence applies to rescuing any person in any place.

The court, in discussing Necessity Defences in Scots law, stated that there was 'no acceptable basis for restricting rescue to protection of persons already known to and having a relationship with the rescuer at the moment of response to the other's danger' [para 44]. Likewise the court saw 'no reason in principle why the defence' of necessity should not be available 'where the place and person or persons under threat from the apprehended danger were remote from the locus of the allegedly malicious damage' [para 45]. These are major clarifications in accordance with common sense and morality and it is good that we will not have to waste time in the future arguing such obvious points.

P3. A specific threat could breach customary international law.

The court does say, 'A State which has a deployed deterrent plainly could and might take some step which turned the situation into one of armed conflict, and involved a sufficiently specific threat to constitute a breach of customary international law' [para 97] even though it does not connect this with the known facts of Trident sailing into the Mediterranean while the air force was bombing in former Yugoslavia and in Iraq.

P4. Intervention against active threat might be lawful under Scots law.

The court makes an implicit admission of the possibility that if the UK were to move from mere general deterrent threat to active threat of use against a target state, then intervention might be legitimate (though not under customary international law). It states 'but any issue of justification would depend not on the mere fact [sic] of any such illegality, but upon the Scots law of necessity, with the requirements *inter alia* of immediacy of danger and prospects of prevention' [paras 105 and 106]. We could use this to argue that present members of the armed forces have a greater possibility of a valid defence in law than we would because they could make more effective plans now to prevent nuclear weapons from ever being launched in armed conflict in the future. We shall be producing a leaflet for the armed forces to encourage them to prevent mass murder by ensuring that our nuclear weapons could never actually be launched – perhaps by inserting hidden instructions in the computer targeting programmes that in the event of a real launch would prevent it from occurring. This would not be incitement to disaffection but encouragement to uphold international law and a practical refusal to be complicit in actual war crimes.

Negatives

N1. Disposition and armament of the Armed Forces is non-justiciable.

The court brought up the tired old doctrine of Royal Prerogative according to which any issue of national security and defence cannot be questioned by the courts [paras 56, 57 and 113]. Can blatant illegalities and criminalities be hidden in this devious manner? We argued that any government policy and action that is outside the law can and must be open to challenge by the courts.

any government policy and action that is outside the law can and must be open to challenge by the courts

At no point did the court show the slightest insight into the fact that none of the respondents were against defending people, it was murdering non-combatants and poisoning the globe they objected to. Thus, when citing

none of the respondents were against defending people, it was murdering non-combatants and poisoning the globe they objected to

Lord Reid in Chandler – 'It is in my opinion clear that the disposition and armament of the armed forces are and for centuries have been within the exclusive discretion of the Crown and that no one can seek a legal remedy on the grounds that such discretion has been wrongly [sic] exercised' – they are happy to conflate a principled challenge as to the legality of the course of conduct being pursued by the Crown with a mere political dispute about what is the best or cheapest defence policy or an operational dispute as regards efficiency, etc.

However, they inadvertently undermine their own reactionary retreat to Chandler when at para 59 they quote Simon Brown LJ in *ex parte* Smith: 'only cases involving national security properly so called and where in addition [sic] the courts really do lack the expertise or material to form a judgement on the point of issue' would be ruled strictly beyond the court's purview.

there may be a prerogative for defending the realm but not for mass murder of innocent civilians

And obviously it is not to defence nor to national security 'properly so called' that we object. Put simply, there may be a prerogative for defending the realm but not for mass murder of innocent civilians.

The Court made no attempt to take account of the developments in trans-national accountability implicit in proposals for the International Criminal Court, but instead maintained that the state is above the law. They did not explore in any depth this issue of justiciability – preferring to keep their heads down and defend the status quo. The pointed submissions that we made on the Justices Case at Nuremberg, where the German Judiciary were convicted of putting State law above International law, were not addressed at all.

N2. A person may not commit an offence in order to stop serious crime.

The court invoked Palazzo v Copeland to the effect that it is no defence to malicious damage that the damage was done to prevent another offence, and summarised: 'The principles of our domestic law are general and clear. A person may not take the law into his own hands. A person may not commit an offence in an attempt to stop another.'

The court feared that it would 'invite anarchy' for ordinary people to take the law into their own hands! But if it is the law – and Trident Ploughshares have always stood on that foundation – then surely only a world in which ordinary people feel moral responsibility and social empowerment to take action to uphold, defend and implement the law and frustrate terrorist threats, only such a just world order of responsible civic activism will be truly safe. It is interesting how often our government calls upon people in 'repressive' regimes to act against their government if that government abuses human rights and threatens global security but does not feel able to apply the same principles to its own civic society. The court states clearly that they do not approve of

only such a just world order of responsible civic activism will be truly safe

'self-appointed substitute law enforcers' [para 99]. The court are putting us in double-bind situations and doing everything they can to ensure that our acts of legitimate nuclear disarmament will be seen as completely lawless. They say 'do not take the law into your own hands, tell the responsible authorities', knowing full well that when we do we are ignored or told the whole matter is not justiciable, since defence is exclusively a matter for the executive. When matters of peace and war were purely matters for rulers and soldiers this kind of attitude was more excusable. But in a world where 90% of the casualties in any war are civilians then matters of 'defence' fall very clearly into the normal democratic and civilian spheres of interest and control and must be justiciable.

Significantly the court failed to respond to our motions asking for guidance on any alternative courses of action we could take. By their silence they concede we have none.

The judges found it hard to understand the concept of nonviolence in the context of necessity. They implied that it was valid to act violently in a crisis but not nonviolently to prevent a crisis [para 20]. This is very close to government foreign and defence policy and is one reason it leaves problems in the world until they get to the point where it can justify military intervention and more arms sales. It is very far from current modern thinking on preventative nonviolent conflict resolution – and very far from common sense.

The Opinion shows the judges finding excuses for not addressing issues of the legality of nuclear weapons until it's too late. They do this by stating that in times of peace, international humanitarian law does not apply, and by stating that the threat implicit in nuclear deterrence is not specific enough to be a real threat. But we know that even when the button is about to be pressed and we're at war, some government lawyer will still stand up and say that the naval officers don't know where this warhead is targeted because it's a secret, so they are not making a specific threat, and so it is not a criminal act. According to the judge's logic you can't judge whether the threat to press the button was legal or not until the weapon is in mid-air and on its way to a known target. By which time it is too late! We will continue to try to disarm Trident because we know that now is the time for such action, not some future date, when we are at war, in a national state of emergency, and unable to be very effective.

N3. Rejection of Nuremberg Principles.

The Opinion falsely asserts, in relation to the Nuremberg Principles, that 'the argument based on them was not insisted in' [para 89]. However, this is false, we did insist upon them. The judges dismissed our extension of the Nuremberg Principles which justify citizens taking action to prevent the most serious crimes known to mankind [paras 88-91]. This puts citizens that are concerned about war crimes in a Catch 22 situation – collusion or criminalisation. We do not accept this.

N4. Failure to admit our claim that UK law criminalises Trident too.

The court statement that 'It was not suggested that what the government were doing with Trident would be illegal or criminal apart from customary international law' [paras 32 and 35] is untrue. We specifically did say that preparations and threats to use Trident were criminal in UK law and Scots law. Most importantly we raised and read out whole sections of the Geneva Conventions Act of 1957 and the Geneva Conventions (Amendments) Act of 1995. The court made no attempt to answer our questions of how a Trident 100 kiloton warhead could be used without breaching these Acts.

N5. Failure to admit that we did not concede possession as being lawful.

Likewise the court simply ignored our submissions that specifically did NOT concede that mere possession was lawful [para 62] and misconstrued our position by saying 'The respondents are content to proceed upon the basis that mere possession would not entail any illegality on the part of the Government'. We did not concede it because many of us find it hard to understand how a legal system could accept the lawful possession of an object that could never be used lawfully. The way the government and the court get around this one is to pretend they could be used lawfully but fail to explain how or give any examples.

N6. Failure to distinguish between different necessity cases.

The court also ignored the real situation faced by the respondents. By sticking so closely to the 'normal' sort of case of necessity defences (broken fence around field with dangerous bull in it, dog worrying sheep, lorry rolling down a hill towards people, etc) they completely invalidated the experience and perspective of the defendants. Thus at para 37, we read that 'A danger which is threatened at a future time, as opposed to immediately impending [*sic*], might be avoided by informing the owner of the property and so allowing [!] that person [the MOD] to take action to avert the danger, or informing some responsible authority of the perceived need for intervention' – as if we hadn't spent years informing the authorities. It is irrational to equate the timeline for a run-of-the mill necessity case with the timeline for preventing a nuclear holocaust. It is ridiculous to suppose that one would be able to take action after Trident's warheads have been launched. The court's reasoning here is a classic example of applying a principle taken from one factual context to an entirely different context in which the principle cannot possibly serve the same function.

N7. Failure to distinguish between legitimate self-defence and reckless threats of mass destruction.

The court also ignored our repeated community based analogies that it was one thing for two neighbours to fall out and even come to blows with each other, but that it was another thing entirely, and one abhorrent to our normal moral consensus as a society, for one neighbour to burn the other's house down at dead of night with the death of babies and aged relatives, and for the resulting fires to poison the entire neighbourhood including the first neighbour's own family.

N8. Failure to accept that self-help is a necessity.

Aidan O'Neill QC had likened the respondents' action to that of a community self-help group of mothers who began to campaign to get a heroin dealer arrested. 'Nonsense', the police or Procurator Fiscal say, 'that man is a member of Muirfield Golf Club and can't possibly be doing anything criminal'. So the women wait until the dealer is out one day, break into his flat and destroy his heroin and scales. Would it invalidate their action that another heroin dealer might come into the same area subsequently? But if, being part of a continuing campaign [which the court at para 20 was inclined to hold against the respondents], the same thing happened repeatedly, sooner or later heroin pushers would be deterred from trying to operate in that neighbourhood. Thus the action of the three women at Loch Goil was valid in itself and further justified by being part of a sequence of actions. Just because the arrest of a dealer doesn't by itself immediately terminate all hard-drug crime in an area, doesn't mean to say that the action isn't capable of leading towards the ending of the dangerous crime complained of. Once again, the court failed to respond. Maybe because they see Trident deployments as lawful and as a victimless non-crime, they see no basis for 'self-appointed law enforcers' to intervene to uphold the law or to prevent harm.

N9. Failure to understand the nature of the risk.

The court completely failed to understand the vital concept of risk as involving not only the likelihood of a particular event but also the level of catastrophe of the event. The risk increases the greater the badness of the outcome of an event even if the likelihood of an event happening remains constant. They also completely failed to show that they had any sense of the unimaginable horrors of even one nuclear explosion, let alone a nuclear campaign or war, let alone nuclear winter or the possible end of human life on earth. Accordingly, they assumed deterrence was an acceptable policy. No consideration was given to the ongoing risks of accidental explosion or war which nuclear deployments impose on others willy-nilly. 'In the present case, there is no question of the alleged danger arising from contingencies such as natural disasters' [para 35]. 'The actor must have good cause to fear that death or serious injury would [sic – not might] result unless he acted' [para 42]. 'Merely making a danger less likely might not be regarded as justified by necessity at all' [para 46]. Note the use of the word 'merely' – as in merely reducing the likelihood of the dog savaging some sheep. Yet the worst case scenario Trident could bring about is the end of human life on earth. 'The conduct carried out must be broadly proportional to the risk' they admit at para 47 – but still they have no sense that even a tiny likelihood of the end of the world happening is a huge risk. And yet again at para 46: 'If there were no prospect that the conduct complained of would affect the danger anticipated the relationship between the danger and the conduct would not be established. ... if the action could achieve no more [!] than, say, postponement or interruption of danger ... or some lessening of its likelihood ... the assessment of any necessity would be less simple.'

The court also assumes nuclear deterrence is a harm-free policy. Thus they completely fail to understand the point that Trident is being used all the time in the sense of being used to instil fear. They refer to 'a danger which is threatened at a future time, as opposed to [sic] immediately pending ...' [para 37]. There is no awareness that nuclear deterrence is a threat made to everyone, that puts

nuclear deterrence is a threat made to everyone, that puts non-combatant people and neutral nations all over the world in fear of their existence

non-combatant people and neutral nations all over the world in fear of their existence. It lowers the moral water-table in international society and violates our right to freedom from fear, as well as the right of all nations, not only neutral ones, to international security.

This takes us to the court's view of deterrence as not representing a real threat, merely a general display of military might like tanks in Red Square, quoting Lord Murray [para 98]. But the whole point is that tanks in Red Square or wherever – although they might be asked to fire much too close to schools and hospitals, or might be used directly in a terrorist mode – could at least be used lawfully, discriminately. In contrast, nuclear deployments represent a standing threat to all third parties and non-combatant categories in the world – neutral nations, peaceful civilians, children, the old, pregnant mothers, patients, medical workers and hospitals, the environment, the unborn generations. These people are being given notice that should any nation attack a nuclear nation (or its protected ally) the UK reserves the right to defend itself not merely by the legitimate use of force (defined as some focussed extension of fist, sword, spear, etc) but also by setting chemical fires, vandalising electronic equipment across a continent (electro-magnetic pulse effects) and spreading uncontrollable, undirectable poison persisting in cumulative genetic damage through thousands of generations.

And yet domestic law is so clear. If someone becomes afraid of his neighbours and announces that he has a gadget, which if he is attacked, he will not hesitate to use, a gadget which will, or merely may, poison the entire neighbourhood, the criminal law would step in immediately. Whether the defendant had actually named a particular neighbour or not would not help his case, nor whether he was in dispute with any of them, or whether it was likely that he would ever 'have to' use it. The law would step in because every last person in the entire neighbourhood could legitimately be said to be afflicted by the risk which that person's diseased reasoning and physical preparations represented. It would not matter that the person concerned did not intend to attack children in the next block. That this would be the inevitable result of his action if he ever carried it out if attacked would be enough to render his preparations and plans and deployment threatening and unlawful.

By contrast with the precautionary principle which would be employed *vis a vis* our paranoid defendant – or a polluting company – the Appeal Court seemed only too happy to accept the reassurances of the UK government that the use of tactical nuclear weapons in submarine warfare could 'easily' be lawful and did not mention the 'profoundly pernicious effects in space and time' which all out strategic nuclear war might involve [para 83].

Because the court sees nuclear weapons as basically ordinary weapons, which do not menace the entire civilian world, they are incapable of considering that deployment is both itself illegal now (harming people around the world already) and threatens a future catastrophe. The court cannot admit that the damage the defendants did was capable of assisting in the reduction of the danger of both sorts of harm, especially when viewed as part of a sequence of deterrent acts against illegal terrorism. We have no such problem.

N10. Failure to respect the International Court of Justice.

The Appeal Court indicates a profound lack of respect for the foremost judicial authority in the world whose members unlike Scottish judges were specialists in international law, and had the benefit of many months of study, research, argument, submissions from dozens of nations, etc before bringing their landmark judgement of 8 July 1996 that 'the threat or use of nuclear weapons would generally be contrary to the rules of international law applicable in armed conflict, and in particular the principles and rules of humanitarian law' (Dipositif E).

We are confronted by an astounding contradiction within a single paragraph (para 66). We are told in line 2 that the ICJ Opinion 'is an advisory opinion, not a judicial determination of customary international law' and in line 8 that 'the advisory opinion may be regarded as confirmatory of the then rules of customary law.' It is easy to agree with the second statement, but not with the first. Since the ICJ Advisory Opinion is indeed confirmatory of customary law, how can it not be a determination of that very same law?

If the High Court chooses to rubbish the ICJ Advisory Opinion in such a disrespectful way then we could say they are giving us a precedent for doing the same with their own Opinion!

An ICJ Advisory Opinion is given to the United Nations General Assembly in much the same way as the High Court's own Opinion can be said to advise the Lord Advocate. If the High Court chooses to rubbish the ICJ Advisory Opinion in such a disrepectful way then we could say they are giving us a precedent for doing the same with their own Opinion! The ICJ advises on the law, which is binding on all states. The ICJ speaks of 'intransgressible principles of customary international law' at para 79, quoted by the Appeal Court at para 76. Thus it ought to bind nations in almost as direct a way as the Lord Advocate's Reference is now supposed to bind all lower courts in Scotland.

The Appeal Court greatly exaggerates the divisions within the ICJ and fails to register that although Dispositif E was only passed by 7-7 on the casting vote of the president, the actual underlying majority is 10-4, since 3 of the minority seven believe that the court did have enough factual and legal material to conclude that nuclear weapons would be illegal to use and threaten even in the tiny residual area of *non licet* (not deciding, not ruling) which the court majority saw fit to leave – and which the court president stressed as strongly as he could must not be seen as any kind of loophole for permitted use of nuclear weapons.

The clearest reading of the International Court's Opinion has been that it did not wish to rule on this residuum area of uncertainty because it lacked knowledge about the possibility of making and using micro and mini nuclear weapons of 0.1 to 1 kiloton which would be relatively 'clean'. The ICJ did observe that no nation had denied that nuclear weapons would have to be used in conformity with international law; that merely having the right to defend oneself according to Art 2.4 and Art 51 of the Charter (*jus ad bellum*) did not exempt nations from exercising that right in lawful ways (*jus in bello*); that nuclear weapons seemed 'scarcely reconcilable' with norms such as discrimination, non-combatant immunity, neutrality, and not causing unnecessary suffering; and that no nations had advanced concrete scenarios of ways and circumstances in which nuclear weapons might be used lawfully (merely assertions that they could be). Yet this scrupulous hesitancy to 'conclude with certainty' concerning a possible category of 'clean' small, tactical nuclear weapons is exploited by the Appeal Court as a loophole to suggest that Trident 'warheads' of 100 kilotons could also be used lawfully! At para 86 the Appeal Court openly suggests that there might be some circumstances which would arise which would mean that Trident could be used lawfully 'even if seen as inevitably indiscriminate'.

In reaching this shameful conclusion the Appeal Court rely on another strand which prevented the ICJ Court majority seven from wishing to 'conclude with certainty' that every use of nuclear weapons must necessarily be illegal. This concerns the different views in the world community concerning *opinio juris*. It talks about an emerging norm of non-use and non-threat of use of nuclear weapons but the court majority seven cannot say that it has definitely emerged, in view of the nuclear nations repeated statements that they could use nuclear weapons lawfully. However all these nations have long upheld the various norms of non-combatant immunity, neutrality, not causing unnecessary suffering, non-use of poisonous devices, etc which the use of nuclear weapons, above all ones of 100 kilotons, would surely transgress. The question is what status is to be given to the claim of would be criminals who do not openly say they reserve the right to break the law so long as they use x or y, but rather, against all scientific and common sense evidence, and in violation of the public conscience of the world community, blithely claim that using x wouldn't necessarily break the law. There are some circumstances, which they refuse to divulge, in which they say they could use x without violating the norms to which they remain committed (and which they most certainly make a big protest about if other criminals violate them!)?

The court could also have examined whether in the intervening timespan (between the ICJ Opinion of 1996 and the LAR Opinion of 2001) the embryonic opinio juris to which the ICJ referred had crystallised into an unequivocal rule of customary law. It could, for instance, have drawn some conclusions from the 'unequivocal undertaking' given by the nuclear powers, including the UK, at the end of the NPT review conference last year, 'to accomplish the total abolition of their nuclear arsenals.'

N11. Failure to criminalise Trident deployment.

By rubbishing the authority of the ICJ, exaggerating the divisions on the bench, and exploiting the ICJ's hesitancy to 'conclude definitively' regarding a small residual area having to do with different views held by different nations concerning mini-nuclear weapons and an extreme circumstance of self-defence, in which the very survival of a state would be at stake, the Appeal Court claims that

Trident could be used lawfully. It then claims that our case concerning Trident deployment has two fatal flaws.

At para 95 it claims that 'the relevant rules of conventional and customary international law and in particular the rules of international humanitarian law, are not concerned with regulating the conduct of States in time of peace.' Belligerents and neutrals (they ignore peaceful civilians world-wide) may be entitled to protection under the law of armed conflict, but only when armed conflict breaks out! Yet the basic proposition that a threat to do something is unlawful if the action would be unlawful was not challenged – which is the obvious link between pre-armed conflict and armed conflict.

They get round this problem by claiming that routine deployment of Trident does not really amount to a threat in normal times (though they usefully admit, at para 97, that a given disposition of Trident could amount to a threat in certain circumstances). But they see broadly deterrent conduct, with no specific target and no immediate demands as something quite different from a particular threat of practicable violence, made to a specific 'target', perhaps coupled with some specific demand or perhaps simply as the precursor of an actual attack.

It is giving the peaceful people of the world notice that, so long as the UK or another nation it defends is being attacked, the UK reserves the right to poison the world, cause genetic malformations in untold generations to come, possibly trigger nuclear winter, etc.

Trapped within the outdated traditional view of war as being merely between our own army and the enemy's army, and therefore not anybody else's concern (not even their own people – hence the lack of democratic accountability) they cannot see that any deployment of Trident at all is making a terrible and obscene statement to the rest of the world. It is giving the peaceful people of the world notice that, so long as the UK or another nation it defends is being attacked, the UK reserves the right to poison the world, cause genetic malformations in generations to come, possibly trigger nuclear winter, etc. In this sense it is an illegal deterrent threat however remote or immediate, radically different from the UK saying to the world: 'we have guns and tanks and we will use them to defend ourselves against the military forces of any invading nation if we are attacked'.

N12. Absurd suggestion that civilians have less protection in times of peace than in times of war.

The court's novel theory, in para 95, that humanitarian law does not apply in time of peace is not only surprising but dangerous. The obvious distinction must be drawn between those parts of humanitarian law, like the mistreatment of prisoners, which by definition apply only to the conduct of hostilities, and preparations for war, including the manufacture and deployment of illegal weapons.

Further, the court did not refer to the evidence brought during the LAR proceedings that the UK has been engaged in armed conflict throughout the life of Trident Ploughshares. Evidence, from *Hansard*, was actually put before the three judges during the LAR proceedings about the continuing bombardment of targets in Iraq. These bombardments are still continuing at the time of writing.

N13. Failure to believe our motivation.

The court states that 'in taking the alleged criminality of the Government's actions in relation to Trident as a cornerstone of their argument, the respondents appeared to us ... to be treating the Government's alleged criminality in this respect not merely as something which had to be established in order to succeed in the defence of necessity and justification, but as itself the primary issue, with the respondents' actions at Loch Goil, and their subsequent trial, amounting to no more than a slightly complicated mechanism for bringing the Crown's conduct in relation to Trident indirectly before a court, for scrutiny and, if possible, condemnation as criminal' [para 19]. However, we had made it quite clear we were not using our action in order to bring a test case. Our action was designed to disarm a part of the nuclear weapons system and our actions will continue to do so.

The Scottish judges cannot be allowed to negate international humanitarian law, especially the UN Charter and the Nuremberg Principles. They have given no convincing arguments at all. I think it is worth repeating our rebuttal of their position and explaining once again why the deployment of Trident by the UK is illegal and also criminal in peacetime:-

1) The use of Trident nuclear weapons would be illegal in armed conflict, because the explosive power of each warhead (100 kilotons, equivalent to 8 times that of the weapon which devastated Hiroshima) makes them incapable of use without violating international humanitarian law.

2) In its 8 July 1996 Advisory Opinion, the International Court of Justice (ICJ) concluded [para 47], 'If the envisaged use of force is itself unlawful, the stated readiness to use it would be a threat prohibited under Article 2, paragraph 4 [of the UN Charter].' The UN Charter is applicable at all times and thus the argument that international humanitarian law only applies in armed conflict is irrelevant with respect to threat of use. It is only applicable to use, when by definition there is a situation of armed conflict.

3) UK Trident is deployed under a policy of 'stated readiness to use', in order that nuclear deterrence is credible.

4) By definition, deployment in peacetime fails to meet the ICJ criteria of 'an extreme circumstance of self-defence, in which the very survival of a state would be at stake', even if the Trident warheads could be replaced by ones so small that they complied with international humanitarian law.

5) Nuremberg Principle VI states: 'The crimes hereinafter set out are punishable as crimes under international law: (a) Crimes against peace: (i) Planning, preparation... of a war... in violation of international treaties, agreements or assurances; (ii) Participation in a common plan or conspiracy for the accomplishment of any of the acts mentioned under (i).'

Conclusion

That the High Court answered all four questions in the negative and was so scathing about global citizens' rights to try to prevent the dangers and crimes associated with the use of Trident nuclear weapons means that the Scottish legal system has failed us. This means there will be a continuation of the conflict of interests between the State and ordinary people. Even after our acquittal at Greenock the lower courts continued to find Trident Ploughshares Pledgers guilty, so it will not lead to much change there.

there will be a continuation of the conflict of interests between the State and ordinary people

We see this ruling as a perverse ruling that flies in the face of reason and humanity. A legal system can be supported by people if, and only if, it remains firmly grounded in natural justice and morality. Crime prevention is natural and as long as it is done nonviolently, safely and accountably forms a recognised right in the vast majority of cultures, societies and nations, many of which have incorporated it directly within their judicial systems.

Trident Ploughshares Pledgers act to prevent war crimes, crimes against peace and crimes against humanity. Mass murder is the most heinous wrong known to mankind. The Trident nuclear weapon system is a conspiracy to commit mass murder.

The specious arguments of the Opinion muddy the water and attempt to put the actions of the military beyond judicial questioning. But although these judges may have the last say on how Scots law is interpreted in the courts, this is not the end of the debate. We have already been sent an article by Charles J. Moxley (a well-known respected practising New York attorney and author of *Nuclear Weapons and International Law in the Post Cold War World*) which concludes with this damning sentence,

Scotland is a democracy, and a democracy cannot function if judges make a mockery of the law, dealing with small crimes while leaving the major crimes undealt with.

> The Scots High Court of Justiciary is in error – and does damage to the rule of law...

The full text of Moxley's article, entitled 'Unlawfulness of the

United Kingdom's Policy of Nuclear Deterrence – Invalidity of the Scots High Court's decision in Zelter' can be found on our website (www.tridentploughshares.org)

Scotland is a democracy, and a democracy cannot function if judges make a mockery of the law, dealing with small crimes while leaving the major crimes undealt with. People's Disarmament will continue because murder is murder whether committed by an individual for personal motive or by a state for political motives. If Scots law cannot protect citizens acting to prevent state crime then it has failed us all; we need to reclaim the law for ourselves and insist that it changes so that it bears some relation to the human values contained within the international humanitarian law which we still rely upon.

Decent human beings will continue to try to do all they can to prevent mass murder. Trident Ploughshares will continue.

Letter to the Court
by David Mackenzie, *Local Heroes Affinity Group*

10 May 2001
Depute Clerk of Justiciary
High Court of Justiciary
Lawnmarket
Edinburgh
EH1 2NS

Appeal Against Conviction
Accused: David Mackenzie

I refer to your letter of 1 May with notice of the court's refusal of my appeal against the refusal to grant leave to appeal (your ref 257/01/DL). I guess that it is not open to me to appeal against the court's refusal of my appeal against the refusal to grant leave to appeal, if you follow me. On the slim chance that it is please let me know. If it isn't don't waste any paper or postage.

I would be grateful if you would pass on to Lord Prosser the following poem with my genuine good wishes for his retirement.
David Mackenzie

My case is over – so that is that.
Lord Prosser decrees the earth is flat.
I'm glad your fiat will not extend
From John O'Groats to the world's end
But can mark its vires only there,
On a moist lamp-post in Parliament Square;
While out in the wind and the booming street
Where thoughts are live and arguments meet
People will wonder why up is down
Why anything goes if it's done by the Crown;
Why white is black and short is long
Why murder is fine and stopping it wrong;
Why you only can check Trident's legal status
In that rather limited hiatus
Between firing the missile and seeing it land.
So I gently ask you to understand
The time is coming (best stay out of range!)
For a quite inescapable climate change
That will flood these questions right back to your Hall
And there won't be any more room at all
For those who mangle the ancient saw
And make such a horrible arse of the law.

The Dragonrider

by Kreb Dragonrider, *Druids Against Trident Affinity Group*

Hello, I'm Kreb Dragonrider, a Buddhist Druid, deaf, and actively engaged in nuclear disarmament in Trident Ploughshares, against nuclear crime.

Sorry, I didn't hear you, please speak up clearly. Ah, thank you, that's better, I can hear your questions.

That's why I'm wearing a white robe, because I'm a Druid. The embroidered green dragon was made for me by a friendly Newbury woman in 1996, and I stitched it onto my robes. Oh, yes, I made my own robes. Why am I carrying the buddha? I'm a Buddhist Druid. All in good time, as my tale will unfold.

In the dark warmth of my kind mother's womb, I became ill

catching pre-natal rubella, and the world became silent. On 27 January 1958, I was born in London, and named David John Townsend. Two years later, still not speaking, I was found to be deaf, and since then have worn a hearing aid. At four, I was taught to speak. My intelligence shone, and I was educated at Mary Hare Grammar School, where sign language was not encouraged. I left with 9 'O' levels and 2 'A' levels, and later passed HNC Chemistry at Croydon College.

How deaf am I? My good speech belies my severe deafness. Without my hearing aid I cannot hear anything except for the loudest sound, such as jet engines, road drills, and loud music in night-clubs. With my hearing aid, I can hear music, conversation in a quiet place with one other person, and use the telephone. However I am unable to hear conversation in a group – including meetings – and therefore get left out. I am therefore able to converse, if you speak slowly and clearly. I am proficient in other means of communication, such as written English, lip-reading, and British Sign Language.

I worked eight years as a production chemist, and four years a computer programmer, before being made redundant in July 1992. Since then, I have either been unemployed, or have worked as a cleaner, hearing aid technician, and process operative. These days I fancy myself as a nuclear disarmer, knight errant, peace pilgrim, and bodhisattva.

When did it all begin? I began nonviolent direct action (NVDA) in September 1995, when I camped with eco-protestors in Snelsmore Common, on the path of the infamous Newbury Bypass. I became very concerned about new roads destroying the environment and the Bypass was routed to sweep past my old school by 400 metres.

On 21 November 1995 I changed my name by deed poll to Kreb Dragonrider, after a stupendous magic mushroom trip when I became aware of the Earth Goddess and of her appearance as a green dragon, and of my vow of enacting 1000 years of peace. Kreb is from the *Clan of the Cave Bear*, a stone-age novel written by Jean Auel, and my surname of Dragonrider I composed to mean 'to live in harmony with nature', for the dragon symbolizes many useful spiritual ideas, one of which being the forces of the natural universe. Instead of trying to tame or master nature, as rulers and industrialists try to do, we should be living in harmony with the environment.

My first arrest was on 10 January 1996, near Newbury, for aggravated trespass. I attempted to climb an apple tree to prevent it from being cut down, when two policemen stopped me. I was later found guilty and fined £20.

There I met Galahad, who told me about King Arthur Pendragon and his Druid knights, Loyal Arthurian Warband (LAW). I met King Arthur on 20 June 1996, and was knighted into his order. On the 30 September 1996 I was raised to Shield Knight and Battle Chieftain. Since then I have closely followed King Arthur, and have worn my Druid robes at ecological and peace demos.

On 11 January 1998 I founded South Downs Dragon Order of Druids, and joined the Council of British Druid Orders. Guiding a small Druid order, but allowing the members to pursue their own religious faiths in their ways, I became well known within Druidic circles.

My quest for the best spiritual path involved a pilgrimage to Glastonbury where I discovered some Buddhists from the New Kadampa Order (NKT). They are known as a teaching order, and for granting initiations. I preferred to be initiated than enrol on long courses, and so ended up taking the Bodhisattya Vow and Avalokiteshvara (Buddha of Compassion) Empowerment on 10 April 1999. However, NKT disapproved even of nonviolent direct action, preferring to show the way to peace by good example.

I became involved with Trident Ploughshares in 1999, and signed the Pledge to Prevent Nuclear Crime on 9 August that year, after completing a two day workshop on nonviolence. I formed a small affinity group, 'Druids Against Trident', and did minor arrestable actions, such as sit-downs and fence cutting.

Year 2000 was eventful for me. I obtained a 30cm high Buddha statue, filled with mantras and lovingly painted by a Buddhist artist. On 24 June during a dream I became a direct disciple of Buddha Shakyamuni. I left my last job as a process operative to go on a peace walk, robed, and carrying the Buddha. At the front of the walk were monks and nuns of Nipponzan Myohoji, beating Japanese prayer drums and chanting NAMU

MYOHO RENGE KYO all the way from Aldermaston to Faslane. They were followed by a motley band of peace walkers of various faiths, languages, and abilities, but with the same heart of peace.

496 miles (794 kilometres) and 5 weeks later, at 7am on I August 2000, we arrived at the north gate of Faslane naval base. Peace walkers sat down and were arrested. Excellent photos were taken of Buddhist nuns being arrested and carried off, and made front-page news.

Our affinity group renamed ourselves as 'Wo/men from UNCLE', a nuclear inspection team. During the summer disarmament camp I gave sign language workshops, did a 24 hour peace vigil and fast outside Faslane North Gate on Hiroshima Day, also joined the 'Hobble Hobble into Trouble' affinity group and racked up five arrests before being remanded in custody for 20 days before trial. Despite offering the defence of preventing the greater crime of genocide, I was found guilty of four charges including malicious mischief and breach of bail, and fined £850 pounds. This stonking fine is currently subject to appeal, so I legally don't have to pay yet, whether I want to pay or not!

What now? The 'Wo/men of UNCLE' have now dispersed to other affinity groups. I am currently forming a new affinity group, consisting of Trident Ploughshares Pledgers living in London and south east England. I remain an Arthurian knight, Buddhist Druid, and a direct disciple of Buddha Shakyamuni.

Despite my communication difficulties at meetings (I promise in future not to interrupt so much!) (What was that? Please can you speak clearly so I can hear you. Ah that's much better thank you!) I have tremendously enjoyed the company of fellow

Kreb at Coulport, August 2000.

Credit: McColl

pacifists and nuclear disarmers. Whatever your backgrounds, if you are a pacifist and speak up clearly (or sign) then it's a pleasure knowing you! I look forward to more sign language workshops, disarmament camps, arrestable nonviolent direct action for peace, and to a nuclear-free world (and extrapolating, to a world of peace and love).

Blessed Be.

Disarming the Bases with Music

by Emilia Benjamin, *Venus' Birds Affinity Group*

My involvement with Trident Ploughshares 2000 began when I came home one evening after a concert to find Angie Zelter sitting at our kitchen table. This was a big thrill for me because it was not long after the jury in Liverpool had acquitted her and three others. Having also heard a couple of radio interviews, I was rather in awe of her. Her unexpected materialisation at the table was the doing of one of my housemates, a filmmaker, with whom Angie was discussing the making of a video to recruit Pledgers.

By the end of the evening I was fired up with enthusiasm to become a Pledger and actually DO some direct action rather than simply condoning it from afar. Angie was marvellously reassuring about it, stressing that my 'group' could do as much or as little as it pleased, and just one concert was better than no concert. Since then, the only pressure to continue disarming the bases with music has come from within – a mixture of desire and guilt.

And so Venus' Birds, the affinity group, was born. Originally a consort of viols named after a song by Purcell, Venus' Birds plays music from the 17th and 18th centuries written for viol consort. The viol is a beautiful instrument, immortalised in the pictures of Vermeer, which died out by the end of the 18th century, its nose put out of joint by the louder cellos and violins. The group is composed of professional musicians, and none of us had done any direct action before. In fact, only two members of the group besides myself, Sarah Cunningham and Sarah Groser, were willing to become Pledgers but, since consort music can accommodate from two to eight parts, this was OK.

Our idea was to stage a concert in front of the main gates of

Faslane as part of a mass blockade. In the event of arrest, we thought it prudent to have another member of the group who could whisk away our valuable instruments before the police man-handled them. This was Wendy Vale, who came up with her two year old daughter and her partner. Having a small child with us was possible but not ideal. Mingka had a strong aversion to all the mud around and insisted on being carried everywhere.

After a day of organising, rehearsing, and banner-stitching on the loch shore (filmed closely by the police in their helicopters!), the day of the blockade dawned. It is a bit of a shock to musicians to have to give a concert at 7am in Scottish drizzle after a broken night in a cold tent, but the presence of Angie and her multi-coloured umbrella holding up the traffic for us as we set up in front of the gates was inspiring, and the concert began. It was strange and a bit frightening to ignore the policemen as they asked us to refrain from playing. Baroque musicians are used to being 'law-abiding'. But somehow, it worked, and they let us play the concert to its end. And so Bach, Gibbons and Byrd were put to work as disarmament facilitators, a job new to them, I'm sure. It suited them. And I hope it had some effect on the unharmonious mindsets of the amassed forces guarding the submarines. It is dif-ficult to bring music to such an ugly place, but rewarding – par-ticularly when it uplifts the spirits of our fellow disarmers.

I was finally arrested, after playing on doggedly for some time with cold fingers, charged with breach of the peace(!) and taken to a police cell for 10 hours. My instrument was safely taken by Wendy. The others need not have worried about arrest – it took perseverance to provoke!

Many of my colleagues express an interest in playing concerts for Trident Ploughshares 2000, but the fear of arrest is the stum-bling block. A criminal record makes it a lot harder to get into America, where we go often to work. Since Faslane, I have man-aged to get together one more group (Sonnerie, directed by Monica Huggett) to play at Aldermaston. This was not a blockade, simply a concert outside the base for the benefit of Trident Ploughshares and the guards, who all seemed to appreciate it. I would have liked to have blockaded, but of course, I couldn't guarantee to the oth-ers that they would not be arrested.

Venus' Birds playing Bach. Emilia is 3rd from the left

I went on to get arrested the next day as part of a mass blockade, and I found it far less alarming than my first arrest, simply because I now knew the ropes. It was just a matter of being herded from one holding pen to another – quite humdrum really. I was put in a cell with a woman called Cat who told me she had moved here from the US specifically to do direct action, because, even if the charges against you are upheld (and they are often dropped, as both mine have been), the prison sentences and penalties are very minimal. She wondered why on earth the people in Britain aren't on the streets in their masses, upholding international law. It is so easy here, compared to the penalties imposed in the US.

After my two experiences of disarming Trident, I feel far less nervous about arrest, and quite enthused, work allowing, to continue. Convincing my fellow musicians will always be the difficult part. Work commitments, apathy, and fear of arrest, even simple fear of not doing what a policeman has asked you to do – flagrant disobedience! – are all big stumbling blocks. I would like them to experience the ordinariness of arrest, and also the feelings of community and peace in sharing the whole process, knowing that you are contributing to something good and great – a positive movement towards peace.

'Strike the Little Bell!' (From Adomnan's 'Law of the Innocents')

by Maire-Colette Wilkie, *Adomnan of Iona Affinity Group*

Conversation dwindled. The gloom deepened. The view across the desolate Scottish moor quickly faded as the fog tightened its grip on the vehicle. Soon, as they crawled along, only the low purr of the car's engine and the susurrations of the tyres on the damp road could be heard, occasionally interspersed with the whimpers of Saucy Sally's trembling dog. (But he slept on!).

Inside the car, Emcee (Wide-Boy Wilkie's Moll) wondered if she should get out into the cold and dark to try to guide the driver, Wide-Boy Wilkie, but she quickly discarded the idea. There were too many intriguing questions to ponder. Were they being followed or was the car close behind bearing Dauntless David and Trusty Tony? Had they even left the safe house? Would the Glasgow contingent make it back to the railway station? Would the beautiful young Japanese photographer deliver her goods and turn up again at the next rendezvous? Would Marauding Morag and Jaunty James drive home by another route? Would Doughty Douglas and Joyful Jean get our Trident Missile armable in time for the action? Would the kind, thoughtful officers from Lothian and Borders Criminal Investigation Department bring lots more chocolate cake on their next visit? Where would it all end? What lay ahead?

Who were these people and what could be driving this band of desperadoes? What could have forced anyone to write such drivel as the above?

Dear Reader, what lay ahead was, in space, the outskirts of Edinburgh and, in time, a mere ten days away on 12 February 2001, the Big Blockade of the Faslane naval base. And the 'desperadoes', these were members of the Adomnan of Iona Affinity Group of Trident Ploughshares returning from one of their regular meetings at which they plan their disarmament actions and practice their tactics. And the reason for the writing was simply a request from Angie. How could that be refused!

The Adomnan Affinity Group was formed in preparation for the formal launch of Trident Ploughshares in May 1998. Originally we consisted of eight members, most of whom are either Members or Associates of the Iona Community. This pre-existing common Christian link no doubt inspired and strengthened the bonding of the Group, which has a reputation of having one of the most stable memberships in the Trident Ploughshares movement. During the last three years eight more activists have joined, all committed Christians, most with links to the Iona Community.

Of the current 16 members all but three are willing to risk arrest. Inevitably, not everyone gets arrested at every action or on all possible occasions! One member is now in Germany and has had to curtail his direct actions for the time being but instead regularly preaches to US senior military staff; two live in England and devote some of their energies to working with other affinity groups. Even in Scotland we have often joined with other groups when circumstances require some ad hoc arrangements.

Our very even mix of gender, age and Christian denomination has enriched our deliberations and creativity, producing both more serious actions as well as events that were designed mainly for fun. Many of our actions have begun with a service of worship. To date we reckon to have secured several dozen arrests between us. The consequent trials at Helensburgh District Court have resulted in a mix of verdicts, sometimes 'guilty and admonished', or 'case dropped', or 'not proven', with many remaining unresolved in the legal pipeline.

Apart from the deep bonding process that has taken place within the Group, as well as with the other members of Trident Ploughshares, we have all gained in terms of learning so much. Some of this has been practical skills such as lock-on devices, spotting weak points in fences, and the like. But much more have been learnt about international and domestic law and the processes of the criminal justice system. However, we remain baffled as to how the Procurator Fiscal selects the indictments he decides to take to trial, having experienced episodes when seven or more of us were all locked together and arrested together, but only one was subsequently taken to court!

The Wilkies have enjoyed their regular three-monthly visits from officers of Lothian and Borders CID. Courtesy, mutual respect and friendship have grown with each meeting but we still wonder why they come. Each visit has supplied the local police with no more than a repeat of the information currently published in 'Speed the Plough' and on the Ploughshares website, plus a free lecture on aspects of the illegality of Trident! Since the visitors are always most generous with the cakes they bring the visits have also contributed to Alan's expanded waistline!

Of course, there have been times when we have been disgruntled, wet, cold or weary. It is often exhausting just trying to keep up with the flow of mail, court cases and education opportunities. Sometimes we are all so busy it is difficult to arrange meetings. Many in our Group have been in the anti-nuclear movement for years. They are sometimes depressed that we still have to go out onto the streets to put across the message that to base our national security on our willingness to use Trident to commit the mass murder of innocent people is immoral, illegal and militarily unsound.

Of course we have got things wrong. Even although Alan is the most meticulous person on the planet, there are free spirits among us who cannot bear boring details, and we do slip up on basic communications sometimes! Overcoming these weaknesses has been part of our learning and bonding process. The resulting Group solidarity has enabled us to organise both the sheer fun of the spoof 'Harry Potter' action at Coulport in August 2000, and the deeply spiritual moments of Holy Communion shared outside the North Gate of Faslane. Each of us has learned a deeper patience – the virtue of long-suffering - as we watch the building blocks go into place to build the final victory that must surely come.

And what of the strange ramblings at the start of this opus? The Group had spent their Sunday afternoon practising locking-on to each other using a mock-up model Trident missile! Ever devoted to the value of symbols, seven of us planned to take our missile to the north gate of the Faslane base. We would 'arm' it by locking our arms to each other through it, and then lie down to blockade as much of the entrance roadway as possible for as long as possible. We expected that it would then be Strathclyde Police, who would, in fact, 'disarm' our missile as they arrested us. They would thus symbolically prefigure the day when the Trident submarine fleet itself will be decommissioned and disarmed by the law because it has been proved to be criminal.

Harry Potter action, August 2000. From left to right – Georgina Smith, Marjen Willemson, Marie-Colette Wilkie, Alan Wilkie, David Heller, Brian Quail, Gabrielle Foulkes.

Credit: Roger Franklin

The practice session produced much laughter and serious work. The journey home was truly through thick cloud and fog! And the dog did sleep throughout! The CID arrived at the Wilkies' house on the Thursday before the Big Blockade bearing a large box of fruit that they reckoned we would be able to share! (Much healthier than cake!)

And the Big Blockade? Guided missiles were never before tended so lovingly! Thrusting ourselves forward through the police line to a vacant spot in the roadway, we had barely sat down when fellow protesters surrounded us. They sat on us, around us and, in one case, in us. (As the nose cone fell off from our missile, a young woman squeezed inside the tube and wrapped her legs around our interlocked arms.) This unexpected attention had the effect of extending and consolidating our blockading position but it wrecked all our calculations for maintaining comfortable manoeuvrability in our cramped lock-ons!

For nearly four hours we sat, thanking God for the wonderful weather. Treasured moments will always be the laughter as the police who had just surrounded us to begin removing protestors from our group, disappeared again to deal with some other miscreants who had sneaked back into the cleared area behind them. Left unattended we sang a verse of 'Where have all the p'licemen gone?' More laughter erupted when completely encircled again by a line of police, shoulder to shoulder with arms linked, the officers suddenly executed a nifty turn. This time a wag in the crowd started the 'Hokey Cokey', which was taken up by all the protesters and even the police were laughing!

Equally memorable was the glorious quietening as our legal observer read in strong tones from Ephesians 6 – the 'Armour of God'. This reverence was repeated in the hush that descended as the police circle opened to let her in to feed us with some of the Communion Bread that had just been offered in a service held a few yards away involving many of our Iona Community friends just before they too were arrested.

And what about the beautiful young Japanese photographer? She was there in the middle of the action and her pictures have already gone around the world on the Trident Ploughshares web site.

And finally our missile was 'disarmed'. The first part to be cut away by the police shears had attached to it a little bell. This is our symbolic reminder of the great bell of our patron, Adomnan, ninth Abbot of Iona who in 697 devised his 'Law of the Innocents' which required the protection of non-combatants in time of war. He enjoined on his successors that they must see that his Law was obeyed and enforced. If they found it had been violated they were to ring his great bell to bring punishment down upon those who had broken the Law. As Adomnan's spiritual heirs our little bell has been rung countless times in the presence of the Trident system because it violates the intransgressible norms of international humanitarian law. We confidently work for the day when it can lie silent beside the disarmed Trident missiles as it did on February 12 2001.

(All seven members of the Group locked-on to the 'missile' were arrested and spent time in custody, some until 4am the following morning. One other member joined the 'Local Heroes'

Affinity Group. They too were arrested and released before midnight. The two southern members blockaded at the South Gate. One got arrested with the 'Woodwoses' Group and the other with the clergy! The four absent members were lighting candles for good weather, managing telephone calls and creating the enormous wall of prayer that sustains the 'Armour of God'.)

CHAPTER 8

Ourstory

LIKE MANY PEOPLE I had been inspired by the Berrigans' Plowshares actions in the USA. I was not a Catholic – when I have to define and pigeonhole what my spiritual beliefs are, rather than just live them, then I usually call myself a multi-faither in search of universal ethics – but I admired the simplicity and directness of their faith-in-action. The idea of disarming oneself and then going on to disarm weapons, to transform them, to turn swords into ploughshares, was very appealing. I like direct practical acts of love but I spent almost twenty years actively involved in civil resistance and nonviolent direct action in the peace and environmental movements before I finally took part in a Ploughshares action in 1996.

I joined a group of ten women in 1995 and together, over a year of planning and getting to know each other, we took part in the disarmament of a British Aerospace (BAe) Hawk fighter plane that was part of a batch being sold to Indonesia. We knew that previous Hawks had been used to bomb innocent civilians in East Timor, that 200,000 East Timorese (a third of the population) had been killed, that whole tribes, with their own unique cultures and languages, had been wiped out by the Indonesians. Our government, along with many others, had provided the weapons that the Indonesians needed because they wanted the oil, timber and gold that Indonesia ravaged from tribal lands. Trade and national interests were more important to our government and corporations than the lives of ordinary people. We determined that if all the conventional means of persuading BAe and the government failed then we would disarm as many planes as we could ourselves. Four of our group of ten were active disarmers able to risk a possible ten-year sentence and six remained unseen as essential supporters. We called ourselves the Seeds of Hope – East Timor – Women Disarming for Life and Justice – Ploughshares. Just before the planes were delivered, on 29 January 1996 our group disarmed one of the Hawk planes and caused one and a half million pounds

Freedom after six months in Risley after the Seeds of Hope acquittal, 30 July 1996 by a Liverpool jury. From left to right – Andrea Needham, Angie Zelter, Lotte Kronlid, Jo Wilson.

Credit: Ricarda Steinbrecher

worth of damage. Jo, Lotte, Andrea and I spent six months in Risley prison on remand before we were released after winning our case at Liverpool Crown Court on 30 July.

Whilst in prison, I had time to wonder why other people were not disarming the rest of the planes and why the Ploughshares Movement as a whole seemed to consist of one-off disarmament actions that took a very long time to prepare for. After prison, I felt the lack of any follow-up disarmament work that I could do with our group as we each went our separate ways. I was also distressed at the easy dismissal by other people of their own involvement by putting us on pedestals and a tendency towards hero-worship, especially the phrase, 'I couldn't do anything like that – you are so brave'. I knew I wasn't brave and certainly did not want to be put on a pedestal from which I would be bound to fall. In any case, although the deeds were inspiring in themselves, I knew that we needed each person's creativity and power if we were going to change ingrained state power structures by such actions. I was also dismayed that people thought that only 'religious' people could do a Ploughshares action, when in our group we had had women with no religious beliefs, women who worked within the anarchist tradition, one who defined herself as a pagan and another as a heathen! It was then that I decided to try to set up a structured campaign that would enable many different kinds of people to take part in Ploughshares actions over a sustained period of time and which would impact on social, political and legal structures. We needed a steady stream of disarmament actions with effective follow-through.

Whilst I had been in prison, on 8 July 1996, the International Court of Justice had issued its Advisory Opinion on nuclear weapons. I had been involved with the Institute for Law and Peace, pushing over many years for this initiative, and was heartened by the ruling and knew that what was needed now was people power to push for its implementation. The nuclear powers would try to sideline this decision and global citizens would need to collaborate with each other to strengthen international law and give it some teeth. I determined therefore to do a nuclear-weapon Ploughshares action but to do it within the context of a fully thought-out campaign that would enable very many people to join in – hence the evolution of Trident Ploughshares.

I therefore sat down and wrote an outline of the campaign, which I sent out, on 1 June 1997, to around a hundred people that I thought might be interested. I called it an 'unsolicited letter' to protect people from possible conspiracy charges and I asked for volunteers to join a Core Group to help organise the campaign and requested donations. I approached my Seeds of Hope group, that was still meeting to sort out unfinished business, for an initial grant of a hundred pounds, which helped to get us started – a true seed of hope. I also started talking to lots of people about the idea and visiting active peace groups to ask for their support and approval. Soon there were seven people in the Core Group and we started serious work. Trident Ploughshares was born.

That autumn we each took on different tasks. I was to write the *Handbook* (which is now into its 3rd Edition and being translated into French and Japanese) and to find someone to work with me to produce a short video to explain the campaign. I ransacked books and articles and persuaded friends to help write bits and pieces, asked Joe to desktop publish the *Handbook*, Ross and Ellen to design the logo, and Frankie to print it at cost. Gaby did the filming for the video free of charge and Charlie in his Glasgow studios edited it for us. Without this amazing support we would never have managed to do so much in such a short time. I also hosted at my home the first training for trainers where the Turning the Tide facilitators worked with their trainers and our Core Group to finalise the contents of the nonviolence and safety workshops that we were insisting on for all Pledgers. It was good to work with so many lovely people, most of whom were new to me. The Core Group was starting to work really well together as we got to know each other better.

We took a trip up to Scotland to meet with Scottish CND, local peace groups and Faslane peace camp. This was done to link with them – so that our campaign would supplement their work and not be seen as a threat or challenge. There we were introduced to Georgina, an ex-Greenham campaigner who owns Peaton Wood. The wood was very large with running streams and a waterfall, a beautiful view over the loch and was only 500 yards from the main gate at Coulport. Georgina generously allowed us to camp there for our first planning weekend in April 1998 when representatives from all the affinity groups met to discuss how to organise our first disarmament camp in August later that year. Georgina has allowed us to use the wood ever since, providing us with a welcoming base to organise from.

That first April camp was set among the bluebells as we talked over the practical arrangements and the ethos we wanted to create for August. We talked about the possibility of a heavy response from the authorities, maybe even conspiracy charges carrying a maximum penalty of ten years in prison arising out of the simple process of signing the Pledge to Prevent Nuclear Crime. These anxieties have to date proved groundless, but it is significant that the potential for such serious consequences did not lead to anyone withdrawing their Pledge.

Parallel to these practical arrangements the campaign set in motion its attempts to engage the UK government in dialogue. In March 1998 the Core Group sent an open letter to the Prime Minister, Tony Blair, stating that we would not begin our disarmament actions before 11 August to allow time for dialogue about the government's possible disarmament intentions and their response to our campaign. The response was that the retention of Trident was a manifesto pledge and that the government was confident that Trident was legal. Just before the August camp we again wrote a final plea for a meeting before direct disarmament began. This time the reply had an additional reason for not meeting us. It was apparently inappropriate to meet with members of a campaign, which was threatening illegal actions. We have kept up this constant communication with letters to the Prime Minister every three months which are all published on our website.

On 2 May 1998 there were simultaneous formal launches of the campaign in Hiroshima, Gent, Gothenburg, London and Edinburgh. Pol, in Gent, set the tone, 'For us as concerned citizens there is no other way but to start nuclear disarmament ourselves.' At the Edinburgh launch a fine banner was unfurled, which listed all the 62 people who had by that time signed the Pledge.

August soon arrived with hundreds of supporters. Twelve different nationalities were present. This welcome international dimension came with the For Mother Earth group who had walked 1,000 kilometres from NATO headquarters in Brussels. They arrived in time to join the march to the north gate, headed by the lively all women's drumming band Commotion, where we held an opening ceremony to start our two-week disarmament camp. The best moment, for me, was the symbolic disarmament of a model Trident submarine into a CND peace symbol. Jo Butler, the blacksmith from Oxford, had brought his mobile forge along and people were queuing up to help him with the bellows and to have a hammer at the sub. The carnival atmosphere was creative and friendly with blow-up plastic hammers, painted faces, and musicians performing from the roundabout, which we had claimed for the day.

Within two days the action and the arrests began, as did the rain, which was heavy and continuous for most of the fortnight. Not long after dawn on 13 August I was arrested along with four members of my affinity group, Woodwoses, as we attempted to cut through the fence at Faslane.

Then a group was arrested for blockading Coulport and at noon the Adomnan Affinity Group conducted a ritual cleansing of

Faslane with gallons of harmless but brightly coloured detergent. The following night Aldermaston Women Trash Trident Affinity Group cut into Coulport, to be followed the next day by three young Swedish church ministers, members of the Corpus Christi Affinity Group.

Jo Butler (left) with Ed Stanton (right) transforming Trident into a peace symbol

Then on Saturday 15 August there was a large rally at Faslane, organised by Scottish CND, involving about 300 people; followed on the Monday by a blockade and fence cutting at Coulport and another intrusion at Faslane.

The highlight of the camp was, howev-

Jo Butler with his model submarine

er, the spectacular swim in the early hours of 18 August by Katri, Krista and Rick, from the Titanic Trident affinity group. Dressed in wet suits, hammers and glue strapped to their bodies, they entered the water at the far side of the Gareloch and got to within ten metres of a berthed Trident submarine before being spotted and arrested. Although they were congratulated by their captors an official MOD spokesman denied they had been anywhere near a submarine.

Arrests reached the 100 mark on 20 August when Katri and Krista repeated their swim on 24 August and again penetrated the high-security waters, getting even closer to the submarine.

There were numerous appearances in the local court and at the end of the camp seven activists were on remand. Jens Light

Fredrik Ivarsson, Church of Sweden
minister entering Coulport,
Summer 1998

(Australian) and Ian Thomson (Scottish) were in Greenock prison and Krista van Velzen (Dutch), Hanna Jarvinen and Katri Silvonen (both Finnish), and Helen John and myself (both English) were in Cornton Vale prison. We were held until trial a month later. This provided an opportunity for peace activists in other countries to write to the UK government demanding the release of their nationals who were acting to uphold international law and helped draw in more supporters.

The experience of so many court appearances, trials and our first prisoners provided the lessons needed to improve the legal support and we established our future pattern. We would provide 24 hour centralised legal support during camps and other direct action events and proactive communication with the custody centres. All in all, the camp had proved a considerable success and people throve on the co-operative energy and the vegan food, provided in the first week by Bumblebee. The main gripe was the condition of the chemical toilets, which were so unpopular that Warren from the Ceilidh Creatures Affinity Group volunteered to build two compost toilets that we have used ever since.

At the end of the camp we filed a citizen's complaint at the Procurator Fiscal's office in Dumbarton, asking for a prosecution against the British government for breaching international law in respect of Trident. The response was that the complaint did not merit further action but it has been helpful to refer to it in court cases as yet another example of our willingness to pursue all conventional routes for nuclear disarmament and shows how ineffective such methods have proved.

Britain's fourth Trident submarine was rolled out of its shed at

Titanic Trident preparing for the swim, 18 August 1998 – from left to right – Rick Springer, Katri Silvonen and Krista van Velzen

Barrow on 19 September. The five of us on remand at Cornton Vale decided to mark the event with a modest protest. We felt that prisoners had as much right as anyone to protest. So, we made two banners by cutting out the shapes of letters from coloured illustrations in newspapers and stuck them on two old prison sheets with toothpaste. We intended to drop them out of our windows on the 19th and to refuse to talk, eat or move from our cells for the whole of that day. We prepared a letter to the prison authorities explaining our action and making it clear that we were protesting about Trident not the prison.

However, the prison officers were suspicious and searched our cells the day before, discovering our banners and notes. We were all separated, strip-searched and punished. I was particularly badly hurt as on the day of our planned protest, I decided to protest anyway and refused to walk to the punishment block and had my wrists and thumbs forced right back, causing excruciating pain. I was then forced face down onto the concrete floor of a punishment cell where my clothes were ripped off and I was left without clothes for a day. My wrists were so badly hurt that they still give me problems two years later.

I reported the matter to the police but they covered up for the prison staff, so once I left prison I wrote a report of the assault to the Scottish Prison Complaints Commission. They have since recommended that prisoners should not be deprived of their clothes in such circumstances and that prison officers should be trained to deal with passive resistance in a better way. With the generous support of Dennis Canavan MP who took up my complaint with the Ombudsman I have now received an apology from the prison service. The whole process took two years.

However, active involvement in prison reform and support is now well established and many of us going into prison feel supported enough to make complaints when they are deserved and to write reports of our experiences. For instance, nearly every time we go to prison we have to make detailed complaints about the lack of our statutory right to exercise and also on the lack of adequate toilet facilities within the Cornton Vale remand centre. Our reports are sent to the prison authorities and prison reform groups as well as going up on our web sites. Another welcome offshoot of the prison experiences has been the involvement of the local Stirling CND group in visiting Trident Ploughshares prisoners. This has led to a wider active and practical concern for all prisoners and for what goes on behind the bars.

The first of the Trident Ploughshares trials was heard at the end of September. Four of the remanded women were admonished as were Jens and Anja Light. Strong defences, founded on international law were mounted and in the case of Katri, Krista and Hanna were backed up by expert testimony from Glen Rangwala of Cambridge University. The Justice of the Peace was clearly impressed but still found them guilty, saying that he had to disregard international law arguments. Helen John was fined £150. This is how David Mackenzie, our press liaison, described Argyle and Bute District Court, 'The attitude of the local magistrates may be summarised as 'You are nice people and we bend over backwards to avoid coming down heavily on you. You argue from international law, but we don't know much about that, and we are pretty sure it does not apply on our patch. These matters are for a higher court but we will still hear the cases and dish out our judgements. We deal with Scots law and under that you are guilty and must be punished'.'

We hardly had time to take a breath before the November camp was upon us. Rupert Eris and Peter Lanyon made a good start on Thursday 12 by cutting into Coulport near the explosives handling jetty. This was no idle attempt. In their heavy bags they carried pliers, bolt-cutters, super-glue, liquid cement, carpets and saw-blades.

The weather was with us too, with sharp, clear sunshine. More actions followed – five women were arrested at Faslane on Friday and on Saturday the Gareloch Horticulturists locked up the main door of the MOD building in Glasgow. At a religious service at Faslane on the Sunday, Scottish church leader Maxwell Craig put Trident firmly in the sin category, and there were more arrests.

Monday saw a new type of drive-in direct action when I gave in to temptation after spotting lax security at the main gate at Faslane. After a quick check with my passengers, 'Shall we drive in?' I drove Peter Lanyon's car right past security and set off the bandit alarm. The security personnel were so embarrassed at this that they arrested us all, confiscated Peter's car (it took us over a week to get it back – I was shamefaced as we were actually en route to support him in court!), and invented a charge of assault on the basis of reckless driving. Krista was also charged with possession of an offensive weapon – her peanut butter knife that was in the boot of the car with the peanut butter. This was rather ironic considering the UK's possession of Trident. We all spent a weekend in isolation in separate police cells until released from court on Monday. I then spent anxious months wondering how I would be able to defend myself against lies especially as they refused to hand over any video material of the actual events. When it finally came to trial in August 1999, one of the security men told the truth and the Sheriff in Dumbarton laughed it out of court, saying, 'It was a frail bark that set sail towards the horizon, disappeared and was never seen again.' This is what this case reminds me of.' Krista also won her knife case.

In December 1998 representatives of the various affinity groups met in Berwick-on-Tweed to look back on five months of activity. There were some concerns. Some of us felt that we had wandered too far from the original blueprint – surely a 'real' Ploughshares campaign would involve more serious attempts to disarm Trident than we had had to date. The two swims to the submarine berths by Titanic Trident were hardly to be balanced by the very many comparatively low level actions, most veering towards the symbolic end of the spectrum. Others of us felt that we should not devalue these more symbolic actions which were all that many activists could manage for various personal reasons.

They were still as serious and came from similar motivations – we were all part of the same movement. In retrospect this discussion was very important for clarifying the character of the campaign. We would not become a campaign in which a small elite of dis-armers was supported by a large group of supporters who did not undertake direct action themselves, but would be a campaign in which everything was underpinned by the concept of what much later came to be called 'people's disarmament' – the undertaking by ordinary citizens of the urgent work of disarming Trident in the absence of any such action by the authorities.

We also discussed our decision-making structure and decided that we would hold twice-yearly Pledgers' meetings where we would make the basic decisions about the direction of the campaign, the yearly timetable, the approach to direct action, the legal strategy, the principles for running camps, etc. A core group would then work within this framework to make sure it all happened.

And the first six weeks of 1999 illustrated just how healthy a spectrum of activities the campaign could sustain, including the 'symbolic', 'maximum disarmament' and the germ of a pattern for involving more and more people.

In January, Margaret Bremner, was in Helensburgh District Court for blockading Faslane in August 1998 and for doing some anti-nuclear graffiti on her cell walls. She told the Justice of the Peace (JP) that as a health professional she knew that the health services could not cope with the results of a nuclear war. Later that month Katri Silvonen told the same court how this was an inter-national matter since the whole world was under threat from Britain's weapons. The court however, seemed to be deaf to any reference to international law. It was if the Nuremberg Trials had never happened. When I appeared before the same court for another of my August camp charges and when I was given no assurance by the JP that he would take international law seriously, I refused to take the court seriously and walked out saying, 'If you cannot give me justice then I might as well leave'. I was arrested and held for contempt of court. The supporters in court refused to rise for the JP and he had to leave with them still seated.

There is still a debate within the campaign as to how much we should respect the courts and legal system while it refuses to respect international law and continues to act as if defence policies are above the law and not to be challenged. Part of the debate centres around making sure that the challenge is still put so that there is an opportunity for the system to change – surely a very nonviolent and necessary aspect of our campaign. We would not be able to win any legal victories if we did not at least put our case. There also seems to be an inconsistency if we based our campaign upon the law and then refused to respect it in any manner. So we had to think hard. Certainly the time had not yet come to boycott the courts. We needed to give the Scottish legal system a chance.

Then, at Barrow-in-Furness, on Monday 1 February 1999, Rosie James and Rachel Wenham, of the Aldermaston Women Trash Trident Affinity Group, swam to and boarded the Trident *Vengeance*. They painted slogans on the sub, draped their banners and damaged test equipment on the conning tower before giving themselves up. Three other members of their group, Janet Kilburn, Helen Harris and Louise Wilder, were arrested when they went to Barrow police station to deliver clothing to the wet-suited swimmers. All of the five women were accused of £25,000 of criminal damage. This was Trident Ploughshares' first 'maximum' disarmament action and it was greeted with great grins of delight.

'The reality of 'Yes, we're really doing it!' hit us when we reached the let-off point', said Rachel. 'We were amazed at how simple it was reaching, getting onto and inside the sub. The action worked on the night due to boldness and luck. If you believe it you can really do it. The funniest thing was the jaw-drop response of the security men round the sub. Saying 'Alright mate' to a man who didn't bat an eyelid at two dripping women with hammers sticking out of their wetsuits was beyond belief. Being in the water with that atrocious construction is something I will never forget.'

Rosie said, 'The message I want to pass on to other Pledgers about this action is of its simplicity. Once we had realised how vulnerable *Vengeance* was from the water, the most difficult thing was getting into our wetsuits. Never underestimate that! We can take heart from how dozy they are when there's not an organised event on. So all you need is to see a way in, buy the tools, borrow the wetsuits, and take the plunge!'

Almost a year passed before Rachel and Rosie first came to

trial and at the time of writing they are still within the toils of the system awaiting their third trial. Their first trial was held in Preston Crown Court, with Rachel and Rosie in a dock with a branding iron nailed to the wall as a decoration, in the very court-room where numerous witches were sentenced to death by burn-ing at the stake. It was a really eerie place. The trial ended in dis-array when the prosecution kept changing their minds about the value of the damage done by the two – it veered from over a hun-dred thousand pounds right down to nothing!

Fortunately they managed to get the second trial moved to Manchester Crown Court. The navy mechanic who accompanied them off the submarine at the time of their action admitted that the vessel had been delayed in sailing after the action. Another Crown witness said that the sub had eventually sailed without its radar surveillance system being in working order because they had not been able to replace the testing equipment disarmed by Rachel and Rosie. They had both been represented but when the judge ruled at the end of the case that the threat or use of Trident did not contravene existing English law, and ruled that the part of the defence founded on that matter could not be put to the jury, Rachel decided to dispense with her barrister. She was then able to appeal directly to the jury to follow their conscience in accordance with the Nuremberg Principles. The two women were found not guilty on the charge of criminal damage relating to the spray painting of peace slogans on *Vengeance* but even after extra time the jury could not reach a verdict on the first charge relating to the damage to the testing equipment. This was a tremendous achieve-ment in the light of the fact that the women had never denied doing the damage. The case had obviously caused the jury a diffi-cult dilemma. The third trial is due sometime in October 2001. Rosie will stay with her solicitor, Gareth Peirce, and Rachel will represent herself throughout the trial this time. The legal process will have taken over two and a half years by the time of the third trial. We have certainly had to learn patience in this campaign and not to let the delays of the legal system stop us from continuing with our disarmament work.

In order to bring in fresh energy and people who might want to help, but could only spare a day, we decided that our next concerted effort at the Clyde bases would not be a camp but a one-day blockade of Faslane on February 15. The Glasgow Quakers generously allowed us to take over their Friends Meeting House the night before and we bussed in to Faslane early the next morning. As a sign that political support was growing, ex-vice-president of the Scottish National Party, Billy Wolfe, was arrested at the blockade along with 48 others, while Dennis Canavan, still at that time a Labour MP and Tommy Sheridan of the Scottish Socialist Party joined Iona Community Leader, Norman Shanks, in giving support to the blockaders. The mixture of a Woodwose, a vehicle and an open security gate was again a potent one as Martin drove the Norwich minibus right inside the base. Max the dog, an innocent occupant of the van, was also held for questioning but was released after the usual paw-print routine.

David Mackenzie was busy with press requests, and Jane Tallents with legal support as they worked from Jim and Jane's living room to develop the logistics for monitoring lots of activists in different police stations while dealing with the Scottish press who had at last realised there was a story here worth telling. Up until

Max being arrested, February 1999.

Drawing by Peter Lanyon

this time, with a few exceptions, only foreign journalists had covered our story with full-length documentaries in Finland, Belgium and Holland.

Two days later, Trident Ploughshares was in action again, this time at Aldermaston, where the nuclear warheads are manufactured. Tigger McGregor and Sam Geall scaled the perimeter fence, hung banners from the barbed wire and decorated the fence posts before being escorted off by MOD police.

Although many days had already been spent on remand, on 4 March Sylvia Boyes was jailed for seven days. She had appeared on three charges, two under military bye-laws and one for cutting a perimeter fence. One of the bye-law charges was dismissed due to lack of evidence but she was fined £50 for the other two and when she made it quite clear that she had no intention of paying was sent off to Cornton Vale. As March rolled on, the same court heard Fredrik Ivarsson, of the Corpus Christi Affinity Group describe nuclear weapons as a blasphemy, and dished out heavy fines on Jo Markham and myself. When I appeared again with my fellow Woodwose Clive Fudge, on a breach of the peace charge from the February blockade we were both simply admonished. David Mackenzie has propounded various theories as to the chronic inconsistency of the prosecution and magistrates in Argyle and Bute District. I like this one best, 'The most likely explanation for the Procurator's whim is that he sorts the charge sheets by throwing them down his back stairs. If you land below the seventh stair, you're for it. Magistrate variability is perhaps best explained by indigestion or the ability of some activists to exert effective magical influence.'

At the end of March, Barbara Sunderland of the Adomnan Affinity Group, also had her wrist slapped for blockading, just as the Northumbrian Affinity Group were dismantling large amounts of fence at the Albermarle Secure Nuclear Vehicle Compound near Newcastle, regularly used by the nuclear convoys carrying nuclear warheads from Burghfield to Coulport. The group spent over half an hour chopping the fence, and painting slogans on the bunkers and concrete. Since no one was around, the group practised thorough accountability by leaving leaflets and the slogan 'Trident Ploughshares 2000 were here'.

Amid all the blur of activity new Pledges were being signed and new affinity groups forming. One such was the Local Heroes, centred in Helensburgh and launched in style on 22 April. Local Hero, Eleanor Stobo, wrote, 'Minutes before the morning shift change some of us donnered up to the north gate at Faslane for a chat. One policewoman gawped in mid-sentence as Eric and David secured a cable across the entrance to the base. Seconds later Brian had to help me lock-on to the cable as my hands were too shaky. There was a pause as we looked at each other and it sank in that we had done it … the traffic was queuing up. The elation was tangible. For most of us this was our first locking-on, for some their first nonviolent direct action and subsequent arrest. After a while a copper took a huge pair of bolt-cutters to the fine cable – but to no avail. Red-faced he left, to return ten minutes later with suitably adjusted croppers. Eventually they gnawed through. One by one we were unthreaded and led off. Brian sat down looking calm and strong. The symbolism left me feeling proud and humble to be part of such a powerful creative group.'

Meanwhile, the attempts to engage the government in meaningful dialogue continued. As the new Trident submarine *Vengeance* finally set off for its base at Faslane an MOD official explained to Trident Ploughshares how the executive would deal with the issue of Trident's legality. Simon Gillespie said that they would take legal advice about Trident only if and when its use was being considered. As David so dryly exclaimed, 'this is known as the SOFAL response – Send Out For A Lawyer'. Our response was somewhat different with Fungus and Tamson swimming out to greet *Vengeance* in their own way – Tamson's kilt fell off and his naked protest was featured in the press the next day.

In the middle of May we were back in numbers at Peaton Wood. Earlier in the month a teletext poll had registered 85% of Scots in opposition to nuclear weapons in Scotland and at the north gate at Faslane the leading Scottish Nationalist, Professor Neil McCormick, gave the same strong message. That day there were 16 arrests and our total topped 200.

Our man on the spot – David Mackenzie – reported it thus, 'One action featured wheelchair users Morag Balfour and Roz Bullen along with the Ceilidh Creatures from Edinburgh. They were variously locked on to the fence and each other, threaded through the fence and generally entangled in such a complex weaving of arms and legs that the tableau looked like the result of a very nasty accident during a wheelchair race. It took ages for the police to sort it all out, which they did with good humour. It was a very colourful weekend. The sun shone. Martyn strode about as Tony Blair on a pair of stilts and the Ceilidh Creatures enlivened everything with their imaginative costumery.'

Later that month, as NATO bombed Serbia from a great height, I joined other Trident Ploughshares activists who were among 500 from around the globe, walking from the Hague to Brussels in protest against NATO's illegal nuclear weapons policy. Brian was there with Babs, putting their language skills to excellent use, chatting away in French, Russian, German and Gaelic. Brian wrote, 'That huge grim stalinistic star so often seen on TV, the rows of water cannon, ranks of riot police with visors, shields and batons, all left no doubt. We had arrived at NATO headquarters. This was the end of the long walk. Blistered, bleeding and exhausted, I slumped to the ground. It was shortly afterwards I was hit full on by a jet from a water cannon and sent spinning across the road. A novel experience indeed for a 61 year old with a heart bypass ... Later, I saw riot police lash out at the arms and wrists of demonstrators approaching the wire. Our crime? Simply being there. Confronting NATO with the illegality of its own nuclear war plans. Peacefully, openly and nonviolently.'

During the walk to NATO headquarters I had also met up with Ulla Roder, from Denmark, to check some final details on the joint statement I was writing for our 'maximum' disarmament action. We had formed an ad hoc affinity group with Ellen Moxley called the Pheasants Union quite some months before and Ulla was soon due to come over to Scotland for the last time before our action. Finally, on 8 June 1999, Ulla, Ellen and I got into our little inflatable and drove across Loch Goil and onto the floating laboratory *Maytime* which is engaged in maintaining Trident's 'invisibility' from surveillance whilst under the water. There we managed to empty the contents of the laboratory into the loch. We then spent five months on remand in Cornton Vale prison, including the month spent arguing our case at Greenock Sheriff's Court. The

Angie Zelter nonviolently confronting NATO troops and water cannon at
NATO HQ, May 1999

acquittal and ensuing Lord Advocate's Reference is covered fully
in other sections of this book so I will leave this story here.

On 30 June 1999 the High Court in Edinburgh permitted
Brian Quail's appeal against his conviction, following his disarmament action at Faslane naval base the previous November, to be
resubmitted on broader grounds. He had been convicted of causing criminal damage 'without reasonable excuse'. The appeal will
consider whether the magistrate was wrong not to take account of
international law in reaching his verdict. Two years later, the
appeal had still not been heard and the local court was still not
considering the international law implications of our actions. An
earlier appeal by Helen John on similar grounds had been rejected
by the High Court. It had been poorly argued by her lawyers who,
in particular, had failed to focus on the specific issue of Trident
and the fact that it is a threat. The judges ruled that her sincere
belief in the illegality of Trident was not a sufficient defence. Apart
from Brian's case there are four other appeals awaiting a hearing.

There had been a feeling for some time that the campaign
should extend its attentions to other Trident related sites in the UK
apart from Coulport and Faslane. The *Maytime* action was a good

example as was the Midlands Affinity Group action in July. Roger Franklin, Sylvia Boyes, Alison Crane and Marlene Yeo (dubbed the 'Magic Four') were able to enter the 'secure' Nuclear Weapons Establishment at Aldermaston but only had time to display their banners before being arrested. They had intended to confront the workers inside the site on the basis of the Nuremberg Principles.

On 13 July Ian Thomson (Tamson) was released from custody after appearing in court on charges related to his action when he celebrated the official opening of the Scottish Parliament on 1 July by attempting to demolish the perimeter fence at Coulport. He was also in bother for his May swim to *Vengeance*. Found guilty on both charges, he was set free without sentence having spent 12 days on remand in Greenock prison.

For August 1999 the disarmament camp infrastructure was much improved, with mains electricity installed in the media and press caravan. Bumblebee again cooked for the first week and then kindly donated valuable kitchen equipment after training a few Trident Ploughshares volunteers to take responsibility for the future camps. David reported, 'The camp was again distinctly international with lots of new faces. The activists were anxious to get on with the work and Joy Mitchell and Joan Meredith set the tone on the first day by blockading the main gate at Coulport. Indeed, not a day of the fifteen passed without at least one arrestable action taking place. Some of them were spectacular such as the swimming actions, involving variously Marcus Armstrong, Louise James, Clive Fudge, Kirsty Gathergood and Josje Snoek. New ground was broken by the Woodwoses and friends who improved the external decoration of the submarine testing station at Cove with appropriate messages such as 'Trident is illegal'. There was a 'pernicious paddling' women's action where the Coulport fence runs into the water. The women carried their banners inside the base by paddling deep along the shoreline. One MOD policeman was heard to say, 'I'm not having them standing there taking the piss.'

This flurry of activity went on right up to the last night of the camp as Marjan Willemsen recounts, 'Monday was the last day of the camp and the people that were still there went to have a ceilidh at the gates of Coulport. It started out with nice music, singing and dancing, and then all of a sudden every one ran a different way in order to be decoys. After most of us got back we heard something and two girls were inside the base! Then we heard another noise and Jenny was on top of the fence, inside the rolls of razor wire! She stayed there for a few hours. Meanwhile David and Emma were arrested for cutting the fence, Teapot for blowing raspberries, Fungus for trying to get into the base by crawling underneath the gate, Anne for blockading a police van, and myself for seeing how they were treating Anne.'

Blockade at Coulport, August 1999

If they thought it was all over, then they were wrong. Just four days later Sylvia Boyes and Anne Scholz swam round the perimeter fence at Faslane and after two hours in the water were intercepted swimming under the jetties where the Polaris submarines were formerly berthed. Anne said, 'My plan was to get onto a Trident sub and lock myself to it. Sylvia had a hammer to use on the exterior and spray paint to use on computer monitors inside the boat. With a bit of luck we would have got there just as Rachel and Rosie did in Barrow.'

Early in September Helen John reminded the people of Edinburgh about the UK's nuclear crime, as well as its illegal use of depleted uranium and its support for the sanctions against Iraq, by painting slogans on imposing public buildings in the High Street. Two weeks later she included Westminster in the process by painting foot-high slogans on the St. Stephens entrance to the House of Commons. The Edinburgh Procurator has not yet been organised

Special relationship – street theatre at Helensburgh, August 1999

enough to bring her to trial. But when she appeared in December 1999 for her work at Westminster a London jury, who had heard from MPs Tony Benn and Alan Simpson, found her guilty of the criminal damage charge but, perhaps uniquely, added a rider that she was justified in what she had done.

October 1999 was the month of the Greenock trial and the Trident Ploughshares legal team worked non-stop supporting us. No sooner was it over than the November camp began with a fresh edge. The acquittal at Greenock had begun to sow doubts in many minds, especially those whose business it was to promote and protect Trident from our crime prevention activities. A letter was handed in to Rear Admiral Gregory at the Coulport main gate, advising him that he was putting his personnel in an unenviable position by inciting them to engage in criminal and immoral activities. We knew we had some sympathy within the Strathclyde police and we publicly expressed our hope that they would get the support they needed as they thought through what it means to be involved in law enforcement in a society which is becoming more openly unhappy about threatening genocide. We began to emphasise more and more our crime prevention role. The action highlight of the weekend was the two gate blockade of Coulport. While one group formed a linked obstruction across the main gate Sylvia

Boyes, Marjan Willemsen and Jenny Gaiawyn locked on to three separate workers' buses at the construction gate.

The trials continued in Helensburgh, keeping the legal team on their toes. No one knows how many hundreds of hours the faithful Helensburgh local volunteers have spent supporting the numerous activists and keeping records of every case. There were no surprises on November 22 when the court brought forth another guilty verdict, this time against the Irish activist Mary Kelly, despite her brilliant summary of the case against Trident. The police witnesses wandered even further away than usual from the truth and claimed they did not know that there were nuclear weapons inside Faslane.

Meanwhile *Vengeance* was back in Barrow waiting its commissioning. It claimed the attention of Sylvia Boyes and River who were arrested inside the dock having intended to swim across to board the submarine. They carried with them hammers, glue, and spray-on varnish. They were filmed by BBC1's *Everyman* team who had been following Sylvia for many months and finally made a very good documentary that was broadcast at the end of January 2001.

Sylvia refused bail and River did not seek it. At their hearing on 2 December Sylvia agreed to the bail conditions and was released but River refused them because they included the condition that he stay at least ten miles away from any nuclear weapons base. River pointed out that the UK was crammed with Trident-related facilities and said he would accept the conditions if he was assured that no nuclear warheads would be within ten miles of *Vengeance*. He was sent back to Preston prison. A week later he argued successfully and significantly that the conditions infringed his basic right to protest peacefully and was also freed.

They had another year to wait before their trial started on 9 January 2001 at Manchester Crown Court. They were charged with conspiracy to commit criminal damage. Gareth Peirce acted as solicitor for Sylvia. She has defended many Trident Ploughshares activists in the English courts and her calm, supportive expertise is greatly valued. River defended himself. On 18 January 2001 after five hours of deliberations the jury were unable to reach a unanimous verdict and were asked to try for a majority verdict which they quickly did. Not guilty was the verdict. What an encouragement it was to all of us! It seemed that whenever we had a chance to put a full case to the British public in jury trials we were either acquitted or had hung juries. There is no doubt that the legal status of Trident is being severely battered in the courts.

From November 1999 some accused activists were developing alternative approaches to their defence in the District Court in Helensburgh in an attempt to break through the impasse there. Local Heroes Barbara McGregor, Brian Quail, Jane Tallents and Eric Wallace put in a claim that the European Convention on Human Rights gave them the right to intervene peacefully and nonviolently when they knew a war crime was being committed. Alan Wilkie of Adomnan made a similar claim as he defended himself against a breach of the peace charge and Pamela Smith challenged the whole concept of breach of the peace. These submissions are known as devolution issues, since they refer to the incorporation of the Convention into Scots law under the Scotland Act of 1999. Alan's plea has been rejected, as has Pamela's though she has appealed. The Local Heroes are waiting the outcome of a similar case elsewhere in Scotland.

In our publicity for the planned blockade of Faslane, jointly organised with CND, on 14 February 2000, we had asked people to make it a priority for the year and the response was most encouraging. The training and briefing events in Glasgow on Sunday 13 went well and emphasised our nonviolence and safety guidelines. At 5.30am the next morning the minibuses and coaches were loaded and took off from the Glasgow centres with a minimum of fuss and delay, while other overnight transport from all over the country was homing in on the base. There were messages of support coming in from celebrities, including Sean Connery, Emma Thompson and Kurt Vonnegut, whose message described the campaign as 'the shock troops of the sane in the war against insanity'. The blockade held the base up for over two hours and 185 were arrested, including Member of the Scottish Parliament Tommy Sheridan, Member of the European Parliament Caroline Lucas and ten Scottish church ministers. Our press man David made a special mention of the weather in his report, 'When some of the cases came to court in October 2000 a police witness, asked if he had his notes from that day, said that due to the weather conditions note taking had been inappropriate. That was putting it mildly. Legal support 'runners' did a brilliant job logging the arrests and dashing to and fro with sheets of paper disintegrating in their hands, and many activists are still carrying around diaries and notebooks with that tell-tale Valentine's Day water stain. The legal support team did an unbroken 26-hour shift monitoring the arrests, updating information about who was in what police station and arranging pick-ups for those released. It was a media event countrywide but the biggest boost was the evidence it gave of more and more people willing to play an active part in nuclear crime prevention.'

On 3 March the 'Magic Four' from the Midlands Affinity Group were found guilty at Newbury Magistrates' Court by a magistrate who said, like his myopic peers in Helensburgh District Court, that he could not consider international law if it was not incorporated by statute. Hefty compensation orders were dished out and Sylvia, in view of her honourable record, was also fined. Marlene Yeo's refusal to pay up led to the bailiffs being set upon her and plenty of opportunities for more local outreach work to explain why she was keeping her doors locked and what Trident cost.

The court in Helensburgh continued to throw up one bizarre hearing after another. In the trial of Marilyn Croser and Helen Harris a police constable from the Gorbals in Glasgow said that if told by a peace protester that international law was being breached in Faslane or Coulport he would take action to investigate that allegation. Testimony by Crown witnesses was a shambles and JP Stirling found them not guilty as Helen put it 'not for the best reasons'. Typically the JP had not allowed the accused to cross-examine Crown witnesses on international law.

Marcus Armstrong and Louise James were fined in Helensburgh on 9 May for their August swim to Trident, when they had made it up to the floating barrier at Faslane. Marcus gave a simple but brilliant summary of the moral case against Trident and ended by saying, 'If anything ever happened and if any of my children, grandchildren or any other person asks me, did you know? What did you do? Although it would give me little comfort, I would be able to say yes, I did know and although I wish I'd found the strength to do more, I did what I could at the time, given the circumstances.' Turning to Justice of the Peace Scullion he asked him directly, 'What would you say to your children or grandchildren?' There was a silence and then the JP said, 'I will not answer that question.'

The May camp was in Aldermaston in the year 2000. We felt that it was essential to start building more support down in the south and to start applying pressure where the nuclear warheads for Trident are actually manufactured. It was also close to Westminster where the decisions about Trident are still being made and where they continue to ignore the upsurge in public protest in Scotland. Trident was an English responsibility and there needed to be an English Trident Ploughshares disarmament focus. This was a hard decision and still is. We had got used to working in Scotland and had already set up our support teams and roles and felt we needed to keep the pressure on in Scotland too.

On May 13 Trident Ploughshares along with Scottish CND therefore arranged a 'Carnival' at Faslane that sent a practical message of solidarity to the action in the south. Barbara McGregor described it, 'MAY carnival: a festival of fertility and earthy eroticism. Traditionally young men and women went to the woods the night before Mayday to find a suitable maypole 'grooving the dark earthy groves vicarless and knickerless' in search of a sturdy trunk. Our El had been on the case though. Up came an erection made with love in Lochgoilhead. More of a totem than a mere pole, with sea creatures, birds, and cute beasts all the way up, crowned by a golden sun. And the revellers danced round it – weaving patterns of creative chaos. At the appointed hour, cleverly liasing with the north gate and a run on the barricades by riot girl Morag, nine whirling dervishes laid the pole to rest across the middle of the road, punched holes into the papier-mâché coating and locked their assorted jewellery onto the centrally running chain inside. A cheer went up, funky music went on, the police roasted, and we toasted under a benevolent sun, chewing on liquorice and succumbing to sloppy kisses from wayward dogs. HOLD ON by the Soulmasters was never so apt. 'Too many to arrest' was the word on the police walkie-talkie – even the bobbies were langorous. At 3 we all traipsed off to catch the bus home. A jolly splendid summer sortie.'

Thames Valley Police (TVP) had written to us in April, hoping to identify the organisers for the planned event at Aldermaston

Maypole Blockade, Faslane, May 2000.
Credit: David Mackenzie

and asking us to confine our activities on the 22 May (the day of the planned blockade) to a designated car park. We pointed out that 'There are no 'organisers' or 'leaders'. Different people take on different responsibilities at different times but the bottom line is always individual responsibility and autonomy along with respect for others.' We also took the opportunity to challenge TVP about their failure to act, in the following terms, 'The Trident system threatens innocent civilians in their millions and presents a long-term and serious threat to the natural environment. What action is Thames Valley Police taking on this urgent and desperately serious matter?' Although TVP had been in touch with Strathclyde to gain from their experience of dealing with our activities they opted for intimidation but relaxed into a more reasonable line when their bluff was called. This extended to an understanding that we would use the informal camping site we had intended. There was also a letter from AWE (Atomic Weapons Establishment) PLC threatening legal action against the campaign should there be any disruption or damage.

We worked with the Aldermaston Women's Peace Camp who maintain a regular monthly vigil at Aldermaston at the Falcon gate. Some of their women had formed the Aldermaston Women Trash Trident Affinity Group, whom we knew well, but it was good to meet the other women and wonderful for some of the other Trident Ploughshares women to experience their first ever women only space. The co-operative camp worked well and began with a concert at the gates by the baroque ensemble Sonnerie with world famous violinist Monica Huggett who said, 'Maybe doing a concert at Aldermaston will present a stark enough contrast to nudge people's minds'. There was a march from Reading the next day and the first arrests, of Ulla, Roger, Joan and Fungus who got into the base. The police bail conditions were that they could not come within five miles of Aldermaston so they set up camp at Burghfield, another Trident related base nearby.

Eric Wallace described the blockade that took place on the Monday, 'The decision to use karabiners and tubes in our action seemed a bit daunting to some of us at first, but Fungus persuaded us otherwise and it all turned out for the best since the equipment stopped the police trying to pull and push us apart and we were able to hold the gate shut for more than three hours. Even when special constables arrived to cut us loose we were able to hold on or let go as individuals, always it seemed the control rested with us. If we had merely linked arms then our line would almost certainly have been broken when one irate motorist decided to call our bluff and drive through the line. Only when it became apparent to him that we were unable to move did he back off. Another advantage of this tubing arrangement was that we were able to move our location at will and indeed police cleared a way for us as required!' There were 46 arrests that day and 55 for the whole weekend. Very few of us were charged – most having been bailed to come back at a later date. The weekend was a great success, it was especially helpful to have those involved who have long targeted that location. As Helen Harris put it, 'Overall, despite some of the usual ill informed hostility, I felt the Trident Ploughshares camp raised the local awareness of Aldermaston, leading to a high level of local interest and support.'

Trident Ploughshares also made more solid links with another important peace group – the Womenwith Hill Women's Peace Camp. On 19 June 2000 I joined Helen John and Anne Lee to cut through the new high-security fence at the US National Security Agency Space-War Spy Base at Menwith Hill in Yorkshire. Menwith Hill contains systems designed for the new US anti-ballistic missile system (ABM) as well as being intimately linked with the command and control network around Trident. We were caught trying to cut through one of the inner fences around the satellite communications 'golf-ball'.

A week later a group of Walkers for Peace set off from Aldermaston to cover the 400 miles to Faslane. The core of the group were the monks and nuns of Nipponzan Myohoji, a small Buddhist order committed to peace. By the time they arrived at Faslane they had formed our latest Trident Ploughshares Affinity Group calling themselves 'Peace Pagoda'. The following Thursday Helen Harris was sent to prison for seven days after refusing to pay a fine and a heavy compensation order. At that time the number of days spent in prison by Trident Ploughshares campaigners was already over 700.

Preparations were now underway for the third August camp at Coulport and for the Faslane blockade on 1 August that would start it all off. David's July press release noted that the UK was defending itself in the High Court against the islanders of Diego Garcia who had been evicted from their island as part of a treacherous Polaris deal with the US in the 1960s. The British government tendency to recognise international law only when conve-

Entering Menwith Spy Base, 19 June 2000. From top to bottom – Anne Lee, (behind centre of gate) Angie Zelter, Helen John.

Credit: Kathyrn Amos

nient has a long pedigree. In the run up to the blockade we wrote an open letter to the Chief Constable of Strathclyde Police, John Orr, asking him not to arrest us or move us forcibly from the scene. This was the beginning of an interesting correspondence in which Orr showed willingness to discuss the issues of legality, at least to a certain point. The Greenock verdict was still having its impact.

The beginning of the blockade was signalled by the arrival of the 30 peace walkers who had been on the road from Aldermaston since 26 June. The walkers, led by the monks and nuns, went right up to the gate and attempted to attach the thousands of paper cranes they had brought with them. This was refused and after a brief ceremony activists blocked the gateway by sitting down or locking on to each other. After warnings police moved in to remove, arrest and charge them. Hoosey and Teapot managed to get up their tripod in record time and remained effectively blocking the south gate for seven hours before they came down voluntarily. Leeds MP Harold Best and writer A.L. Kennedy were present to give their support and encouragement.

The day brought an ironic twist, as many of the women on the Peace Walk from Aldermaston, who had received a warm and high-profile reception from West Dunbartonshire Council on our way through Clydebank, found themselves in the police cells in the same town after being arrested at the blockade. The contrast between the burnt baked bean meal in the cell on the floor and the succulent dishes in the comfy council chambers was rather a stark reminder of official schizophrenia.

The camp itself began with Jenny Gaiawyn being sent to Cornton Vale for refusing to pay a fine. The following days brought a whole variety of actions. People holding placards which each had a separate word on – Shift To Peace Work – and who kept shifting positions until they suddenly formed a blockade of the gate, graffiti for peace, getting into the protected area at Coulport by inflatable boat, fence cutting galore (especially at the sponsored fence cut), and again a swim, this time right up to the ship-lift only a few metres from Trident.

On Hiroshima Day we gathered at Faslane for a moving and extended ceremony, moving through a sequence of emotional

Peace Walk arriving at Faslane, 1 August 2000

responses to nuclear crime, from sorrow, to anger, to hope and empowerment, all symbolised by a giant female puppet who was draped in cloths of different colours. The evening ceremony was on the shore of Loch Long and began with a Buddhist ceremony on the beach. The floating lanterns we had prepared were in danger of being blown inshore so we sought the help of the MOD marine unit. We waded out to the inflatable police boat with the lanterns held aloft – a beautiful sight. I was then allowed in the boat to take them out to the middle of the loch and was touched to find how gently the policemen lit the candles and help set them safely afloat, joining in the commemoration of all those incinerated by the atomic bombs. At that moment we knew true peace as we mourned the thousands who had died together and watched the flickering candles spread across the water.

There were a total of 161 arrests during the fortnight. Several campers had multiple arrests, Marcus Armstrong leading with seven. As well as being an action camp there were also many opportunities for activists old and new to renew their vision and commitment, to develop their skills in a whole range of areas, such as court work, the principles and practice of nonviolence, com-

Peace lanterns on the loch, Hiroshima Day 2000

munication, boat-handling, and to reflect on strategies for the future. At the end of the camp Kreb Dragonrider was sent to Greenock prison on remand. He had failed to turn up for a previous trial and had broken bail conditions. On 4 September, although soundly defended by solicitor Liz Ross he had the misfortune to be before Justice Fraser Gillies in Helensburgh who fined him a total of no less than £850. Our patience with the shenanigans of that court was wearing very thin indeed and Sylvia Boyes showed a proper disrespect for its authority on 11 September when she was up for swimming into Faslane and locking on to a bus at Coulport the previous August. Sylvia refused to give her testimony from the witness box saying that as a Quaker it did not matter where she stood – she would tell the truth. JP McPhaill listened patiently to her powerful summary but said he was not there to judge the legality of Trident. She was fined £100 and said she would not pay and would not leave the court until the question of her unpaid fine was dealt with. The next case was called and Roger Franklin sat down in the dock beside Sylvia. His case was then adjourned and Sylvia was still sitting there. The JP gathered up his papers and he and the Clerk and the Fiscal scuttled out the door, ignoring the fact that neither Sylvia nor the four supporters present had obeyed the instruction to stand up.

4 October was another of those long days that Jane had to sit through and record for us all. There were 24 Trident Ploughshares cases being discussed, and six trials due to take place. Two had to be rescheduled due to lack of disability access to the court. With 40 trials still in the pipeline and reports relating to the 161 arrests at the August blockade still before the Procurator Fiscal it appeared that the local court was seizing up. In David's words, 'In the end none of these trials materialised and we were subjected to the usual chorus of adjournments, stretching well into next year. Late in the afternoon the court rose but our day was far from over. Why not make all our travelling worthwhile? A dozen or so of us made our way westward to Coulport where we set about the perimeter fence. Seven of us were arrested and everyone was out again in a few hours.'

The hearing of the Lord Advocate's Reference began as scheduled on October 9 and involved the help and support of many people in Edinburgh including the members of the St. Augustine's United Church who lent us an office and allowed us to sleep in their church. A regular presence was maintained outside the court with placards and banners and the handing out of leaflets, accompanied by a very tall woman in white, Lady Justice herself, with a Trident in one hand and hospitals and schools in the other. El and Marjan had made her out of plaster and placed her in the square overlooking the High Court of Justiciary. On 13 October after an adjournment of the hearing to 14 November, I was invited to speak at a seminar given by the World Court Project along with Professor Staale Eskeland of Oslo University. Our message was that regardless of the abstruse legal language of the past week, the simple heart of the matter was that it was wrong to threaten to kill millions of innocent people and that direct action and practical disarmament would change things. The City of Edinburgh council then laid on a generous civic reception, which was a welcome relief from the tensions of the High Court. A month later we completed the four remaining days of the Lord Advocate's Reference and were told that we would hear the rulings in a short while.

Meanwhile, Jane, our loyal legal and court supporter, was in

Court support at the Lord Advocate's Reference hearings, October 2000. From left to right; Alan Wilkie, Billy Wolfe and Ian Thomson.

the dock herself for a breach of the peace charge that arose from her blockading the Trident warhead store at Coulport in August. She said she had been acting 'in solidarity with victims of the nuclear chain', such as the Shoshone people of Nevada whose lands had been poisoned by the nuclear bomb testing of the UK and US. She was fined a hefty £300 and immediately appealed both the conviction and sentence saying, 'This is a perverse verdict. The Procurator Fiscal made no attempts to rebut my defence of necessity.'

In the early hours of 3 November 2000 Catholic priest Martin Newell and Dutch Catholic Worker Susan van der Hijden, calling themselves Jubilee Ploughshares 2000, entered Wittering airforce base in Cambridgeshire and disabled a Trident warhead carrier by hammering on the inside and outside. In their statement they said, 'Through the Jubilee 2000 Campaign, the church has committed herself to working for justice for the poor and the oppressed. British nuclear weapons are a central part of the chains of oppression. As Christians we have taken responsibility and acted in solidarity with the 'least of this world'.' They were immediately remanded in custody where they stayed for 7 months awaiting trial for burglary with intent to cause criminal damage. The estimate of the damage was £32,000. Their highly successful 'maximum' disarmament action was very encouraging to us all and is encouraging the Catholic community to more action.

Fungus from Faslane Peace Camp was taken on November 6 to Cornton Vale prison to serve seven days after firmly indicating that she would not be paying any of her fines. This brought to 750 the total number of days spent in prison by Trident Ploughshares activists.

The weekend of the 10 and 12 November saw the return to Aldermaston of the Trident Ploughshares camp. Dr. Rosalie Bertell, the internationally recognised expert in the area of the effects of low-level radiation and a supporter of Trident Ploughshares, spoke at the Tadley community centre on 'Radiation and Health'. Remembrance Day saw a challenge to both ends of the nuclear chain, in Scotland and England, as Trident Ploughshares activists cut their way into the nuclear facili-

ties in Faslane (Jean Oliver and Douglas Shaw) and at Aldermaston (Barbara Sunder-land, Davida Higgin, Peter Lanyon and Simone Chimowitz).

The actions showed our continuing commitment to disarmament work at both ends of the nuclear chain from manufacture at Aldermaston to deployment at Faslane and came just days before the beginning of the examination of the legality of Trident in the High Court.

MSP Tommy Sheridan appeared in Helensburgh District Court on 14 November saying, 'If we don't all take a stand on this one, none of us will be left standing'. Justice McPhail

Tommy Sheridan outside Victoria Halls, Helensburgh, before his trial. Barbara Mauer on right, October 2000.
Credit: David Mackenzie

found him guilty without any explanation and fined him £250. Tommy made it quite clear he would not be paying his fine. He arranged to hand himself into Dumbarton Police station at midnight on 17 December for non-payment of his fine and was sent to Greenock where he spent five days in prison. The fact that a Scottish parliamentarian was willing to back us up in this way showed remarkable solidarity, humanity and integrity not at all common in politicians. It also demonstrated the growing understanding that civil resistance to the shame of Trident is both legitimate and essential.

November had seen other courts dealing with non-payment of fines. Roger Franklin (72) refused to pay his fines in Gloucestershire Magistrate Court on 21 November and Joy Mitchell (67), Joan Meredith (71) and David Mackenzie (56) refused to pay up in Helensburgh on 28 November. Joy asked the court how we could teach our children to uphold the law when our country was so flagrantly breaching it and Joan told the court, 'I will not sit at home knitting, pretending that it's all right when it's all wrong.' At the end of the hearing Joy was arrested by the police and taken to prison for an unpaid fine from a previous conviction.

On 4 December the court at Helensburgh fined Marcus and Brian for their parts in the February blockade. JP McPhail ruled out all the evidence essential to their defence against their charges of breach of the peace and showed his biased opinions by referring to them as 'you people'. Without any apparent attempts at irony the Procurator Fiscal said that Faslane was a dangerous place and it was essential to public safety that its smooth running continued unimpeded. Once again the lower Scottish courts showed their inability to conduct fair trials or to conceive the possibility that what's official might be illegal. The brave independence of Sheriff Gimblett has not affected these lower magistrates.

Clive Fudge was before the same court on 6 December and on cross-examination of the second police witness got him to admit that he was not sure if any traffic had been held up by the blockade. He also argued that the Fiscal's assertion that his behaviour could reasonably be expected to cause alarm had no basis. Justice of the Peace Viv Dance found him not guilty, showing us we should never give up the possibility of victory in the most unexpected quarters. However, two police officers were waiting for him just outside the court where they handcuffed him and took him away to prison for seven days for a previous unpaid fine. Three other activists had their plea of not guilty accepted by the court due to missing Crown witnesses.

The year 2001 is keeping us all fully stretched with scarce a breathing space. As the actions at other Trident related sites around the UK begin to result in court cases, as fines are brought to local courts, as more and more people are getting involved, the work load increases. Luckily, so do the volunteers to do all the work – a real people's campaign.

Thursday 18 January 2001 – the same day River and Sylvia were acquitted at Manchester Crown Court – four activists were found guilty of obstructing the highway outside Aldermaston during the May 2000 blockades. After a truly pathetic prosecution case – with lost exhibits, useless witnesses and questions over the validity of police statements – Ganesh, Andrea Needham and Helen Harris were all fined £50 and ordered to pay £100 costs. One positive outcome of this case however, was the Stipendiary Magistrate's agreement that there was no further case to answer on a further charge of breaking the Section 14 order (directions/restrictions for/on lawful assembly, under the 1986 Public Order Act). He threw out the case because there was insufficient evidence to prove that Andrea had received a copy of the order. He also seemed unhappy that she was the only person to be charged with an offence which stipulates that at least 20 other people be present (why weren't they charged too?).

Ulla was arrested again on 19 January at Coulport with fellow activist Tamson. This was the 12th arrest for the Danish activist but she was soon released. Marcus, another repeat crime-preventer, was sent down on the 24th after refusing to pay his fines and spent seven days in Greenock, bringing our total to 939 days. Ulla had to make her way down south again for her trial at Newbury Magistrates Court on 30 January for the outcome of the charges brought against them for cutting into Aldermaston in May the previous year. She was found guilty along with Joan and Roger and although they were not fined because of their 'honesty and sincerity' nevertheless they had costs of £150 and £200 compensation orders imposed. The Magistrates Court had been treated to the testimony from eminent expert witnesses Professor Frank Barnaby who spoke on the destructive power of Trident, Nick Grief, Professor of International Law who argued that UK courts had to take account of international law and William Peden of Greenpeace who argued about the dangerous nature of the Aldermaston site.

Meanwhile, we were all working hard on the mobilisation and support for the Big Blockade. On 26 January Chief Constable Orr of the Strathclyde Police was urged not to arrest people blockading Faslane on 12 February. The letter said, 'the *prima facie* evidence for Trident's unlawfulness is now ever more firmly in the public domain. This means further that a civil police force, especially one in whose area the operations under question are being conducted, has even less excuse than before for failing to engage in at least preliminary investigations on its own behalf, or for failing to review and revise its current policy of impeding and arresting those who are acting to uphold the law.'

The Big Blockade, jointly organised by Trident Ploughshares and Scottish CND, proved to be a tremendous success. The Faslane base was completely closed down for five hours on Monday 12 February 2001. The South gate was closed by a tripod put up by the Faslane Peace Camp at 1.30 in the morning and it had only just been removed when the main group of blockaders arrived at 7am. A cycle flower blockade suddenly appeared (five cycles locked onto a flower structure and five of us locked into and onto both) which took police over an hour to chop their way through; the Irish contingent sang, chanted and danced, Mancunians and East Anglians held arms and blocked the road completely, and Seize the Day sang and drummed for us. The south gate remained closed until 2pm in the afternoon. At the main gate, the north one, the blockade started at 7am and was not cleared until midday. The majority of people went to the north gate where there were spaceship lock-ons, anarchist chants, Socialist Worker placards, religious ceremonies, woven webs, politicians smiling, a well-respected lawyer sitting on the ground, drummers and musicians, piles of policemen, and a wonderful atmosphere.

Blockade at Faslane main gate, 12 February 2001.

With over 1,000 blockaders, it was the biggest anti-nuclear direct action in Scotland for many years and in total there were 385 arrests including George Galloway MP, Tommy Sheridan MSP, Caroline Lucas MEP and Ian Hamilton QC. Numerous church leaders were arrested along with Reverend Norman Shanks, the leader of the Iona Community, and watched over by the supportive Moderator of the Church of Scotland, the Very Rev Dr Andrew MacLellan. After the blockade had finished six people from the Belgium Titanic Trident Affinity Group managed to break into the base and walk down the main road inside the base, passing base personnel, before getting into the entrance of the Trident jetties where they were arrested.

Everyone felt very energised after the blockade, which was just as well as there was plenty of work to do. Dozens of supporters had been stretched to the limits providing nonviolence workshops, sleeping accommodation, food, transport and legal support for so many people. It was amazing how much we were able to do with so few resources and no paid staff, but there were limits and we were reaching them. We knew we had to encourage as many people as possible to do the 2 day nonviolence workshops and to form sustainable affinity groups so that they could be more autonomous and eventually so they would be able to help with the next wave of new people. Marguerite and Peter updated the computer data files and letters were sent out to all the new people who had been arrested.

We began our planning for the Aldermaston camp and also decided to call another large blockade for 22 October. We decided we needed to keep the pressure up and could not allow another year to go by before mobilising large numbers again. If we wanted to get rid of Trident more and more people had to be encouraged to join in and blockades seemed to be the best way to do this. Hopefully their participation in the blockades would lead to further involvement.

The trials were continuing of course. Ian Thomson was in Dumbarton Sheriff Court on 27 February for his fence demolition work at Coulport on two occasions and for one breach of bail. He had demolished about 12 sections of fence and explained that he was starting to dismantle the base. In court he detailed some of the voluntary projects he had been involved in but said that his most rewarding project was his present one of restoring the beauty to Faslane and Coulport by dismantling the bases. Ian was found guilty and fined £200 for each charge. He had appeared five times for this case and had spent two weeks on remand. He continues with his demolition work. Another Pledger, Marilyn Croser spent two days in Cornton Vale for an unpaid fine after handing herself in.

On 7 March Warren Canham managed in his cross-examination to get the police officers to admit that if they knew someone had a lethal weapon they would do something about it and that they agreed that nuclear weapons were lethal. But he was still found guilty although only fined £20.

On 25 March the Ministry of Defence finally admitted in a letter addressed to Dr Kim Howells MP that 'Nuclear, biological and chemical weapons are indiscriminate weapons of mass destruction, specifically designed to incapacitate or kill large numbers of people'. The letter was in relation to depleted uranium and obviously the truth just slipped out – too late to use in the Lord

Advocate's Reference proceedings but nevertheless we will use it to good effect in future cases.

Father Martin Newell and Susan van der Hijden appeared at Basildon Crown Court on 27 March having already spent over 90 days in custody. Their trial was listed for the end of May at Chelmsford. Vigils and talks have been organised on their behalf and yet another part of the UK is being galvanised by their witness and dedication.

Ian Thomson was back in court a month later, on 27 March, and received his 5th jail sentence for direct action against Trident, when he said, 'With respect to the court, I have to say that hell will freeze over before I pay this fine.' His tenacity reminded us all that the core of our campaign is not complex political or legal arguments but a straightforward determination to do whatever we can with the tools to hand to disarm this awful weapon.

March was also the month when a System 3 opinion poll commissioned by Scottish CND showed that 51% of those questioned in Scotland supported the action taken by people who took part in the blockade of Faslane the previous month.

This was in marked contrast to the Opinion finally given by the High Court in Edinburgh in answer to the Lord Advocate's Questions. The Opinion of Lords Prosser, Kirkwood and Penrose were a disappointment to us all. But I have already written about this in the previous chapter.

As a good antidote to the pro-government stance of the High Court, on 15 April we took our protest directly into the Scottish parliament. We attempted to put Trident on the agenda by a dramatic banner drop during a crowded First Minister's question time. There were 12 of us. We draped banners which read 'COMPASSION, INTEGRITY, WISDOM = NO TRIDENT. WHERE'S THE JUSTICE?' This was a quote from the parliament mace. Some of the Scottish activists shouted out 'The people of Scotland want rid of Trident. What will you do about it?' Most of us tied ourselves to the barrier at the front of the public gallery , drawing applause from quite a few of the MSPs, some of whom joined in our singing and one of whom (Margo McDonald of the SNP) came and supported us by joining us in the gallery. Apparently there is to be an investigation into the behaviour of these supportive MSPs!

Eleven of us were eventually charged with breach of the peace and will have to appear in the Sheriffs Court in Edinburgh – another chance for a high profile political case as we point out that there is no better place to bring our concerns than to the elected representatives of the Scottish parliament. Brian Quail was not released along with the rest of us, he was sent to Barlinnie Prison for a week for non-payment of a fine.

A couple of days later we went back to Faslane for a rally. Around 150 people turned up and after a few short speeches by Helen Steven, Alan Wilkie and Tommy Sheridan, we re-pledged our commitment to continue our disarmament work. I invited others to join me in dismantling the fence at the north gate whilst others had already started cutting in along the perimeter fence. We heard the bandit-alert go off as several people managed to enter the base. In all 18 of us were arrested and charged with malicious mischief.

Just as I was finishing this book, I heard that Ulla had been arrested for the 16th time in the UK. On 27 April 2001 she swam up to two Trident submarines berthed at Faslane, attempting to prise off the anechoic tiles and spray painting 'Useless' on the side of HMS *Vanguard*. So once again, an ordinary woman has breached the high security and started to dismantle the submarines – a feat the Ministry of Defence said was impossible. I have let her tell her story in her own words at the end of this chapter.

The road to peace is not quick or easy, but it is full of life and community, heart and soul. Our story of People's Disarmament is still being written. You are a part of it – whether in support or opposition or just looking on. Why not join us?

Trying to Disarm the Vanguard Submarine

by Ulla Roder, *Douglas Water Affinity Group*

Trident is not disarmed yet – but a little step closer. There is hope and lots of experience to get in every action. How did I do it? It is a mixture of luck, hard work, sweat and patience and a strong feeling that this is the right plan. I started out Tuesday night/ Wednesday morning, but had to give up because the daylight was very early and visibility was just too good. So I left a nice hole in the fence (a very remote place) and hoped it would still be there when I arrived at midnight between Thursday and Friday 26/27 April.

I went to Edinburgh Sheriff Court to plead not guilty (about the action at the Scottish Parliament) in the morning and returned in the afternoon to Glasgow, where I had stayed the last week in the home of a lovely Scottish TP couple in Glasgow, who always are helpful and do a lot themselves to disarm Trident. Bob Sprocket from the Water Babies Affinity Group had visited me a few weeks before and brought a very fine diver's dry suit and other swim stuff. He came up all the way again from the south of England to assist me with all the small details that have to be ready before going into an action at a nuclear submarine base. I felt good the whole day. I was careful to eat and drink the right food all day and I felt physically in top form. I had tried the suit in the local swimming pool and I knew it would be all right and very easy to move in. So everything was ready to take off.

Except for lack of the driver, who could not help this evening, everything had been smooth and I was even dreaming that I would be able to do this action. I had never felt more convinced. At the last minute another nice fellow was found, who was willing to drive me up to the base. He and his dog arrived before midnight and brought me safe to the starting point at the northern end of the base. The dog thought it was on its way for a good night walk, and I was sorry to jump out of the car without the dog. I must remember to apologise with a dog biscuit some day.

I arrived at the site where I had cut the hole. The MOD had repaired it. There was no way in this way any longer. I could not cut another hole, because it had to be cut too high up and it would not be possible to climb through. I sat down for an hour and listened and observed the activities out at the sea and around me. I thought of an alternative way and decided to try. I left some of my luggage at the site and went off.

Now I cannot tell much more. (I do not feel it wise to share my information or any details of how I got my way in). But in the end I reached the high security area. The night sky is very beautiful at Faslane. The stars are bright and you can nearly forget the mission. My swimming suit was perfect, I could not feel any cold at all, and the visibility was affected by just enough mist to give me a little cover. I could see the inflatable police boat in the distance and once I thought they had noticed me when it started to sail towards the place I had hidden myself, but it turned around and disappeared in the direction of the peace camp. The rest of the night I saw it mostly lying in the water just outside the floating boom. The speedboat sailed more quietly up and down than the other night. They might have been suspicious after discovering the hole in the fence.

The most difficult task was inside the high security area. There is so much light that it is impossible to hide. So the only thing is to pray, look like a fish in the water or a packet of rubbish. There is lots of rubbish in the water and the surface is green from petrol and other substances. I will write to the base commander to complain about this. The least they could do is to clean the water and the local beach for the sake of the people who have to live in this awful corner of Scotland and TP activists would be grateful too in their future water expeditions I am sure. Of course the best would be that the MOD moved Trident away once and for all, but it seems like we have to do part of that job first if we want to get rid of Trident.

I took my time and took no risk at all at any time. I wanted to get there. Better late than never. Patience pays off I told myself again and again. And it did. I found myself between *Victorious* and *Vanguard*. I was not happy at all. I had reached my goal and should be, but a very strong and strange feeling overwhelmed me for a while. I was covered and took time to think. Horrible! What could have happened if someone with evil intent was here with a suicide bomb? The huge submarines look scaring and ugly like a monster in the water. Suddenly all I knew about the disaster of Hiroshima went though my head and ugly war pictures of victims and refugees passed in my mind. I thought of the many poor and socially deprived people and some homeless people I had known, I nearly wept but remembered that this was exactly why I was here.

I had to find out how to enter the submarine. And imagine what difficult choice I had. I wanted to disarm both. I could not see the name on *Victorious*, so I chose *Vanguard*, which is the fastest of the submarines. (It is also the one on the stamps by the way). *Victorious* lay more open in the berth 11 than *Vanguard* in berth 10.

I could see and hear three soldiers talking on the bridge of *Vanguard* and at the back of the submarine was a guard walking around. I could have chosen to climb onboard at the back, but why risk to be seen swimming to the back, when I could do the same on the side of the submarine? I knew I would be discovered as soon as I made a noise with my tools.

My original plan was to be able to break the tiles that cover the submarine in order to keep it silent and undetectable. Also, *Vanguard* needed a more up to date name. Since the Navy likes names as 'Tireless' I thought USELESS would be a more appropriate name for a mass killing machine, which is exactly what a Trident submarine is.

As you may know Lord Prosser and Co. of the Scottish High Court have decided that deployment of Trident cannot be seen as a threat in peacetime but if used in wartime the 100 kiloton nuclear warheads would breach the international laws of warfare. This is nonsense and every person with common sense knows that Trident is dangerous every day. Accidents, terrorism, international crises can occur any time. Trident costs a lot of money and the whole production contaminates our air and sea.

If I was very lucky to get onboard I had planned to spread a nice DISARMAMENT SOLUTION (syrup, furniture polish and sand from Iona) where the missiles are launched and then paint ONLY FOR WAR CRIMES over it. Should I be really lucky I would climb to the tower and disarm the inside. I brought an extra bottle of disarmament solution and super glue for that purpose.

To be able to get one hand free I had to find something to hold on. The only choice was direct under the bridge to the submarine. *Vanguard* looked terrible. As far as I know sailors are normally very proud of keeping their vessels clean and well kept, but this submarine was in a very bad condition. Several tiles were broken or fallen out. There were brown squares here and there on the hull. I managed to get out the hammer and chisel and I swam the last few metres to the side of the submarine. I placed the chisel between two tiles. I had just lifted the hammer when a guard heard me and shouted loudly and firmly, 'Get away from that submarine! Get away from that submarine!' I had to look at him and could not hammer. He was a young soldier in camouflage uniform and he pointed the machine gun direct at me removing the safety catch. I shouted back, 'I am a peace protester'. I saw someone running over the deck – probably the guard from the back of the submarine. The Alarm went on and the voice in the public address system said something I could not make out. 'Get away' the guard shouted again, this time sounding nervous. I did not want to risk my life for a tile so I preferred to be co-operative for a little while and moved a metre back; but not for too long. When he looked to be calmer I cut up the bag containing the paint and opened the container that was wrapped in black tape. The container looked precisely like a bomb. I drifted slowly toward the side of the submarine again and managed to spray USELESS on the side. The paint was spread too much so I tried again starting with the S. It is really not an easy task to hit the same place twice when at the same time you have to balance in the water which was now choppy in the wash from the police boat. When I came back to the letter U the police boat stopped me. They took me on board and I had a little rest after a hard night. I tried to shout with my tired voice to the soldier that he should not be proud of his job… preparing for mass murder… A war crime to take part in preparations… that our sons' lives were too important to be wasted in wars…

A well-known face with MOD police dress showed up. 'Hello, Ulla' he said and helped me over to the waiting police car. The other police officer spared me from giving all my details this time. He has all of the info about me in his notebook from our latest fence cutting on 7 April. I confirmed my address and birthday had not changed since then. They were convinced that I was not alone and I did nothing to disabuse them of their belief. The bandit alarm sounded for 2 hours, which means the base was stopped for that length of time.

I was driven to the process center where I waited a little while. They gave me a nice cup of warm coffee. I sat in the warm cell with a blanket and felt I had done what I could. Mr Cassidy wanted to know what route I had taken to the submarines and asked me if I knew anything about a little incident a couple of days ago, which I admitted. He asked for the bolt cutter. I told him I actually had brought it, but it slipped away and was to be found at the bottom of the sea. He did not get information about my way in and neither do you. This information is only to share between the TP activists with serious jobs to do at the Faslane Naval base, but not for the MOD (or other terrorists). I know the MOD really want to know my secret, but they have more secrets themselves they are unwilling to share with the people. They have now started an investigation.

I was charged for the painting, for trespassing without authority and for breach of the bye-laws, then released and driven back to the peace camp, where some clothes quickly were given to me. Later on a good friend brought my own clothes and he drove me to Helensburgh. I went by train to Glasgow to get my luggage, had a cup of coffee and off I went to the train to Lanark and the bus to Wiston. I was safe at home at seven o'clock in the evening. The lovely people at Wiston had made a big meal for me and served it for me immediately. Lovely new energy! I phoned a few people, washed my wet and dirty clothes and went to sleep.

What a busy day, but that is the life of many of the Trident Ploughshares activists who do actions or support others in the effort to stop these dangerous nuclear Trident submarines and hopefully we will be able to save the lives of the next generations too and our environment on our lovely planet.

From out of the Horse's Mouth

by Brian Quail, *Local Heroes Affinity Group*

When reality outruns satire it is a richer source of humour than any fictional efforts of mine. These quotes make an unanswerable comic relief.

'If we have to start all over again with another Adam and Eve, I want them to be American.'
Senator Richard Russell, 1969

'So long as an Adam and an Eve survive in every little hamlet, and

so long as they like each other, we shall have this nation going on again...'
The idyllic post-holocaust scenario as envisaged by Wing Commander Harle

'Protective measures should not be regarded as ineffective because they are simple in concept. The whitewashing of windows can provide very effective protection against fire resulting from heat-blast from nuclear explosions.'
William Whitelaw, British Home Secretary, 1981

'Everybody's going to make it [i.e. survive a nuclear war – ed.] if there are enough shovels to go around ... Dig a hole, cover it with a couple of doors, and then throw three feet of dirt on top. It's the dirt that does it.'
T.K.Jones, Former US Deputy Undersecretary of Defense

'The British people are prepared if necessary to be blown to atomic dust.'
Sir Alex Douglas Home, British Prime Minister

'I can go into my office, pick up the telephone, and in 25 minutes 70 million people will be dead.
President Richard Nixon

'If you saw a frog running about, you would have to wash it to get rid of radioactive dust, cook it and eat it.'
Vice Chairman of Civil Aid

'Go forth into the world in peace; be of good courage; hold fast that which is good; render no man evil for evil; strengthen the fainthearted; support the weak; help the afflicted; honour all men; love and serve the Lord, rejoicing in the power of the Holy Spirit.'
Benediction used in the religious ceremony to commission Britain's first Polaris ballistic submarine.

'My life wouldn't be worth living without dope ... it's really a buzz to be tripping out and know that you're cruising the Arctic with Polaris missiles that could wipe out half of Russia – man, that's a real trip!'
US submariner in interview with Duncan Campbell, November 1981

'A nuclear power plant is definitely safer than eating, because 300 people choke to death on food every year.'
Dixie Lee Roy, Governor of Washington State, 1977

'Not only will this test centre promote French military research, but it will also be highly beneficial from the point of view of the economy of the inhabitants of Polynesia ... I have not forgotten all that you (the people of French Polynesia) have done supporting Free France and this is one of the reasons I have chosen to install this base in Polynesia. '
President De Gaulle

'In order to make the country bear the burden (of arms expenditure) we have to create an atmosphere akin to wartime psychology. We must create the idea of a threat from without.'
John Foster Dulles, US Secretary of State

'If my soldiers began to think, not one would stay in the ranks.'
Frederick the Great

'At the end of the day, if three Americans and two Russians are left alive – we have won!'
General Curtis LeMay

'Anyone who thinks we will ever get rid of nuclear weapons is living in cloud cuckoo land.'
Margaret Thatcher, British Prime Minister, 1987

'My fellow Americans, I am pleased to tell you today that I've signed legislation that outlaws Russia forever. The bombing begins in five minutes.'
President Ronald Reagan making a 'joke' during a radio test broadcast in 1984. This was intercepted by Soviet Intelligence.

Contacts

Trident Ploughshares is a campaign to disarm the UK Trident nuclear weapon system in a nonviolent, open, peaceful and fully accountable manner. We act to uphold international humanitarian law, to expose the illegality of the Trident system, and to disarm it. We have an occasional newsletter called *Speed the Plough* which keeps interested people up to date with the campaign. For more information on Trident Ploughshares please look up our website on www.gn.apc.org/tp2000 or www.tridentploughshares.org or contact us at 42-46 Bethel St, Norwich, Norfolk, NR2 1NR. If you wish to join us then please contact us by letter at the above address or by e-mail at tp2000@gn.apc.org

For texts and transcripts with full references of all the legal submissions and court hearings please see the website or contact us directly.

Acknowledgements

The main acknowledgements have to be made to all the Trident Ploughshares Pledgers whose names appear below. Without their dedication and spirit there would be no People's Disarmament.

A special thank you must also go to all the contributors of the special profiles and to David Mackenzie and Jane Tallents who recorded and wrote up so many of the reports from Pledgers' actions, court appearances and prison experiences. Thanks to David also for comments on various drafts of the book and for Roo for his helpful advice. The photographers, many of whom prefer to remain anonymous, have provided a wonderful record of the campaign, some of which have been gratefully used in this book. Roger and Conor – you both restore my faith in lawyers, thanks for your wonderful support and your thought-provoking forewords.

Then there are the friends and supporters who have advised and provided help with the legal submissions in one way or another. To name just a few: John Ainslie, John Burroughs, Roger Clark, Liz Crocker, George Delf, George Farebrother, Nick Grief, Rebecca Johnson, Peter Lanyon, David Mackenzie, Keith Mothersson, Satomi Oba, Ulf Panzer, Isabel Pickering, Glen Rangwalla, Lorna Richardson, Paul Rogers, Keiko Shimizu, Phil Shiner, Fred Starkey, Jane Tallents, and Alan Wilkie.

Thanks to my Mackenzie Friends, who supported me in the various courts – Ev Brown, who persevered through all four weeks of the Greenock Trial, Phil Shiner and Gareth Peirce – wonderful English solicitors, who at great cost to themselves came up to see me through the first stressful days of the Lord Advocate's Reference, and Jane who covered for the remainder. Alan, an amazingly generous man, for working through all the transcripts and looking after the fundraising with George to pay for the valuable record we now have.

I would also like to acknowledge the lawyers who acted for Ellen and Ulla at Greenock and in Edinburgh – Joanna McDonald, John Mayer, Ian Anderson, Matthew Berlow, Callum Ross, Stephen Fox, Jerry Brown, John McLaughlin, and Aidan O'Neill. The lawyers on the other side (or no side) deserve some thanks too

– Gerry Moynihan (the unwanted amicus curiae), Simon di Rollo and Duncan Menzies who acted for the Crown (I am sure they would really rather have been on our side) – especially for their reading from *Yes Minister* which was appreciated by everyone in the Court at the end of Round One and to their adviser Alastair Brown, for his helpfulness. And for the Clerks who shared their table with us all.

Perhaps this is a good place to also record thanks to the majority of the Strathclyde Police who have respected our right to protest and have mostly arrested us with care and who are finally understanding that we actually have a right to dismantle all weapons of mass destruction as well – maybe they will soon be joining us in this crime prevention work.

Sheriff Gimblett deserves major recognition and thanks for her brave decision that jerked the Scottish legal profession out of their complacency. I hope she found more support than criticism for her Greenock decision from her colleagues. It is always hard to be the first to break the status quo. Without her decision there would have been no Lord Advocate's Reference and I doubt if this book would exist.

Gavin, of Luath, thanks for your support and faith that this was a good book to publish.

And for my family and friends who have had to be so patient with my single-minded passion and abstractedness, I wish you to know that it is your love that keeps me going. Thank you Alex, Zina and Camilla especially.

Names of Trident Ploughshares Pledgers on 30 March 2001

River, England
Mark Akkerman, Netherlands
Justin Alexander, England
Stephen Allcroft, England
Kathryn Amos, England
Emma Appleton, England
Marcus Armstrong, England
John Baker, Ireland
Morag Balfour, Scotland
Gaynor Barrett, England
Emilia Benjamin, England
Johanna Berking, England
Duncan Blinkhorn, England
Hazel Bloor, England
Anna Boll, Netherlands
Amanda Booth, England
Rachel Boyd, England
Sylvia Boyes, England
Betty Brown, England
Liz Brown, England
Roz Bullen, Scotland
Stuart Burbridge, England
Janet Cameron, Scotland
Una Campbell, Scotland
Warren David Canham, Scotland
Kay Carmichael, Scotland
Viv Carnea, England
Martina Caruso, England
Maggie Charnley, England
Anna Coldham, Scotland
Adam Conway, England
Vanessa Cope, England
Maxwell Craig, Scotland
Alison Crane, England

Cat Crone, England
Emily Crosby, England
Marilyn Croser, Scotland
Sarah Cunningham, England
Pol D'Huyvetter, Belgium
Susan Davis, England
Bernard De Witte, Belgium
Stuart Dennis, England
Paul Dolman, England
Mog-Ur Kreb Dragonrider, Scotland
Hugh Drummond, Scotland
Rowland Dye, England
Klaus Engel, Sweden
Keeley Morris, England
Roo Eris, England
George Farebrother, England
Claire Fearnley, England
Marguerite Finn, England
Iona Fisher, Scotland
Roger Franklin, England
Clive Fudge, England
Jenny Gaiawyn, England
Myra Garrett, England
Kirsty Gathergood, England
Martha Goddard, England
Colin Goldblatt, England
Andrew Gray, England
Alison Greenhalgh-Watson, England
Hannah Griffin, England
Sara Groser, England
Dirk Grutzmacher, Australia
Gyosei Handa, Japan

Anthony (Teapot) Hannigan, Scotland
Helen Harris, England
Tracy Hart, England
David Heller, England
Davida Higgin, England
Dougald Hine, England
Tim Hinton, England
Robert House, Scotland
Mike Hutchinson, England
Fredrik Ivarsson, Sweden
Rosie James, England
Louise James, Ireland
Hanna Jarvinen, Belgium
Sid Jefferies, Wales
Petter Joelson, Sweden
Helen John, England
Terry Johnson, England
Margaret Jones, England
Ruth Jones, England
Sian Jones, England
Tarna Kannisto, Finland
Mary Kelly, Ireland
Martyn Kelly, Ireland
Paul Andrew Kelly, Scotland
Jutta Kill, Germany
Ganesh Bruce Kings, England
Carol (Kez) Kirby, England
Leeron Koren, Israel
Andrea Kuhnke, Germany
Hans Lammerant, Belgium
Peter Lanyon, England
Sarah Lasenby, England
Mark Leach, Scotland
Martin Lee, England
Annette Lee-Forrester, England
Kristel Letschert, Netherlands
Richard Lewis, England

Anja Light, Australia
Jens Light, Australia
Anne Livingstone, Scotland
Angela Loveridge, Wales
Debbie Mace, England
Babs Macgregor, Scotland
Tigger Macgregor, England
Sheila Mackay, Scotland
David Mackenzie, Scotland
Jacinta Manning, England
Yoshie Marute, Japan
Barbara Maver, Scotland
Eoin Mccarthy, Scotland
James Mclachlan, Scotland
Kath Mcnulty, Wales
Kate Mcnutt, England
Joan Meredith, England
Joan Miller, Scotland
Mika Minio, England
Joy Mitchell, England
Koen Moens, Belgium
Janet Moir, England
Ellen Moxley, Scotland
John Myhill, England
Martin Newell, England
Grace Nicol, Scotland
Bill North, England
Allen O'Keefe, England
Yuko Ohara, Japan
Jean Oliver, Scotland
Igge Olsson, Sweden
Tara Ann Plumley, England
Frances Judith Pritchard, England
Brian Quail, Scotland
Hazel Rennie, England
Ian Richardson, Scotland
Natasha Jane Ritchie, Scotland
Ian Roberts, Scotland

Ulla Roder, Denmark
Koen Roggen, Belgium
Dave Rolstone, England
Anne Scholz, Germany
Amy Scott, England
Norman Shanks, Scotland
Douglas Shaw, Scotland
Katri Silvonen, Belgium
Lou Smith, England
Rick Springer, USA
Robert Peter Sprocket, England
Helen Steven, Scotland
Eleanor Stobo, Scotland
Barbara Mary Sunderland, England
Robban Sundstrom, Sweden
Jane Tallents, Scotland
Alan Thornton, England
Anna Tuominen, Finland
David Turner, Scotland
Astrid Ubas, Netherlands
Wendy Vale, England

Susan Van Der Hyden, Netherlands
Iskander Van Spengen, Scotland
Krista Van Velzen, Netherlands
Eric Wallace, Scotland
Agnes Walton, Scotland
Stokely Webster, Wales
Zoe Weir, Scotland
Rachel Wenham, England
Louise Wilder, England
Maire-Colette Wilkie, Scotland
Alan Wilkie, Scotland
Marjan Willemsen, Netherlands
Erica Wilson, England
Ben Wincott, Scotland
Raga Woods, England
Marlene Yeo, England
Becqke Young, England
Angie Zelter, England

179 Pledgers from 15 countries

Index

Anderson, Ian 177, 302
Armstrong, Marcus 127, 129, 272, 276, 283, 304
Barnaby, Frank 289
Bedjaoui, Judge 105, 107, 141, 185
Benjamin, Emilia 244, 304
Benn, Tony 123, 273
Bertell, Rosalie 286
Best, Harold 281
Boag, Jack 68, 106
Boyes, Sylvia 76, 267, 271, 273, 274, 283, 304
Boyle, Francis 68
Canavan, Dennis 161, 163, 260, 266
Case, Justice 186
Clark, Roger 302
Cook, Robin 111
Crane, Alison 75, 76, 271, 304
Day, Dorothy 56
Davis, Sue 124
De Witte, Bernard 212, 213, 304
Di Rollo, Simon 176, 303
Farebrother, George 62, 64, 302, 304
Falk, Richard 50
Finn, Marguerite 71, 72, 304
Franklin, Roger 76, 169, 171, 205, 249, 271, 283, 287, 304
Gaiawyn, Jenny 167, 274, 282, 304
Galloway, George 50, 290
Gearty, Conor 50
Gillies, Justice Fraser 283

Gimblett, Sheriff 66, 69, 70, 98, 148, 184, 187, 220, 287, 303
Greenwood, Christopher 107
Grief, Nick 93, 289, 302
Hamilton, Ian 50, 290
HARDIE, LORD 66, 79, 161
Harris, Helen 129, 130, 264, 276, 280, 288, 304
Heller, David 166, 167, 212, 213, 249, 304
Hijden, Susan van der 286, 292
John, Helen 148, 259, 261, 270, 273, 279, 280, 305
Johnson, Rebecca 68, 302
Kennedy, A.L. 281
Kirkwood, Lord 84
Lanyon, Peter 60, 71, 83, 176, 261, 262, 265, 286, 302, 305
Lord Advocate 50, 79, 82, 98, 99, 100, 101, 110, 123, 132, 139, 146, 155, 156, 159, 161, 163, 164, 176, 191, 198, 199, 203, 215, 217, 220, 221, 233, 270, 284, 285, 292, 302, 303
Leach, Mark 88, 305
Lucas, Caroline 50, 275, 290
Lyell, Sir Nicholas 107, 114, 222
Macgregor, Tigger 305
MacKay, Sheila 85, 305
Mackenzie, David 70, 77, 150, 152, 239, 240, 261, 266, 267, 268, 277, 285, 287, 302, 305
McCormick, Neil 268

McGregor, Barbara 275, 277
McLaughlin, John 68, 82, 302
McLellan, Andrew 290
Maurin, Peter 56
Mayer, John 68, 82, 177, 218, 302
Menzies, Duncan 177, 303
Meredith, Joan 159, 272, 287, 305
Mitchell, Joy 272, 287, 305
Moxley, Ellen 66, 67, 270, 305
Moynihan, Jerry 84, 177
Murray, Lord 110, 231
Newell, Martin 286, 292, 305
O'Neill, Aidan 177, 229, 302
Panzer, Ulf 68, 302
Peden, William 289
Penrose, Lord 84
Potter, Harry 175, 249, 250
Pritchard, Judith 77, 78, 173, 305
Prosser, Lord 84, 191, 215, 217, 218, 240, 296
Quail, Brian 249, 270, 275, 293, 298, 305
Quinlan, Michael 117
Rifkind, Malcolm 110
Robertson, George 111
Roder, Ulla 66, 67, 218, 270, 293, 305
Rodger, Lord 82, 84
Rogers, Paul 68, 93, 111, 302
Schwebel, Judge 111, 117
Shahabuddeen, Judge 105
Shanks, Norman 137, 138, 266, 290, 305
Shawcross, Sir Hartley 132, 140, 187

Sheridan, Tommy 50, 127, 150, 266, 275, 285, 286, 290, 293
Shi, Judge 97
Simpson, Alan 119, 273
Spaight, J.M. 178
Stobo, Eleanor 268, 305
Tallents, Jane 150, 266, 275, 302, 305
Ubas, Astrid 205, 206, 305
Wallace, Eric 275, 279, 305
Weeramantry, Judge 141, 144, 164, 188, 190, 194
Wenham, Rachel 94, 95, 264, 305
Wilkie, Maire-Colette 247, 305
Willemsen, Marjan 272, 274, 305
Wolfe, Billy 160, 284
Yeo, Marlene 76, 173, 174, 271, 276, 305
Zelter, Angie 93, 98, 100, 101, 132, 175, 177, 218, 244, 253, 269, 279, 305

GENERAL

Abolition 124, 208, 235
Accident 68, 145, 147, 156, 182, 184, 187, 202, 230, 269, 296
Acquittal 53, 54, 70, 79, 96, 98, 124, 159, 161, 162, 220, 238, 253, 270, 273
Advisory Opinion 54, 84, 101, 103, 118, 120, 124, 141, 148, 180, 191, 192, 204, 219, 231, 232, 233, 237, 255
Aerial bombardment 140
Aldermaston 52, 53, 71, 74, 76,

94, 95, 119, 129, 130, 169,
173, 211, 243, 246, 258, 264,
267, 271, 277, 278, 279, 280,
281, 282, 286, 288, 289, 291
Answer 50, 63, 74, 79, 80, 108,
113, 123, 125, 131, 132, 137,
138, 139, 142, 148, 149, 151,
153, 159, 161, 162, 164, 193,
199, 203, 217, 227, 277, 288,
292
Anti-Ballistic Missile Treaty 184
Arrest 47, 51, 61, 88, 89, 90,
91, 92, 96, 125, 127, 137,
150, 167, 170, 211, 212, 229,
242, 243, 245, 246, 248, 258,
259, 278, 281, 288, 289
Attorney General 50, 123, 155,
156
Authorisation 139
Bailiff 169, 170, 171, 172, 174,
175, 276
Barrow-in-Furness 95, 264
Belief 264, 270, 297
Berrigans 253
Blockade 47, 50, 52, 88, 89, 91,
124, 138, 168, 207, 212, 213,
245, 246, 247, 250, 258, 266,
267, 273, 275, 278, 279, 280,
281, 284, 287, 289, 290, 291,
292
Buddha 206, 207, 241, 243,
244
Bully 179
Burghfield 58, 200, 267, 279
Cardinal Principles 103
Casualties 63, 114, 115, 226
Chemical Weapons Convention
191
Citizen's Inspection 71, 74

Civilian 49, 59, 95, 102, 103,
104, 105, 106, 108, 110, 112,
114, 115, 140, 144, 155, 157,
158, 163, 178, 191, 225, 226,
231, 232, 235, 236, 254, 278
CND 50, 85, 87, 88, 89, 126,
168, 210, 256, 258, 261, 275,
277, 290, 292
Complicity 142, 157
Conflict 55, 77, 103, 106, 107,
108, 110, 112, 113, 114, 122,
149, 157, 161, 163, 164, 166,
167, 190, 192, 203, 222, 223,
224, 226, 232, 235, 236, 237,
238
Controllability 103, 105
Convoy 52, 56, 58, 59, 150,
210, 267
Cornton Vale Prison 66, 259,
270, 286
Coulport 47, 49, 52, 82, 86,
127, 140, 149, 167, 170, 173,
200, 250, 256, 258, 261, 267,
270, 271, 272, 273, 276, 280,
282, 283, 284, 285, 288, 291
Crime Prevention 52, 67, 100,
155, 158, 162, 164, 186, 200,
201, 238, 273, 276, 303
Crimes Against Humanity 238
Crimes Against Peace 102, 143,
144, 238
Criminality 100, 101, 139, 143,
147, 155, 159, 164, 191, 199,
236
Customary International Law
101, 132, 133, 134, 135, 136,
137, 138, 143, 146, 158, 189,
217, 222, 223, 224, 227, 232,
233, 235

Danger 68, 95, 106, 109, 122, 147, 154, 166, 180, 184, 185, 202, 217, 223, 224, 228, 230, 232, 283

Declaration of St. Petersburg 48, 101, 196

Deployment 199, 200, 204, 209, 229, 231, 232, 235, 236, 237, 286, 296

Desert Fox 94, 97

Dialogue 49, 62, 63, 137, 256, 268

Disarmament 47, 48, 49, 50, 51, 52, 54, 55, 62, 67, 81, 89, 98, 99, 100, 102, 119, 120, 125, 137, 143, 145, 147, 149, 151, 156, 163, 164, 166, 167, 168, 175, 184, 189, 190, 200, 201, 202, 203, 204, 206, 207, 209, 210, 215, 216, 222, 226, 239, 240, 243, 244, 246, 248, 253, 254, 255, 256, 260, 263, 264, 266, 270, 271, 277, 285, 286, 293, 296, 302

Discrimination 103, 105, 141, 148, 178, 199, 206, 233

Dresden 178

East Timor 201, 254

Edinburgh 68, 86, 87, 89, 98, 100, 101, 132, 137, 177, 215, 217, 239, 247, 257, 268, 270, 273, 285, 292, 293, 294, 302

Environment 48, 55, 63, 71, 74, 94, 97, 102, 109, 113, 141, 178, 231, 241, 242, 278, 298

European Convention on Human Rights 137, 275

Evidential basis 198, 199

Faslane 47, 49, 50, 52, 82, 86, 87, 88, 90, 91, 92, 115, 124, 137, 140, 149, 150, 159, 166, 167, 168, 210, 211, 212, 213, 215, 217, 222, 243, 245, 246, 247, 250, 258, 262, 263, 266, 268, 270, 273, 274, 275, 276, 277, 280, 282, 283, 286, 287, 289, 291, 292, 293, 295, 298

Faslane Peace Camp 87, 167, 168, 213, 214, 256, 286, 290

Fence cutting 52, 77, 243, 258, 282, 297

For Mother Earth 166, 208, 209, 211, 212, 257

Fudge 106, 215, 267, 272, 287, 304

Fungus 268, 272, 279, 286

Ganesh 288, 305

General Lee Butler 180, 181, 185, 202

Geneva Conventions 102, 123, 227

Glasgow Quakers 266

Global 2000 50

Global citizen 47, 48, 49, 80, 82, 99, 154, 164, 187, 216, 238, 255

Greenock 54, 66, 69, 79, 80, 82, 84, 88, 89, 91, 98, 100, 106, 111, 124, 135, 136, 142, 146, 147, 148, 151, 154, 159, 161, 163, 164, 180, 184, 187, 193, 198, 199, 220, 238, 259, 270, 271, 273, 281, 283, 287, 288, 302, 303

Hague Convention 48, 101

Halabja 142

Handbook 200, 255

Helensburgh 127, 150, 168, 170, 173, 222, 248, 263, 268, 274, 275, 276, 283, 286, 287, 298

High Court 79, 96, 98, 100,
  101, 132, 137, 161, 162, 163,
  164, 176, 177, 215, 216, 217,
  219, 221, 232, 238, 239, 270,
  280, 285, 286, 292, 296
Hiroshima 54, 96, 106, 113,
  114, 116, 145, 178, 207, 209,
  237, 243, 257, 282, 295
Hoozie 166
Hostages Case 122
Human Rights 98, 102, 116,
  145, 156, 158, 185, 215, 226
Humanitarian Law 301
Hypothetical 63, 121, 179
Imminence 68
Immunity 103, 105, 136, 141,
  146, 178, 233, 234
Individual responsibility 278
Intention 111, 116, 117, 118,
  119, 139, 148, 192, 193, 195,
  196, 256, 267
International Court of Justice
  54, 101, 103, 104, 106, 107,
  111, 114, 116, 117, 119, 120,
  121, 124, 134, 139, 141, 143,
  144, 148, 158, 180, 189, 191,
  192, 193, 199, 203, 204, 208,
  212, 222, 232, 233, 234, 235,
  237, 255
International Covenant on Civil
  and Political Rights 158, 162
International Criminal Court
  112, 115, 225
International Criminal Tribunal
  104
Intervention 183, 184, 185,
  186, 187, 188, 223, 226, 228
Justification 142, 147, 151,
  152, 155, 160, 185, 186, 221,
  224, 236

Katri Silvonen 208, 210, 212,
  213, 259, 263, 305
Kees Koning 57
Koen Moens 152, 305
Kreb Dragonrider 240, 241,
  283, 304
Krupp trial 122
Lakenheath 180
Lawful excuse 64
Liverpool 244, 254
Loch Goil 46, 52, 66, 67, 88,
  229, 236, 270
Lock-on 290
London 137, 169, 178, 206,
  241, 243, 257, 273
Manchester 77, 96, 124, 265,
  274, 288
Martens Clause 101, 144, 200
Mass Destruction 201, 203,
  208, 209, 215, 221, 228, 291,
  303
Maximum disarmament 263
Maytime 39, 40, 52, 66, 67, 68,
  143, 149, 200, 202, 270
McPhaill 283
Menwith Hill 280
Ministry of Defence 40, 45,
  291, 293
Missile 296, 299
Moderation 103
Morality 140, 163, 164, 202,
  220, 221, 223, 238
Moscow 106, 115, 184
Motions 203, 204, 226
Murder 238, 239, 240, 250,
  297
Music 241, 244, 245, 246, 272,
  278, 290
Mutually Assured Destruction
  183, 196

Nagasaki 207, 209

NATO 44, 49, 94, 106, 111, 166, 180, 184, 208, 209, 210, 212, 257, 269, 298

Nazi 143, 146, 185, 187, 191

Necessity 200, 202, 204, 216, 217, 223, 224, 226, 228, 229, 230, 236, 286

Non Combatants 104

Non-Proliferation Treaty 27, 98, 120, 189, 235

Nonviolent Resistance 158

Nuclear Deterrence 185, 187, 194, 197, 209, 222, 227, 230, 238

Nuremberg 65, 101, 102, 104, 113, 115, 122, 123, 132, 140, 142, 143, 144, 145, 146, 157, 162, 185, 186, 204, 216, 218, 225, 227, 237, 238, 263, 271

Opinio juris 191, 222, 234

Outer Space Treaty 184

Pinochet case 133

Pledge to Prevent Nuclear Crime 243, 256

Police 260, 262, 264, 266, 267, 268, 269, 272, 273, 274, 275, 276, 278, 279, 281, 283, 287, 288, 289, 291, 295, 297, 303

Possession 69, 79, 99, 117, 125, 136, 138, 139, 147, 148, 170, 175, 189, 190, 191, 194, 195, 199, 228, 262

Preston 265, 274

Prime Minister, Tony Blair 256

Prison 259, 260, 261, 271, 274, 280, 283, 286, 287, 288, 293, 302

Prohibition 108, 139, 189

Proportionality 199

Quaker 210, 266, 283

Question 1 132, 151, 159

Question 2 138, 149

Question 3 151

Question 4 153

Radiation 286

Reasonable force 139, 143, 155, 179

Red Cross 107

Reservation 108, 192

Right to Intervene 216, 275

Risk 295, 296, 297

River 76, 77, 96, 173, 274, 288, 304

Ruling 69, 70, 98, 124, 157, 180, 199, 202, 203, 217, 219, 233, 238, 255, 285

Russia 299, 300

Rwanda 104, 123

Saddam Hussein 111

Scots Law 135, 142, 149, 151, 153, 163, 164, 216, 217, 222, 223, 224, 227, 238, 239, 261, 275

Scottish judiciary 80, 100, 101, 176, 215, 217, 218

Seeds of Hope 254, 255

Self-defence 98, 104, 105, 106, 107, 108, 109, 111, 112, 194, 196, 220, 228, 235, 237

Serbia 269

Shimoda case 54, 114

Sofal response 268

St. Augustine's United Church 285

Star Wars 53

State practice 101, 178, 191, 197

Strategic Defence Review 109, 119, 181
Strathclyde police 88, 163, 250, 273, 281, 289, 303
Symbolic 251, 258, 262, 263
Targets 48, 95, 103, 104, 105, 106, 113, 114, 115, 180, 182, 183, 221, 236
Teapot 166, 272, 281, 304
Threat 237, 256, 263, 265, 270, 278, 285, 296, 300
Tokyo Tribunal 104, 123
Tripod 168, 281, 290
UN 102, 110, 117, 118, 120, 158, 190, 208, 209, 237
United Nations 48, 104, 158, 194, 197, 232
Uncertainty 108, 111, 130, 233
Universal jurisdiction 133
Unnecessary suffering 233, 234
USA 68, 94, 149, 203, 209, 253
Valentine's Day 276

Vanguard 293, 295, 296
Vengeance 52, 94, 149, 200, 264, 266, 268, 271, 274
Vital Interests 109, 194
War crime 202, 224, 227, 238, 275, 296, 297
Warhead 49, 53, 74, 76, 98, 99, 101, 104, 105, 106, 108, 109, 110, 113, 115, 118, 119, 120, 147, 148, 149, 174, 181, 182, 187, 191, 193, 200, 202, 203, 204, 210, 221, 227, 228, 233, 237, 238, 267, 274, 277, 285, 286, 296
Warning shot 110, 118, 193, 194
Warsaw Pact 182
Wittering 286
World Court Project 285
Yugoslavia 104, 123, 212, 223
Zyklon B 142, 146

Some other books published by **LUATH** PRESS

Broomie Law
a collection of cartoons by
Cinders Mcleod
ISBN 0 946487 99 5 PBK £4.00

'Cinders is a great cartoonist and
helps us to see the truth behind the
facade'
TONY BENN, MP

'Broomie Law is the only thing since
the halcyon days of Steve Bell I've been
interested in buying'
PHILL JUPITUS

'Your work is so sharp and unusual
(in these politically surreal times), and
above all, powerful. I'm a fan!'
JOHN PILGER

'Broomie's handbag packs as great a
punch as Lobey Dosser's revolver once
did in the Evening Times'
ELSPETH KING, Stirling Art Gallery
and Museum

'One of the better memories of the Lord
Advocate's Reference hearings in
the High Court last year was listening
to weighty and wordy arguments on
both sides of the question and at the
same time as passing from hand to
hand Cinders' sharp images catching
the complete phallacy of Trident. Dip
into Broomie Law for that same edge.'
DAVID MACKENZIE, Local Heroes
Affinity Group

'Broomie Law is fab'
ALEX SALMOND, MSP MP

'Content, personal political comment,
what you might call genuine social
comment based on observation is rare'
STEVE WAY

'Broomie Law's brilliant. Just the right
lightness to drill home the point'
GEOFF THOMPSON

'... wonderful'
GEORGE MONBIOT

'Broomie Law is so unique and breaks
such new ground'
DR MAEWAN HO

'No blood but plenty of bite. And a
twist of lemon from the fact that all
the characters are female'
AMANDA SEBESTYEN, Red Pepper

'Cinders creations are perceptive and
touch the raw essence of today's big
social issues'
JAMES DOHERTY, The Big Issue in
Scotland

'Let's get married'
JEREMY HARDY

[Un]comfortably Numb: A Prison Requiem

Maureen Maguire

ISBN 1 84282 001 X PBK £8.99

'People may think I've taken the easy way out but please believe me this is the hardest thing I've ever had to do.'

YVONNE GILMOUR

It was Christmas Eve, the atmosphere in Cornton Vale prison was festive, the girls in high spirits as they were locked up for the night. One of their favourite songs, Pink Floyd's *Comfortably Numb*, played loudly from a nearby cell as Yvonne Gilmour wrote her suicide note. She was the sixth of eight inmates to take their own lives in Cornton Vale prison over a short period of time.

[Un]comfortably Numb follows Yvonne through a difficult childhood, a chaotic adolescence and drug addiction to life and death behind bars. Her story is representative of many women in our prisons today. They are not criminals (only 1% are convicted for violent crimes) and two-thirds are between the ages of sixteen and thirty. Suicide rates among them are rising dramatically. Do these vulnerable young girls really belong in prison?

This is a powerful and moving story told in the words of those involved: Yvonne and her family, fellow prisoners, prison officers, social workers, drug workers. It challenges us with questions which demand answers if more deaths are to be avoided – and offers a tragic indictment of social exclusion in 21st century Britain, told in the real voices of women behind bars.

'Uncomfortably Numb is not a legal textbook or a jurisprudential treatise... it is an investigation into something our sophisticated society can't easily face'

AUSTIN LAFFERTY

Scotland - Land and Power
the agenda for land reform

Andy Wightman

foreword by Lesley Riddoch

ISBN 0 946487 70 7 PBK £5.00

What is land reform?

Why is it needed?

Will the Scottish Parliament really make a difference?

Scotland – Land and Power argues passionately that nothing less than a radical, comprehensive programme of land reform can make the difference that is needed. Now is no time for palliative solutions which treat the symptoms and not the causes.

Scotland – Land and Power is a controversial and provocative book that clarifies the complexities of landownership in Scotland. Andy Wightman explodes the myth that land issues are relevant only to the far flung fringes of rural Scotland, and questions mainstream political commitment to land reform. He presents his own far-reaching programme for change and a pragmatic, inspiring vision of how Scotland can move from out-moded, unjust power structures towards a more equitable landowning democracy.

'Writers like Andy Wightman are determined to make sure that the hurt of the last century is not compounded by a rushed solution in the next. This accessible, comprehensive but passionately argued book is quite simply essential reading and perfectly timed – here's hoping Scotland's legislators agree.'

LESLEY RIDDOCH

Listen to the Trees

Don MacCaskill

ISBN 0 946487 65 0   £9.99 PBK

Don MacCaskill is one of Scotland's foremost naturalists, conservationists and wildlife photographers. *Listen to the Trees* is a beautiful and acutely observed account of how his outlook on life began to change as trees, woods, forests and all the wonders that they contain became a focus in his life. It is rich in its portrayal of the life that moves in the Caledonian forest and on the moorlands – lofty twig-stacked heronries, the elusive peregrine falcon and the red, bushy-tailed fox – of the beauty of the trees, and of those who worked in the forests.

'Trees are surely the supreme example of a life-force stronger than our own,' writes Don MacCaskill. 'Some, like the giant redwoods of North America, live for thousands of years. Some, like our own oaks and pines, may live for centuries. All, given the right conditions, will regenerate their species and survive long into the future.'

In the afterword Dr Philip Ratcliffe, former Head of the Forestry Commission's Environment Branch and a leading environment consultant, discusses the future role of Britain's forests – their influence on the natural environment and on the communities that live and work in and around them.

'Listen to the Trees will inspire all those with an interest in nature. It is a beautiful account, strongly anecdotal and filled with humour.'
RENNIE McOWAN

'This man adores trees. 200 years from now, your descendants will know why.'

JIM GILCHRIST, THE SCOTSMAN

But n Ben A-Go-Go

Matthew Fitt

ISBN 0 946487 82 0 HBK £10.99

The year is 2090. Global flooding has left most of Scotland under water. The descendants of those who survived God's Flood live in a community of floating island parishes, known collectively as Port.

Port's citizens live in mortal fear of Senga, a supervirus whose victims are kept in a giant hospital warehouse in sealed capsules called Kists.

Paolo Broon is a low-ranking cyberjanny. His life-partner, Nadia, lies forgotten and alone in Omega Kist 624 in the Rigo Imbeki Medical Center. When he receives an unexpected message from his radge criminal father to meet him at But n Ben A-Go-Go, Paolo's life is changed forever.

He must traverse VINE, Port and the Drylands and deal with rebel American tourists and crabbit Dundonian microchips to discover the truth about his family's past in order to free Nadia from the sair grip of the merciless Senga.

Set in a distinctly unbonnie future-Scotland, the novel's dangerous atmosphere and psychologically-malkied characters weave a tale that both chills and intrigues.

'after a bit – not a very long bit – I was plunged into the particular language of this book just as I'm plunged into that of Chandler or Asimov... you can read this novel because it's very well-written, and it also tells a good story.'
W N HERBERT, SCOTLAND ON SUNDAY

'not a traditional rustic tale... I could understand quite a lot of that!' SUE MACGREGOR; *'the last man who tried anything like this was Hugh MacDiarmid'* MICHAEL FRY,
TODAY PROGRAMME, BBC RADIO 4

'will wean young Scots off reading Harry Potter'
RODDY MARTINE, DAILY MAIL

'a bit of a cracker. I have no Scots... and tend to avoid books with long passages in dialect. But I can, with occasional hiccups, read Fitt's offering and am doing so with much enjoyment. He has found the key, which is to eschew linguistic pedantry in favour of linguistic vigour. To hear him reading aloud at the book launch, giving the Scots language a modern literary voice without selfconsciousness or pretentiousness, was a mesmerising experience.'
KATIE GRANT, THE TIMES

'Easier to read than Shakespeare – twice the fun.'
DES DILLON

On the Trail of John Muir

Cherry Good

ISBN 0 946487 62 6 PBK £7.99

Follow the man who made the US go green. Confidant of presidents, father of American National Parks, trailblazer of world conservation and voted a Man of the Millennium in the US, John Muir's life and work is of continuing relevance. A man ahead of his time who saw the wilderness he loved threatened by industrialisation and determined to protect it, a crusade in which he was largely successful. His love of the wilderness began at an early age and he was filled with wanderlust all his life.

Only by going in silence, without baggage, can on truly get into the heart of the wilderness. All other travel is mere dust and hotels and baggage and chatter. JOHN MUIR

Braving mosquitoes and black bears Cherry Good set herself on his trail – Dunbar, Scotland; Fountain Lake and Hickory Hill, Wisconsin; Yosemite Valley and the Sierra Nevada, California; the Grand Canyon, Arizona; Alaska; and Canada – to tell his story. John Muir was himself a prolific writer, and Good draws on his books, articles, letters and diaries to produce an account that is lively, intimate, humorous and anecdotal, and that provides refreshing new insights into the hero of world conservation.

> John Muir chronology
> General map plus 10 detailed maps covering the US, Canada and Scotland
> Original colour photographs
> Afterword advises on how to get involved
> Conservation websites and addresses

Muir's importance has long been acknowledged in the US with over 200 sites of scenic beauty named after him. He was a Founder of The Sierra Club which now has over $\frac{1}{2}$ million members. Due to the movement he started some 360 million acres of wilderness are now protected. This is a book which shows Muir not simply as a hero but as likeable humorous and self-effacing man of extraordinary vision.

'I do hope that those who read this book will burn with the same enthusiasm for John Muir which the author shows.'
WEST HIGHLAND FREE PRESS

CURRENT ISSUES

Old Scotland New Scotland
Jeff Fallow
ISBN 0 946487 40 5 PBK £6.99

**Notes from the North
Incorporating a Brief History of the
Scots and the English**
Emma Wood
ISBN 0 946487 46 4 PBK £8.99

**Some Assembly Required: behind
the scenes at the rebirth of the
Scottish Parliament**
David Shepherd
ISBN 0 946487 84 7 PBK £7.99

POETRY

Poems to be read aloud
Collected and with an introduction by
Tom Atkinson
ISBN 0 946487 00 6 PBK £5.00

Scots Poems to be Read Aloud
Collectit an wi an innin by
Stuart McHardy
ISBN 0 946487 81 2 PBK £5.00

Blind Harry's Wallace
William Hamilton of Gilbertfield
introduced by Elspeth King
ISBN 0 946487 43 X HBK £15.00
ISBN 0 946487 33 2 PBK £8.99

Men & Beasts
Valerie Gillies amd Rebecca Marr
ISBN 0 946487 92 8 PBK £15.00

The Luath Burns Companion
John Cairney
ISBN 1 84282 000 1 PBK £10.00

'Nothing but Heather!'
Gerry Cambridge
ISBN 0 946487 49 9 PBK £15.00

FICTION

Grave Robbers
Robin Mitchell
ISBN 0 946487 72 3 PBK £7.99

The Bannockburn Years
William Scott
ISBN 0 946487 34 0 PBK £7.95

The Great Melnikov
Hugh MacLachlan
ISBN 0 946487 42 1 PBK £7.95

FOLKLORE

Scotland: Myth Legend & Folklore
Stuart McHardy
ISBN 0 946487 69 3 PBK £7.99

The Supernatural Highlands
Francis Thompson
ISBN 0 946487 31 6 PBK £8.99

Tall Tales from an Island
Peter Macnab
ISBN 0 946487 07 3 PBK £8.99

Tales from the North Coast
Alan Temperley
ISBN 0 946487 18 9 PBK £8.99

ON THE TRAIL OF

On the Trail of Mary Queen of Scots
J. Keith Cheetham
ISBN 0 946487 50 2 PBK £7.99

On the Trail of William Wallace
David R. Ross
ISBN 0 946487 47 2 PBK £7.99

On the Trail of Robert Burns
John Cairney
ISBN 0 946487 51 0 PBK £7.99

On the Trail of Bonnie Prince Charlie
David R. Ross
ISBN 0 946487 68 5 PBK £7.99

**On the Trail of Queen Victoria in the
Highlands**
Ian R. Mitchell
ISBN 0 946487 79 0 PBK £7.99

On the Trail of Robert the Bruce
David R. Ross
ISBN 0 946487 52 9 PBK £7.99

On the Trail of Robert Service
GW Lockhart
ISBN 0 946487 24 3 PBK £7.99

LUATH GUIDES TO SCOTLAND

Mull and Iona: Highways and Byways
Peter Macnab
ISBN 0 946487 58 8 PBK £4.95

South West Scotland
Tom Atkinson
ISBN 0 946487 04 9 PBK £4.95

**The West Highlands: The Lonely
Lands**
Tom Atkinson
ISBN 0 946487 56 1 PBK £4.95

**The Northern Highlands: The Empty
Lands**
Tom Atkinson
ISBN 0 946487 55 3 PBK £4.95

**The North West Highlands: Roads to
the Isles**
Tom Atkinson
ISBN 0 946487 54 5 PBK £4.95

WALK WITH LUATH

Mountain Days & Bothy Nights
Dave Brown and Ian Mitchell
ISBN 0 946487 15 4 PBK £7.50

The Joy of Hillwalking
Ralph Storer
ISBN 0 946487 28 6 PBK £7.50

Scotland's Mountains before the Mountaineers
Ian Mitchell
ISBN 0 946487 39 1 PBK £9.99

LUATH WALKING GUIDES

Walks in the Cairngorms
Ernest Cross
ISBN 0 946487 09 X PBK £4.95

Short Walks in the Cairngorms
Ernest Cross
ISBN 0 946487 23 5 PBK £4.95

HISTORY

Reportage Scotland: History in the Making
Louise Yeoman
ISBN 0 946487 61 8 PBK £9.99

Edinburgh's Historic Mile
Duncan Priddle
ISBN 0 946487 97 9 PBK £2.99

SOCIAL HISTORY

Shale Voices
Alistair Findlay
foreword by Tam Dalyell MP
ISBN 0 946487 63 4 PBK £10.99
ISBN 0 946487 78 2 HBK £17.99

Crofting Years
Francis Thompson
ISBN 0 946487 06 5 PBK £6.95

A Word for Scotland
Jack Campbell
foreword by Magnus Magnusson
ISBN 0 946487 48 0 PBK £12.99

BIOGRAPHY

Tobermory Teuchter: a first-hand account of life on Mull in the early years of the 20th century
Peter Macnab
ISBN 0 946487 41 3 PBK £7.99

The Last Lighthouse
Sharma Kraustopf
ISBN 0 946487 96 0 PBK £7.99

Bare Feet and Tackety Boots
Archie Cameron
ISBN 0 946487 17 0 PBK £7.95

Come Dungeons Dark
John Taylor Caldwell
ISBN 0 946487 19 7 PBK £6.95

MUSIC AND DANCE

Highland Balls & Village Halls
GW Lockhart
ISBN 0 946487 12 X PBK £6.95

Fiddles & Folk: a celebration of the re-emergence of Scotland's musical heritage
GW Lockhart
ISBN 0 946487 38 3 PBK £7.95

FOOD AND DRINK

Edinburgh & Leith Pub Guide
Stuart McHardy
ISBN 0 946487 80 4 PBK £4.99

SPORT

Over the Top with the Tartan Army (Active Service 1992-97)
Andrew McArthur
ISBN 0 946487 45 6 PBK £7.99

Ski & Snowboard Scotland
Hilary Parke
ISBN 0 946487 35 9 PBK £6.99

Pilgrims in the Rough: St Andrews beyond the 19th hole
Michael Tobert
ISBN 0 946487 74 X PBK £7.99

NATURAL WORLD

Wild Lives: Otters – On the Swirl of the Tide
Bridget MacCaskill
ISBN 0 946487 67 7 PBK £9.99

Wild Lives: Foxes – The Blood is Wild
Bridget MacCaskill
ISBN 0 946487 71 5 PBK £9.99

Wild Scotland: The essential guide to finding the best of natural Scotland
James McCarthy
Photography by Laurie Campbell
ISBN 0 946487 37 5 PBK £7.50

Scotland Land and People An Inhabited Solitude
James McCarthy
ISBN 0 946487 57 X PBK £7.99

The Highland Geology Trail
John L Roberts
ISBN 0 946487 36 7 PBK £4.99

Rum: Nature's Island
Magnus Magnusson
ISBN 0 946487 32 4 PBK £7.95

Red Sky at Night
John Barrington
ISBN 0 946487 60 X PBK £8.99

Luath Press Limited
committed to publishing well written books worth reading

LUATH PRESS takes its name from Robert Burns, whose little collie Luath (*Gael.*, swift or nimble) tripped up Jean Armour at a wedding and gave him the chance to speak to the woman who was to be his wife and the abiding love of his life. Burns called one of *The Twa Dogs* Luath after Cuchullin's hunting dog in *Ossian's Fingal*. Luath Press grew up in the heart of Burns country, and now resides a few steps up the road from Burns' first lodgings in Edinburgh's Royal Mile.

Luath offers you distinctive writing with a hint of unexpected pleasures.

Most UK and US bookshops either carry our books in stock or can order them for you. To order direct from us, please send a £sterling cheque, postal order, international money order or your credit card details (number, address of cardholder and expiry date) to us at the address below. Please add post and packing as follows: UK – £1.00 per delivery address; overseas surface mail – £2.50 per delivery address; overseas airmail – £3.50 for the first book to each delivery address, plus £1.00 for each additional book by airmail to the same address. If your order is a gift, we will happily enclose your card or message at no extra charge.

Luath Press Limited
543/2 Castlehill
The Royal Mile
Edinburgh EH1 2ND
Scotland
Telephone: 0131 225 4326 (24 hours)
Fax: 0131 225 4324
email: gavin.macdougall@luath.co.uk
Website: www.luath.co.uk